Paris

**Megacities**
Series Editor: H. V. Savitch

As drivers of economic growth, demographic change and consumption, hyper-conurbations offer unique opportunities to their hinterlands and national economies, as well as huge challenges of governance, planning and provisioning. Each book in this series examines the political and economic development of a specific megacity and explores how and why they have evolved and how policy decisions, couched in geopolitics, have shaped their outcomes. The series covers both paradigmatic mature megacities of the developed world, as well as the fast-growing emerging megacities of South and East Asia, and Latin America.

*Published*

*Paris*
Christian Lefèvre

# Paris

Christian Lefèvre

First published in 2022 by Agenda Publishing

Agenda Publishing Limited
The Core
Bath Lane
Newcastle Helix
Newcastle upon Tyne
NE4 5TF
www.agendapub.com

ISBN 978-1-78821-140-6 (hardcover)
ISBN 978-1-78821-141-3 (paperback)

**British Library Cataloguing-in-Publication Data**
A catalogue record for this book is available from the British Library

Typeset by Newgen Publishing UK
Printed and bound in the UK by CPI Group (UK) Ltd, Croydon, CR0 4YY

# Contents

# Preface and acknowledgements

On 16 March 2020 the French national government imposed a national lockdown that lasted for several weeks in an attempt to contain the spread of the Covid-19 pandemic. In the seven days around that date more than 1.2 million people in the Île-de-France left the largest French metropolis for the countryside. A year on, as I write this preface, the pandemic persists, and the duration of the measures imposed to contain the health crisis have had a devastating effect on the economy and society of the region.

It is too soon to offer an interpretation of the recent changes incurred by the pandemic, simply because it is uncertain whether the transformations it has entailed will be structural (having a durable effect on the structures of the regional economy and society) or merely temporary. It is worth pointing out here some of the major changes caused by the pandemic, however, without taking a position on their medium- or long-term impact on the Paris region.

First of all, the urban economy has suffered serious damage. Although no data are yet available for the 2020 regional economy, it is very likely that they will mirror the downward trend experienced at the national level, with an 8.3 per cent decrease in French gross domestic product (GDP). Considering the high degree of internationalization in the Île-de-France economy, it is very likely that the economic impact will be higher in the region than in the rest of France (Institut Paris Région 2020b).

For instance, as tourism, and notably foreign tourism, constitutes a significant source of revenue for the region, the closure of borders and the decline of air traffic have decimated the sector. The most recent data suggest a 72 per cent drop in revenue for the tourist industry in Île-de-France. Symbolically, the Louvre – the most visited museum in the world – welcomed only 2.7 million visitors in 2020, as opposed to almost 10 million in 2019. Moreover, whereas 75 per cent of the visitors are usually from abroad, they accounted for only 25 per cent in 2020. The aeronautics industry, one of the leading sectors of the regional economy, was similarly affected. With a 70 per cent decrease in air traffic in 2020, this sector has been seriously hit. Not only has the crisis precipitated significant lay-offs at the major airlines such as Air France, it has also impacted the rest of the sector, with the cancellation of contracts for suppliers such as Airbus, one of the two major passenger aircraft manufacturers in the world.

Second, the pandemic-induced recession has had a tremendous impact on national and regional society with a sharp increase in unemployment. The region has been hit hard, with an 8.6 per cent increase in total unemployment in 2020 against "only" 4.8 per cent at the national level – and all this in spite of the considerable support put in place by the national government and local authorities. In addition, the crisis has significantly exacerbated the pre-existing high social and territorial inequalities. The areas where the poorest populations are located, where unemployment was already higher and conditions of employment were bad have been hardest hit by the pandemic.

Finally, one of the most visible impacts of the pandemic has been on urban mobility. Public transport has been seriously hit, not only because metro and bus lines were almost closed during the first lockdown, in March 2020, but also because commuters have deserted what they considered "dangerous" modes of travel, reflecting the higher risk of contagion from using public transport. In addition, the increase in home working has automatically reduced the number of commuters. In the region's peripheries travel has shifted to the car, but in Paris and its adjacent municipalities the use of soft modes of all kinds, though mainly bicycles, has boomed.

Of course, only time will show how all these changes affect the future of the Île-de-France metropolis, as with most other big cities in the world. It is also too soon to tell whether the current health crisis will force the regional players to think of an alternative mode of economic development, which has been called for by some of the regional organizations (IAU 2021).

First of all I would like to thank my research lab, LATTS (Laboratoire Techniques, Territoires, Sociétés) for its academic and financial support. I am also deeply indebted to my friend Pierre Mansat, who was deputy mayor of Paris and special advisor of the Paris's mayor in charge of territorial cooperation between 2001 and 2019. And of course, all my thanks to the many colleagues, researchers, officials in the various institutions and organizations dealing with the Paris and Île-de-France metropolitan area without whom I could not have achieved the writing of this book. Finally, I want to express my warmest wishes to Professor Hank Savitch, editor of the Megacities series with whom I have collaborated for many years around the world.

Christian Lefèvre
Paris, March 2021

## Abbreviations and acronyms

| | |
|---|---|
| AFTRP | Agence foncière et technique de la région parisienne (the state land agency regarding Île-de-France) |
| ANRU | Agence nationale pour la rénovation urbaine (the state agency in charge of urban renewal and policy for cities) |
| APUR | Atelier parisien d'urbanisme (the planning and studies agency of the municipality of Paris) |
| CCI | chambre de commerce et d'industrie (in France, CCIs are public bodies representing business interests) |
| CCIP | Chambre de commerce et d'industrie de Paris |
| CDTs | contrats de développement territorial (contracts between the state and municipalities [or groups of municipalities] established by the Grand Paris Act of 2010) |
| CEA | Commissariat à l'énergie atomique (a state agency) |
| CESER | Conseil économique, social et environnemental régional (previously CESR [Conseil économique et social régional]; the second regional assembly, representing economic and social forces) |
| CGPME | Confédération générale des petites et moyennes entreprises (the national federation of small and medium-sized enterprises; previous name of the present CPME) |
| CNRS | Centre national de la recherche scientifique |
| CPER | contrat de plan État–région (document signed between each region and the state setting up the shared priorities of development for the regional territory) |

| | |
|---|---|
| CPME | Confédération des petites et moyennes entreprises (national federation of small and medium-sized enterprises) |
| CRCI | chambre régional de commerce et d'industrie (regional chamber of commerce) |
| CRIF | Conseil régional d'Île-de-France (Île-de-France regional council) |
| DATAR | Délégation à l'aménagement du territoire et à l'action régionale (the national regional development agency, established in the 1960s, in charge of national and regional planning policies) |
| DIRECCTE | Direction régionale des entreprises, de la concurrence, de la consommation, du travail et de l'emploi (regional directorate for enterprises, competition, consumption, labour and employment, depending on the regional prefecture) |
| DRIEA | Direction régionale et interdépartementale de l'équipement et de l'aménagement (regional directorate for infrastructure and planning, depending on the regional prefecture) |
| DREIF | Direction régionale de l'équipement d'Île-de-France (previous name of DRIEA) |
| DRIHL | Direction régionale et interdépartementale de l'hébergement et du logement (regional directorate of housing, depending on the regional prefecture) |
| DSU | Dotation de solidarité urbaine (urban solidarity grant; a financial equalization scheme at the regional level) |
| EDF | Électricité de France (national public company in charge of production and delivery of electricity) |
| EGT | Enquête générale des transports (national transport survey) |
| ENL | Enquête nationale de logement (national housing survey) |
| EPA | établissement public d'aménagement (public development corporation) |
| EPAD | Établissement public d'aménagement de la Défense (La Défense public development corporation) |
| EPCI | établissement public de coopération intercommunale (intermunicipal joint authority) |

| | |
|---|---|
| EPT | Établissement public territorial (the new EPCI covering the Métropole du Grand Paris [MGP]) |
| ERDF | European Regional Development Fund (one of the most important European Union structural funds) |
| FSRIF | Fonds de solidarité de la région Île-de-France (a financial equalization instrument between municipalities in Île-de-France) |
| GDF | Gaz de France |
| GHG | greenhouse gas |
| GPE | Grand Paris Express (the 200 km automatic metro intended to serve the Île-de-France area) |
| GPSO | Grand Paris Seine Ouest (an EPT of MGP) |
| HLM | habitat à loyer modéré (social housing) |
| IAU | Institut d'aménagement et d'urbanisme de la région Île-de-France (urban planning and development institute of the Île-de-France region) |
| IAURIF | Institut d'aménagement et d'urbanisme de la région Île-de-France (the previous name of the IAU) |
| IdF | Île-de-France |
| INSEE | Institut national de la statistique et des études économiques (national institute of statistics and economic studies) |
| (Loi) MAPTAM | Loi de modernisation de l'action publique territoriale et d'affirmation des métropoles (Modernization of Territorial Public Action and Strengthening of Metropolitan Areas Act) |
| MEDEF | Mouvement des entreprises de France (organization of national firms; the most important business organization at the national level) |
| MGP | Métropole du Grand Paris (Greater Paris metropolitan authority) |
| (Loi) NOTRe | Loi de nouvelle organisation territoriale de la République (New Territorial Organization of the Republic Act) |

| | |
|---|---|
| OMNIL | Observatoire de la mobilité en Île-de-France (an observatory of mobility in Île-de-France, depending on DRIEA) |
| PADOG | Plan d'aménagement et d'organisation générale de la région parisienne (the regional master plan of 1960) |
| PCF | Parti communiste français (the French Communist Party) |
| PDUIF | Plan de déplacements urbains d'Île-de-France (Île-de-France mobility plan) |
| Périphérique | Boulevard périphérique (the first ring road around the city of Paris) |
| PICE | Paris Île-de-France Capitale Économique (Greater Paris Investment Agency, a business association of big firms) |
| PLH | Plan local de l'habitat (local housing plan) |
| PLU | Plan local d'urbanisme (local land use plan) |
| PNRU | Plan national de rénovation urbaine (national urban renewal plan) |
| PRE | Paris region entreprises (the regional promotion agency) |
| PRIF | Préfecture de la région Île-de-France (the regional state administration) |
| PS | Parti socialiste (the French Socialist Party) |
| QPVs | quartiers prioritaires de la politique de la ville (the most deprived urban neighbourhoods, regarded as priority areas for policy for cities) |
| RATP | Régie autonome des transports parisiens (the major public transport operator of Île-de-France) |
| RER | Réseau Express Régional (regional express rail network) |
| SDAURP | Schéma d'aménagement et d'urbanisme de la région parisienne (the regional master plan of 1965) |
| SDF | sans domicile fixe (homeless people) |
| SDRIF | Schéma directeur de la région Île-de-France (Île-de-France master plan) |

| | |
|---|---|
| SGP | Société du Grand Paris (state company in charge of building the Grand Paris Express) |
| SNCF | Société nationale des chemins de fer (the national railway company) |
| SRDE | Schéma régional de développement économique |
| SRDEI | Schéma régional de développement économique et d'innovation |
| SRDEII | Stratégie régionale de développement économique, d'innovation et d'internationalisation |
| (Loi) SRU | Loi de solidarité et renouvellement urbain (Solidarity and Urban Renewal Act) |
| STIF | Syndicat des transports d'Île-de-France (regional public transport authority) |
| STP | Syndicat des transports parisiens (the previous name of the STIF) |
| WHO | World Health Organization |
| ZUP | zone à urbaniser en priorité (area to be developed as a priority; a planning instrument of the 1960s) |
| ZFU | zone franche urbaine (urban enterprise zone) |
| 75 | administrative number of the municipality and *département* of Paris |
| 77 | administrative number of the *département* of Seine-et-Marne |
| 78 | administrative number of the *département* of Yvelines |
| 91 | administrative number of the *département* of Essonne |
| 92 | administrative number of the *département* of Hauts-de-Seine |
| 93 | administrative number of the *département* of Seine-Saint-Denis |
| 94 | administrative number of the *département* of Val-de-Marne |
| 95 | administrative number of the *département* of Val-d'Oise |

# Introduction

The subject of this book is the Paris-Île-de-France region. Its first objective is to provide a relatively full account of the social, economic, political and spatial history of this area up to the present day, with a more precise description of the recent period, broadly since the year 2000. Its second goal is to look critically at the actions of the main protagonists, particularly the public actors, taking into account certain salient features of the history of this region and of the relations between the stakeholders. In this respect, the book takes the view that, despite the recent phenomena of globalization and decentralization, which have impacted and continue to affect Île-de-France and which in many ways contribute to the problems and challenges that this territory faces, the historical factors are crucial to an understanding of the present situation.

From this perspective, it is important to bear in mind several points that have had a long-term structural effect on the economic, social and political development of the region, both in the emergence and perception of the problems and challenges it faces, and in the behaviours and actions of the actors responsible for recognizing and resolving them. There are at least four such points to emphasize.

The first is the historical dominance that Paris and, more recently, Île-de-France have exercised over the rest of the country. This dominance takes many forms. It is demographic, in so far as Paris is by far France's most populous city and Île-de-France its most populous region. Unlike the countries that surround it, such as the United Kingdom, Germany, Italy and Spain, France's urban hierarchy is overwhelmingly dominated by Paris and its conurbation. The other big metropolitan regions, whether Lille, Lyon or Marseille, have populations of barely 2 million compared with six times this number in Île-de-France. The difference between London and Birmingham or Manchester, between Madrid and Barcelona, between Rome and Milan or Naples, and between Berlin and Hamburg or Frankfurt is markedly smaller. Second, this dominance is also economic, with an extremely high concentration of economic and research sectors in Île-de-France. The same is true in terms of culture, since Paris and, to a lesser degree, its region are home to the biggest museums, opera houses, exhibition spaces, conferences, sports facilities and other large infrastructures. Finally, Paris has been the political and administrative capital of France for several centuries. In this capacity, it enjoys a political and symbolic status to which no other city can aspire. This status, as we shall see, is a product of history and in particular of the process of state construction. It gives it a role apart, above France's other cities and population centres. At the national level, it has no rivals.

The second point concerns the role of the state in the construction and development of its capital and the surrounding region. France is well known internationally for its centralized political and administrative system, which in many ways invites comparison with so-called developmental states such as Japan and South Korea. Although France is not the only centralized state in Europe – countries such as the Netherlands and the United Kingdom are also centralized – it differs from them in having a powerful technical and administrative apparatus despite the process of decentralization, what is generally called the "Napoleonic model". This is particularly true of Île-de-France, because of its political and economic importance. As a result, the history of Paris is intimately connected with the history of the state, since central government is – as we shall see – omnipresent and very often in control of its development.

The third point relates to France's political culture, whereby the conduct of public affairs is almost exclusively a matter for the public authorities. This means that central and local government have primary responsibility for the enactment and management, development and implementation of public policies, and are perceived as the only legitimate entities in this role. Other actors, whether from the business sector or civil society, contribute at the discretion of the public authorities, at least as far as is apparent. Under these circumstances – and this is developed in Chapters 1 and 3 – it is central government that decides who can legitimately take part in the conduct of public affairs and on what conditions. As a result, over the centuries a neocorporatist system has developed in which the economic sector and civil society are stakeholders in governance through specific structures, established by the state, and therefore possess a monopoly in the representation of the interests they embody. This is notably the case for the chambers of commerce and industry, which in France are public institutions funded out of taxation, and legally represent the world of business. In this capacity, they are the privileged interlocutors of the public authorities. This system just briefly described certainly holds true for Île-de-France, as we shall see.

Finally, the relationships between all the actors, whether public or private, bear the stamp of often profound ideological divergences that have developed gradually over time. These differences have led to the sharp divisions that sustain the persistent conflicts that can be seen in perceptions of Île-de-France's problems and challenges and of the policies needed to tackle them. I outline their historical development in Chapter 2 and their current expression in the final two chapters. This situation raises a recurrent question about the governance of big metropolitan regions: the question of the construction of the collective actor (Lefèvre 2020).

Taken together, all these factors largely explain an aspect of Île-de-France that distinguishes it from most of the world's other big metropolitan regions in their relationship to globalization. Île-de-France seems to be following a trajectory that is slightly different, in particular from that of its big rivals, such as London or New York, in terms of perceptions and of how to respond to the current phase in the development of capitalism. Although issues of competitiveness and attractiveness are obviously present in the debate, they do not dominate it, and the problems of social and territorial inequalities, now combined with environmental questions, are at least equally salient. If this is the case, it is because – as we shall see in Chapters 5, 6 and 7 – they emanate from different coalitions of actors, of relatively equal strength, which draw their legitimacy and their resources from the history of the region.

This book consists of seven chapters. The first chapter gives a survey of the geographical, economic, social and cultural places of Île-de-France at the end of the second decade of the twenty-first century. It clarifies the geographical area that is discussed throughout the book, briefly presents the international dimension of this region and gives an overview of its system of governance, focusing on the presentation of the main players (the state, local governments and economic actors).

The second and third chapters examine the history of Paris and of Île-de-France. Chapter 2 looks at the spatial, demographic, economic and social aspects of the development of Île-de-France since the emergence of Paris at the beginning of our era. It is divided into three main periods: before the French Revolution of 1789; from the beginning of the nineteenth century to the Second World War; and the contemporary period. It describes the development and rise of this region, the factors that have contributed to its position among the modern world's premier regions. It also places special emphasis on the structural factors that will help to better understand and explain the problems and issues that Île-de-France faces at the present time.

Chapter 3 deals with the political dimension of the history of Paris and Île-de-France. It covers the same period as Chapter 2 up to 2001, when the region and the municipality of Paris were controlled by the left. It shows the importance of the state and of centralization in the development of Île-de-France, emphasizing the tensions that have existed between the national and local levels from the start. This makes it easier to understand both the importance of the decentralization that began in the early 1980s and the obstacles that this process has faced, and thereby to obtain a perspective on its impact.

Chapter 4 gives an overview of the economic transformations of Île-de-France. It shows the dominance of the region over the whole country as well as the emergence of a global metropolis. Focusing on the last two decades, it stresses the major aspects that make the Paris region unique with its own particular economic strengths and weaknesses.

The last three chapters cover the contemporary period, starting in 2000. Chapters 5 and 6 tackle the main problems affecting Île-de-France. Whereas Chapter 5 concentrates on identifying these problems, defining their scale and analysing them both quantitatively and qualitatively, Chapter 6 describes the main policies implemented in trying to resolve them. Problems and policies are then presented in terms of the tensions between two priorities: on the one side, making Île-de-France more competitive and attractive; on the other, countering social and territorial inequalities. Chapter 6 also emphasizes the limitations and difficulties in assessing these policies and their relative failure in the light of the persistence, or even exacerbation, of the problems the region faces.

Finally, Chapter 7 looks at the system of governance of Paris-Île-de-France. Drawing on the historical characteristics previously described in Chapter 3, it shows their continuing relevance today, analysing the changes in the relations between political forces, institutions, the local authorities and central government. The governance of Île-de-France is approached in particular through the study of large infrastructure projects, big urban development projects and strategic planning.

The book ends with a conclusion that highlights both the similarities and the singularities of Île-de-France in a comparison with other big metropolitan regions around the world.

# 1

# Paris and Île-de-France

The aim of this chapter is to briefly present the Île-de-France region at the end of the decade 2010–20 and to set out the politico-institutional framework within which the actors and the ongoing public policies operate. First, however, I need to clearly define the territory that we are discussing.

There is heated debate about the geographical boundaries of the Paris metropolis, because there is a strong political dimension to these boundaries – as will be evident throughout this book. That is why, before developing our analysis of France's leading metropolitan region, it will be helpful to briefly specify its contours and to explain the choice of our territory of study. The Institut national de la statistique et des études économiques (INSEE) defines the functional territory of French cities through the notion of the "urban area" (*aire urbaine*), which it defines as

> all the municipalities forming an integral whole without enclaves, consisting of an urban centre (urban unit providing at least 1,500 jobs) and of so-called unipolar municipalities, i.e. municipalities in which more than 40 per cent of the population works in that urban centre or in another municipality already monopolized by that urban centre.

Under this definition, the Paris urban area comprises almost 12.5 million inhabitants distributed across some 1,800 municipalities and an area of land of a little more than 17,000 sq. km. It extends over almost the entire Île-de-France region (98.8 per cent of municipalities) and over a very small part of the seven *départements* surrounding it.

In this book, the choice is to focus almost exclusively on the Île-de-France region, thus treating it as equivalent to the Paris urban area. The reasons for this choice are, first, that there is a fairly good match between the territory of Île-de-France and the Paris urban area (see Map 1.1) but, above all,

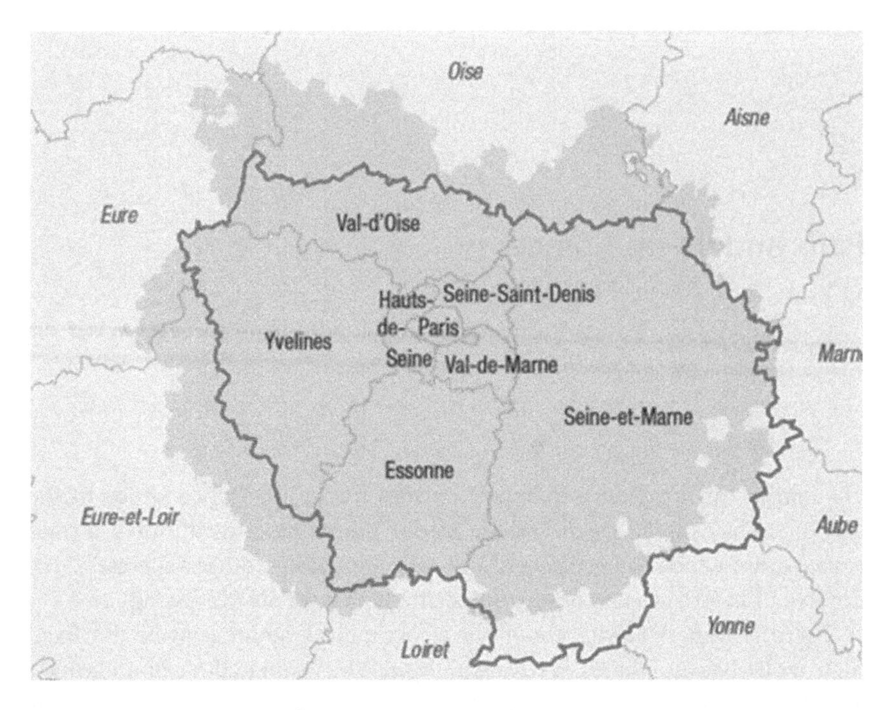


**Map 1.1** Paris urban area and Île-de-France region (with the *départements*)

because Île-de-France is the scale used by the authorities – and, in particular, by the government – in applying its policies, and it corresponds to the scope of the decision-making and consultative structures not only of the political institutions but also of the economic community and civil society. In other words, it is the yardstick territory and makes sense for all the actors concerned with the smooth operation and development of the Paris metropolis.

## Population, society and economy of Île-de-France today

As of 2019 the population of Île-de-France was some 12.3 million people. They represent 19 per cent of the national population in a space of 12,000 sq. km – i.e. only 2 per cent of the area of the country. The core of the territory, the most built-up, most populous and densest part, is home to some 6.8 million people, namely 56 per cent of the population of Île-de-France in an area of only 760 sq. km – in other words, in just over 6 per cent of the land area of the region. It corresponds to what is called the "inner ring", by contrast with the "outer ring", which is much less densely populated and more rural, especially

**Table 1.1** Population of the *départements* of Île-de-France, 2019

| | Surface area (sq. km) | Population | Population density (pers/sq. km) |
|---|---|---|---|
| Paris | 105 | 2,148,300 | 20,460 |
| Seine-et-Marne | 5,915 | 1,423,600 | 241 |
| Yvelines | 2,284 | 1,448,600 | 634 |
| Essonne | 1,804 | 1,319,400 | 731 |
| Hauts-de-Seine | 176 | 1,613,800 | 9,169 |
| Seine-Saint-Denis | 236 | 1,670,100 | 7,077 |
| Val-de-Marne | 245 | 1,406,000 | 5,739 |
| Val-d'Oise | 1,246 | 1,248,400 | 1002 |
| Île-de-France | 12,012 | 12,278,210 | 1,022 |

*Source*: CCI Paris Île-de-France, Institut Paris Région & INSEE Île-de-France (2020).

in its southern and eastern parts. In other words, just 27 per cent of Île-de-France consists of built-up areas, as against 48 per cent farmland and 24 per cent natural zones.

Île-de-France is made up of eight *départements*. Broadly, four of them (Paris, Val-de-Marne, Hauts-de-Seine and Seine-Saint-Denis) represent the inner ring and four others (Essonne, Yvelines, Val-d'Oise and Seine-et-Marne) the outer ring (see Map 1.1).

The city of Paris, which was both a municipality and a *département* until 2018,[1] has a population of slightly under 2.2 million in an area of 105 sq. km. It is the most heavily populated *département*. With a density of 20,460 people per square kilometre, it is one of the world's densest municipalities (New York: 7,100; Tokyo: 6,300; London 5,600). It is by far the largest municipality. The other "big" municipalities in the region range in population size around just 100,000 inhabitants (Boulogne: 119,000; Saint-Denis: 111,000; Argenteuil: 108,000; Montreuil: 108,000; Nanterre: 94,000).

In social terms, Île-de-France is characterized by an apparently paradoxical situation that can be found in many big world cities. It is a rich region where poor populations nevertheless constitute a large proportion of its inhabitants. So, with disposable per capita income of some €24,190 in 2017, it leads the way among the regions of France, where the national average stands at €21,415, and €19,378 excluding the Île-de-France region (INSEE). Almost 64 per cent of the region's inhabitants pay income tax, as compared with only 52 per cent nationwide. On the other hand, poverty levels there are higher, affecting

1. Since February 2018 Paris has become a new local authority with the merger of the municipality and the *département* and a few additional responsibilities.

almost 15.3 per cent of the population in 2017, as compared with only 14.5 per cent for the country as a whole.

With respect to income, jobs and qualifications, therefore, there are sharp inequalities – both social and territorial – in Île-de-France, and notably a substantial disparity between the east and west of the region (see Chapter 2).

In terms of economic power, Île-de-France is by far France's leading region. With a GDP of almost €710 billion in 2018 (Choose Paris Region 2020), it accounts for almost a third (31.1 per cent) of national wealth. Its per capita GDP is €58,300, well above the French national average of €32,900. It is France's richest region. Its economy has shifted sharply towards services in recent decades, with almost 87 per cent of added value coming from the service sector (much more than the national average), in this respect following the trend of most of the world's other metropolises. It retains a fairly dynamic industrial sector, however, which accounts for about 9 per cent of regional GDP (see Chapter 4).

This economy is not evenly spread across the region, however. There is a sharp disparity between the east and west of the region, with jobs concentrated in Paris and in Hauts-de-Seine, which together provided almost a half of the region's employment in 2018, confirming a trend that goes back several decades (see Chapter 2). This situation causes a recurrent problem for the development of the region in so far as the gap between the location of the jobs (more to the west) and the location of populations (more to the east) is steadily growing, a problem we shall return to in Chapters 5, 6 and 7.

Île-de-France is one of the world's most powerful metropolitan areas, whose economic, political, scientific and cultural influence owes more and more to its integration into the global community (see Chapter 4). As such, it is the only French global city.

## The politico-institutional organization of Île-de-France

In order to manage this global metropolis, Île-de-France possesses a complex politico-institutional structure, to which we shall return in the chapters that follow. In this chapter, the objective is to present the main institutions and political players, as well as the major economic and social actors who participate in the governance of the region. How they interact will be analysed in subsequent chapters.

First, central government has a strong presence, much more so than in France's other big cities, notably because its territory encompasses Paris, the national capital. The presence of central government is revealed first of all through its administration, both central administration with the ministries,

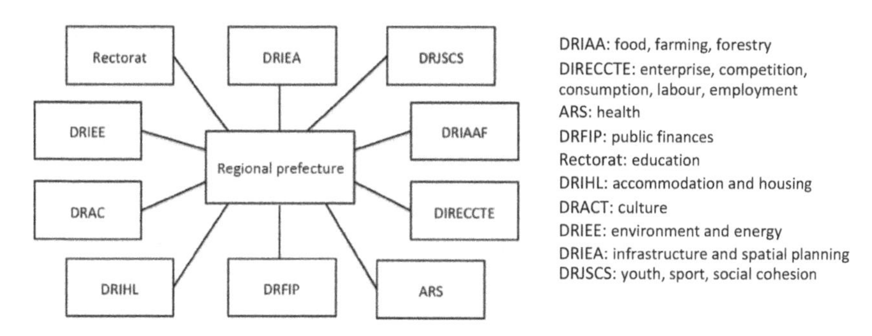


**Figure 1.1** The main administrative directorates of the regional prefecture of Île-de-France

but also at local level with a regional prefecture and seven prefectures of *départements*. The prefect of the region is also the prefect of Paris. The regional prefecture employs several thousand civil servants who are spread across some ten regional directorates, notably covering agriculture and food, infrastructure and spatial planning (see organization chart in Figure 1.1), social cohesion, culture, the economy and employment, the environment and energy, education, housing, health, etc. Some of these directorates also exist at the level of the *départements*. This local administration of the state is very powerful. It is in charge of implementing state policies, monitoring state monies and subsidies to local authorities. It is also significantly involved in local policies; for instance, the regional master plan is elaborated in parallel by the regional council and the regional prefecture.

In addition to the regional prefecture and its directorates, the state is present through the Préfecture de police de l'agglomération parisienne, which is in charge of the policing and security of the 6.8 million people of the inner ring. Established in 1800 on the sole territory of the Paris municipality, the *préfecture*'s jurisdiction was extended to encompass the whole inner ring in 2009. It is composed of about 44,000 staff, including some 25,500 police and 8,400 firefighters.

In addition, central government is present through its control over many public institutions, agencies and enterprises, mainly in the fields of energy, transportation, communications and spatial planning. Its presence is also felt as the main landowner through several public entities, such as the national railways (SNCF) and the army. Here again, we will return to these different structures in the course of the book. The state is therefore a powerful and essential player in the governance of Île-de-France.

For their part, the local authorities are represented by the region, the *départements*, and the municipalities. The region, established in 1982 by the most important laws on decentralization, has a deliberative body, the regional council, elected by direct universal suffrage under proportional representation with a majority bonus system. The regional executive (the president and the vice-presidents) is elected by the council from the regional councillors. The political situation means that the majority on the council, as on the executive, arises from party coalitions. The region has a budget of some €5 billion. Its powers cover public transport, the management of *lycées* (secondary schools that teach up to university), vocational training, planning, the environment and economic development. It also manages European structural funds. To carry out its responsibilities, it has some 10,000 staff, slightly over 8,000 of them assigned to the *lycées* alone.

Île-de-France is also made up of eight *départements* (see Map 1.1), among which Paris is both a municipality and a *département* – or, at least, was until 2018 (see footnote 1). Paris is the biggest of all of them, in demographic (as we have seen) and economic terms (see also Chapter 2) and for its financial power and its expertise. It has a budget of some €10 billion and a workforce of around 40,000. The other two largest *départements* are Hauts-de-Seine and Seine-Saint-Denis, with budgets of around €2 billion. The *départements* are mainly responsible for social affairs and for the *collèges* (secondary schools that teach up to *lycée* level).

Finally, at local level, there are no fewer than 1,281 municipalities, including the largest, Paris. In France, the municipalities have a deliberative body, the municipal council, elected by direct universal suffrage under proportional representation with a majority bonus system. The mayor is elected by and from within the municipal council. He or she is generally the leading candidate from the party that won the elections. In Paris, the executive (the mayor and his or her deputies) is a product of coalitions, either of the right or the left. In the hands of the right until 2001, Paris has since been led by a left-wing coalition, and the mayor is a member of the Socialist Party. The strength of the municipalities lies in their legitimacy thanks to their long existence and their numerous powers, which have been reinforced by decentralization; urban planning, housing, and social affairs are among the most important.

The politico-institutional organization of Île-de-France is thus characterized by significant fragmentation. This fragmentation is partially offset by the cooperation between local authorities, and particularly by intermunicipal cooperation. This has led to the creation of what have come to be called établissements publics de coopération intercommunale (EPCIs: public corporations of intermunicipal cooperation), which can take different legal and political forms, but are in some cases highly integrated (with municipalities, for example, sharing powers, resources and significant taxation). There are several dozen of them in Île-de-France, some very powerful. The most recent is the Métropole du Grand Paris (MGP: Greater Paris metropolitan authority), created in 2014 in the central part of Île-de-France. We shall return to intermunicipal cooperation, and particularly to the Métropole du Grand Paris, in the final chapter, on governance, because the creation of this public institution had the effect of to some extent crystallizing the debates and conflicts between the state and local governments and between public and private actors in Île-de-France.

The political system is controlled by highly ideological parties, in which no single party is able to win a majority. Consequently, executive powers, be it at the municipal (Paris), *départemental* or regional level, are the result of coalitions, as we will see in Chapter 7. On the right, two political parties represent the liberal and Gaullist (slightly more state interventionist) positions. On the left, the main parties are the Socialist Party and the Greens. The Communist Party, once very strong (see Chapter 3), is today practically insignificant, except in certain bastions such as the Val-de-Marne *département* or several municipalities of Seine-Saint-Denis. The far right is represented by the National Front, which so far remains very weak in Paris (taking 6 per cent of the vote in 2014 but less than 2 per cent in 2020) while progressing at the Île-de-France level (about 10 per cent of votes in 2010 but 18 per cent in 2015).

## Economic players

### *The neocorporatist system*

France's political culture prefers public affairs to be conducted almost exclusively by the public authorities. This means that central and local government have primary responsibility for the enactment and management, development and implementation of public policies, and are perceived as the only legitimate entities in this role. Other actors, whether from the business sector or civil society, contribute at the discretion of the public authorities, at least as far as is apparent. Under these circumstances – and this will be developed in Chapter 3 – it is central government that decides who can legitimately take part in the conduct of public affairs and on what conditions. As a result, over the centuries a neocorporatist system has developed in which the economic sector and civil society are stakeholders in governance through specific structures, established by the state, and therefore possess a monopoly in the representation of the interests they embody. This is notably the case for the chambers of commerce and industry, which in France are public institutions funded out of taxation, and legally represent the world of business. In this capacity, they are the privileged interlocutors of the public authorities.

In Île-de-France, this neocorporatist system is illustrated by two main types of institutions: chambers of commerce and the Conseil économique, social et environnemental régional (CESER: regional economic, social and environmental council).

There are eight chambres de commerce et industrie (CCIs) in the Île-de-France (one for each *département*), coming under the umbrella of the regional chamber of commerce (CCI Paris Île-de-France). By law, all enterprises must join a chamber. As a consequence, the CCI Paris Île-de-France has a membership of about 840,000 firms. It had a budget of about €400 million in 2019 and employed more than 3,000 people.

Among the eight chambers, the most important is the Chambre de commerce et d'industrie de Paris (CCIP), which represents about 250,000 enterprises. As the only legal entity of business representation in its territory, it is in charge of the commercial register, but it has also many more competences, mainly in professional training (about half its staff work in its 17 professional schools). In addition, it manages congress centres and participates in the elaboration of most policies regarding economic development and planning. It is a *de jure* member of all councils and committees in charge of those policies, and its seats on these are mandatory (but advisory), as we will see in Chapter 7.

Chambers of commerce and industry are run by assemblies representing their three economic sectors: commerce, industry and services. These assemblies elect their boards, which are generally composed of representatives from the major business organizations (see below). In general, and in Île-de-France more particularly because of its economic importance, presidents of CCIs are important business officials. The president of the regional chamber, CCI Paris Île-de-France, has direct access to the most important political leaders, including ministers. It is very common for the CCI to host international events and official dinners when foreign heads of state visit Paris.

The CESER is the second regional assembly (after the regional council). CESERs were established by the first decentralization act of 1982 in all regions. They are composed of representatives from business and social associations. Their membership comprises three categories of organizations on an equal basis: enterprises, trade unions and the third sector. CESER Île-de-France is one of them. It represents regional civil society.

CESER Île-de-France is an advisory council, but most of its "advice" is mandatory. For instance, it must give advice on the regional budget and on most of the regional policies and official documents, such as the regional masterplan or the regional economic strategy (see Chapter 7). Although it claims to represent regional civil society, its role in the governance of the region is weak, however, and business voices are better expressed by business organizations.

### *Major business organizations*

In Île-de-France, enterprises are represented by two main business organizations: the Confédération des petites et moyennes entreprises (CPME: confederation of small and medium size enterprises) and the Mouvement des entreprises de France (MEDEF: movement of the enterprises of France), which are also the two major organizations at the national level. These two organizations are heavily represented in the neocorporatist system, since both occupy significant positions on the boards of CCIs and CESER. As an example, over the last 20 years most CESER presidents have been members of MEDEF and most high executives of CCIs either members of CPME or MEDEF. They are also important players in the various national and regional structures dealing with social and economic issues (pensions committees, commercial courts, labour courts, etc.).

MEDEF and CPME are organized on both a territorial basis and a sectoral basis. Thus, each has a regional general structure (CPME Île-de-France; MEDEF Île-de-France) and several regional structures by sector (chemical industry, construction, etc.). The sectoral organizations are the powerful ones, the regional general structures serving more as a voice to defend business positions on national and regional issues, such as transport problems, housing or tourism (see Chapter 7). MEDEF also has territorial structures in each of the eight *départements* of the region. Usually CPME represents the small- and medium-sized firms whereas the members of MEDEF are bigger firms.

### *Other economic players*

Beside the major business associations, the Île-de-France economic landscape contains many more organizations, some with significant influence. In this myriad of structures (local business groups, big firms, banks, utilities companies, clubs, think tanks, etc.) one stands apart: the Paris Île-de-France Capitale Économique (PICE), which calls itself the Greater Paris Investment Agency on its English-language website.

PICE was created in the 1990s by the Paris chamber of commerce but has gradually become more independent from its founder. Today it represents about 100 economic players coming from the private as well as the public spheres. PICE members are big public or private enterprises (public and private banks such as Caisse des Dépôts or BNP Paribas; big utilities companies such as Veolia – the second largest utilities company in the world; realtors and builders such as Bouygues and Vinci – among the top firms in this sector in the world; big consulting agencies, such as EY, Accenture and PWC; and large public companies in the mobility and transport sector, such as Air France, RATP, etc.).

PICE acts as a lobbyist and promotional agency of the Paris region at the international level. It organizes road shows for French firms in various cities all over the world (Shanghai, Dubai, Seoul, Singapore, New York, Moscow), welcomes international delegations and provides them with information regarding investment opportunities in the region and funds and disseminates comparative studies and international benchmarks to assess Greater Paris's ranking in the competition between global cities. It also tries to influence national and regional decision-makers regarding economic policies in Île-de-France through reports and selective forums.

As a conclusion to this chapter, some major features of the Île-de-France are sketched out that I will develop in the subsequent chapters. First, the role and place of the state in decision-making and public policy-making is important. Second, the system of players (in the public sector as well as in the private) is very much fragmented but also highly conflictual. Finally, Paris is a political capital, and, over the centuries and particularly today, has become a great world metropolis. Like its peers, it is characterized by a combination of economic development and social and territorial inequalities. The following chapters, which form the core of the book, show how this metropolis grew up and how the problems and challenges it has faced have been dealt with by the regional actors. The emphasis will be placed on their successes, their failures, and the reasons behind them.

# 2

# Social, economic and spatial history of the Île-de-France metropolis

The site of the modern Paris has been inhabited since the Stone Age, the period between around 4000 and 3000 BC. In the third century before our era various tribes – in particular the Parisii – settled in a place called Lutetia. Conquered by Julius Caesar, it then became an important base for the maintenance of the Roman Empire. In the fourth century Lutetia was declared a bishopric and renamed Paris. Historians estimate the population of Paris at around 10,000 at this time.

Paris would gradually go on to become the capital of the kingdom. In the sixth century Clovis, king of the Franks, settled there and made it his royal seat. He was followed by the Capetians, who proclaimed themselves dukes of France and kings of Paris. At the end of the eleventh century Philippe Auguste developed his capital and built the first fortified wall. By then Paris had between 25,000 and 50,000 inhabitants.

The term "Île-de-France" appeared in the tenth century, in reference to the royal domain. Its primary meaning remains uncertain. Sometimes it referred to the piece of land between the rivers Marne, Oise and Seine. At other times it was used in reference to Liddle France, "Little France" in the Frankish language; in other words, the area where the Franks had their roots in Gaul.

In the Middle Ages Paris enjoyed significant cultural and intellectual renown, notably in the fields of theology and the arts and in particular through the University of Paris, whose most prestigious college – the Sorbonne – was built in 1253. A few centuries later François I added the humanities and the exact sciences and created the Collège de France. Breaking with his Capetian predecessors, who had established their domains in the Val de Loire, François I settled in Paris in 1528, thereby restoring the city's status as capital of the kingdom of France. Some 150 years later, however, King Louis XIV quit Paris in the aftermath of the Fronde,[1] establishing himself in his new palace in Versailles, which would remain the seat of national political power until the French Revolution, a century later.

In the sixteenth century Paris was already a big city, with a population estimated at around 300,000. Its demographic growth was largely a result of immigration from the rest of France, the so-called "Province", because the natural rate was negative. During the seventeenth century the nucleus of the city around Île de la Cité became urbanized, as did the area of Invalides. The historic section of the city around the Marais gradually declined, becoming home to the lowest and poorest classes, while the first suburbs (Saint Germain, Saint Honoré) were built and developed fine aristocratic homes.

The eighteenth century saw a continuation of the demographic and economic expansion of Paris. On the eve of the revolution the capital boasted a population of some 650,000. One of Europe's biggest cities, alongside London and Vienna, it was also an important intellectual centre, open to new thinking and, notably, the cradle of the ideas of the philosophers and Encyclopedists.

## Paris Île-de-France: the birth of a metropolitan region, 1800–1945

### *Demographic and suburban expansion*

The French Revolution emptied Paris of its inhabitants. The first official census carried out in 1801 indicates a loss of some 100,000 inhabitants, leaving a population of 547,000. As a whole, however, Île-de-France was home to more than 1.3 million people.

As can be seen in Table 2.1, in 150 years the population of Île-de-France increased fivefold, as did that of Paris. The numbers in the inner city increased remarkably throughout this period, but the main increase, which took place between 1851 and 1881, is primarily explained by the geographical expansion of the municipal territory. In 1860 Paris annexed the areas that fell between the Thiers wall (see Map 2.1), built between 1841 and 1844, and the Fermiers Généraux wall, built just before the revolution (Grenelle, Belleville, Vaugirard), and parts of several suburban communities, such as Aubervilliers, Bagnolet, Clichy, Issy-les-Moulineaux and Ivry. The number of *arrondissements* in the city grew from 12 to 20.

1. The Fronde was a period of civil war in which the nobility came into conflict with the king. It took place between 1648 and 1653.

**Table 2.1** Demographic trends for Paris and Île-de-France, 1801–1946 (in millions)

| | 1801 | 1851 | 1881 | 1901 | 1921 | 1946 |
|---|---|---|---|---|---|---|
| Paris | 0.547 | 1.053 | 2.269 | 2.714 | 2.906 | 2.725 |
| Île-de-France | 1.353 | 2.239 | 3.726 | 4.735 | 5.682 | 6.597 |
| Paris/Île-de-France (%) | 40 | 47 | 61 | 57 | 51 | 41 |

*Sources*: INSEE, IAURIF, Ville de Paris.

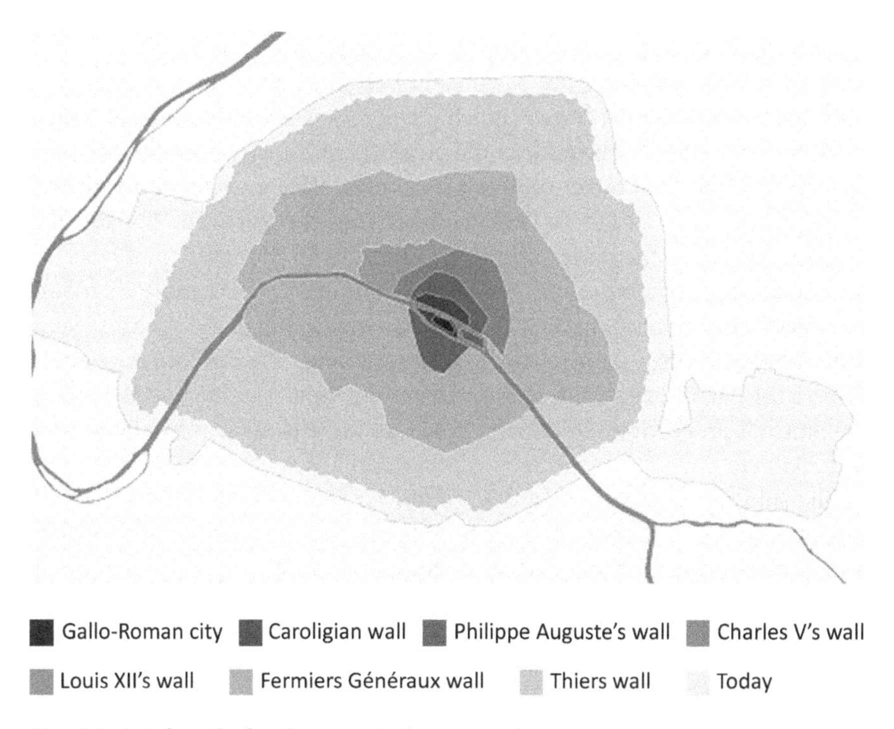


**Map 2.1** Paris from the fourth century to the present day

By the beginning of the twentieth century, therefore, Paris had become the third most populous city in the Western world, behind London (7.2 million) and New York (4.8 million). Demographic growth in Paris and Île-de-France came first from immigration from the provinces, mainly the north, Brittany and the Auvergne. Indeed, the beginnings of industrialization, notably with textiles such as cotton, attracted a working-class population that, from 1830, began to settle in the centre of Paris, in miserable living conditions. During the Second Empire (1852–70), migratory flows increased with the acceleration of the industrial revolution. It was also this period that saw the beginnings of immigration from abroad (Lillo *et al.* 2009). Whereas, during the revolution, the foreign population had fallen by some 3 to 5 per cent (Lillo *et al.* 2009), it increased significantly from the middle of the nineteenth century onwards. From the early twentieth century these essentially economic migrants were joined by populations of refugees, from Spain, Morocco, Algeria and Indochina in the fallout from the First World War, from the Armenian genocide of 1915 and 1916, or from the Russian Revolution of 1917; then, in the interwar period, they were followed by political refugees from the Italian, German, Portuguese and Spanish dictatorships, who came to settle in France, and in many cases in the Paris region.

Until 1870 Île-de-France was mainly a rural area with Paris at its centre, and a few big towns such as Meaux, Melun and Versailles. The suburban phenomenon began with Baron Haussmann's big projects, which drove part of Paris's working-class population towards the outskirts of the city: first the external *arrondissements*, then the current inner suburbs. This movement intensified in the pre-war period (1880–1914) and between the wars. The Italians, for example, settled in the inner suburbs in Saint-Denis, Montreuil and Nogent, the Russians in Alfortville and Issy-les-Moulineaux. In 1931 more than half the 100,000 Italians and the 30,000 Spaniards were living in the suburbs (Lillo *et al.* 2009). Although some refugees and immigrants crowded into the central districts of Paris, such as the Marais, Faubourg Saint Antoine and Belleville, a significant proportion settled in towns close to Paris, such as Boulogne and Aubervilliers.

The suburbs were not just a destination for the working classes and foreign immigrants, however. Some parts were also vacation areas for the wealthy middle classes, such as Maisons-Laffitte, built in the 1830s, or Le Vésinet, which came into existence at the beginning of the Second Empire.

### *Industrialization*

In the course of the nineteenth century Paris would become France's biggest industrial centre. Industrialization began in 1830, but was mainly confined to the main city and its centre. Under the Second Empire, for example, between 1860 and 1872 the working-class population increased by almost 20 per cent (Larroque & Jigaudon 1980). Yet it was also in this period that companies began an initial drift towards the outer boulevards of the capital. In the 1850s and 1860s the big polluting industries (chemicals, foundries) moved to the edges of Paris.

From the 1870s onwards the deindustrialization of inner Paris would accelerate. First, the textile firms and traditional industries left Paris for the suburbs. As a result, the capital, which was home to 489 big firms in these sectors in 1872, housed only 307 by 1914 (Marchand 1993). In the early twentieth century heavy industry, even its most modern sectors, definitively left the city centre, and Paris became a city dedicated to services. The only significant "industries" that remained in the capital (e.g. clothing and the graphic arts) were more like craft activities than genuine industry.

By 1914 Paris was free of essential but highly space-intensive functions; warehouses, prisons, marshalling yards, etc. had moved to the suburbs. The south was mainly home to the chemicals industries, the north to heavy industries such as machinery, and Seine-Saint-Denis to gas plants and glassworks. With the economic recovery at the end of the nineteenth century, the northern and western suburbs became centres for the creation of cutting-edge firms (machinery, cars, aeronautics, electrical equipment, energy). In the words of Pierre Merlin (1982), it might be said that "the formation of the suburbs up to the beginning of the twentieth century was linked with the location of jobs". Nevertheless, although Paris lost much of its industry, a functional differentiation was already apparent, since companies generally maintained their head offices in the capital while locating their production plants in the suburbs. Before 1914, however, the suburbs remained primarily rural and agricultural, with significant market garden production and forests. Industrialization mainly took place in the inner suburbs, as well as in big towns (Meaux, Melun, etc.) further out, which became home to some of these industries.

In this simultaneously geographical and economic process, the railways played an essential role. First, Paris's position as the hub of rail development partly explains the city's growth, since the radiating national network with Paris at its centre considerably reinforced the attractiveness of the capital and its hinterland. Second, industries essentially settled along communication routes, first rivers and roads, then railway tracks, which developed rapidly from the middle of the nineteenth century and generated suburbanization in a radial or glove pattern. After the construction of the big Paris stations, which began with Gare Saint-Lazare in 1837, it was the suburban stations that proliferated from the early days of the Third Republic, broadly in the last third of the nineteenth century. People followed, settling outside the capital in areas that were further from the centre but served by the railway. They avoided the industrial inner suburbs, and the wealthiest moved to areas that were still rural, such as Saint Quentin, Versailles or Sceaux. As a result, some zones – such as the banks of the Seine and the north (the northern suburbs became the region's main industrial centre, and would remain so until 1950) – became industrial, while others became residential.

Industrialization continued after the First World War. With the war, the factories – in particular in metallurgy – were converted to armaments production. Between 1906 and 1921 the numbers working in this sector doubled, from 165,000 to 330,000 (anon. 1960). After the war these factories reconverted, especially in the automobile industry, which already employed more than 100,000 people in 1931. Sectors such as aeronautics and radio-electronics also developed, however. In the interwar period Parisian industry grew more rapidly than French industry overall, and Paris was undoubtedly the country's leading industrial centre.

### *The first planning policies*

The best-known episode of public intervention in Paris in the nineteenth century is of course the work of Baron Haussmann, prefect of La Seine under the Second Empire. This covered almost 20 years between 1852 and 1870 and almost exclusively affected inner Paris, although the latter grew significantly with the annexation of 1860 (see above and Chapter 3). Haussmann's effort was colossal and encompassed urban utilities in addition to spatial development, housing, monuments, etc. The big projects began in 1852. Haussmann opened up the big boulevards, Saint Germain, Saint Michel, Sébastopol or Port Royal and Voltaire. It was his idea to link "Louis-Philippe's stations", so called because they were built during the latter's reign (Gare du Nord in 1846, Gare de Lyon in 1847 and 1855, Gare d'Austerlitz in 1840). He also undertook the construction of sewerage and water systems, as well as public amenities and monuments such as les Halles, neighbourhood markets, the Opéra, theatres (Chatelet and Théâtre de la Ville) and big parks (Montsouris, Buttes-Chaumont) and neighbourhood squares.

However one views Haussmann's intervention, it profoundly altered Paris. The work involved large-scale demolition and had the effect of driving working-class populations towards the outskirts of the city, mainly to the north and to the east, while the wealthier classes opted for the western *arrondissements*. The result was an increase in the polarization between east and west (Marchand 1993), which continues to this day.

The development of the suburbs that took place at the end of the nineteenth century was anarchic and, notably, had the effect of introducing a cultural and moral divide between the central city and its periphery. For Paris, the word "suburb" was pejorative, because it represented the zones inhabited by populations perceived as "backward". Paris would feel a certain contempt for these surrounding areas, and the suburbs would grow in indifference and anarchy (Marchand 1993). A symptom of this divide was the planning and construction of the Metro: when the first line was inaugurated in 1900, it stopped at the municipal boundaries of the central city. The suburbs continued to grow anarchically in the early twentieth century, and the phenomenon of the "ill-housed", the multitude of housing estates built by the private sector with no public transport provision and a perilous shortage of services, is the best-known illustration (Merlin 1982). Between 1920 and 1930, for example, 15,000 hectares of such housing estates – i.e. twice the surface area of Paris – were produced; others sprung up often in industrial towns (Aubervilliers, Aulnay, Blanc-Mesnil, Boulogne-Billancourt) from the 1930s up to the Second World War. The same period saw the anarchic development of detached housing.

The authorities only really began to think about the suburbs after the First World War, by which time their development was already well advanced. Ad hoc operations were thus conducted for social purposes, such as the construction of *habitations bon marché* (HBMs: low-cost dwellings). Eighty of these were built in the 1930s, mainly rented accommodation primarily for working-class populations. Likewise, some 15 garden cities sprang up between 1928 and 1934, with the aim of reducing population density in Paris. They were located at varying distances from the capital, in such places as Champigny, Gennevilliers, Stains and Suresnes.

The authorities, and central government in particular, intervened through planning, which would gradually be applied to the whole of the "Paris region". Just after the First World War, in 1919, an act was passed on the plans for the expansion and development of municipalities, with the aim of anticipating and managing their demographic growth. In 1928 a state body, the Comité supérieur d'aménagement et d'organisation générale de la région parisienne (CSAOGRP: higher committee for the development and general organization of the Paris region), was set up. For the first time a "Paris region" was created, not an administratively defined unit but a reflection of the need for spatial planning (Merlin 1982). The deliberations of this committee led to the passing of the 1932 act on the development of the Paris region, defined as encompassing a circle with a radius of 35 km from the centre of the capital. This territory – whose radius corresponds roughly to one hour of travel using the transport modes of the time – contained 657 municipalities covering an area of 3,800 sq. km.

The 1932 act established two types of plan: the municipal plans and a coordinating "regional plan". This, then, was how the first Paris region plan was prepared in 1934, called the Prost plan after its main author, architect and urbanist Henri Prost. It would not be ratified until 1939, on the eve of the Second World War, and would therefore be applied only partially. Malthusian in its inspiration, since its aim was mainly to contain the growth of the region by restricting land use and limiting construction plots, it assigned a big role to the construction of transport infrastructure, in particular roads and motorways. It provided for the building of five motorways, an orbital bypass and some 15 extensions of the Metro into the suburbs. Only the western motorway, the A13, would be built in 1941, as well as a few extensions to the Metro. The "Sceaux line", serving the southern suburbs, would also be modernized, a forerunner of the first line of the Réseau Express Régional (RER: regional express network), although this would not see the light of day until the late 1960s.

## *Paris, "City of Light"*

Paris, "City of Light", Paris, "City of Enlightenment"! The nickname given to the French capital covers two meanings: it was the city that came to be celebrated in the seventeenth century for its public lighting, probably the first in the world and the most extensive for a city of such a size; but it was also the city that is the symbol of the philosophy of the Enlightenment, which in the eyes of the whole world represents the legacy of the *Encyclopédie*, of the political philosophy of eighteenth-century intellectuals such as Montesquieu, Voltaire and Rousseau, and the universal values of democracy encapsulated in the rallying cry of "Liberty, equality, fraternity".

Although this was in many respects a myth, partly exported by the French Revolution to Europe in opposition to dictatorships and monarchies, or indeed to the United States of America (which France aided in its war of independence against Britain), it was a powerful myth, and from that time on Paris stood for the Enlightenment in international perceptions. Its status as the capital of one of the world's largest colonial empires, alongside the British Empire, favoured the spread of this myth, largely among the elites and upper classes.

It was at the turn of the twentieth century, however, that the myth of Paris really took flight. In the words of Bernard Marchand (1993: 206): "The French capital attached its name to the Belle Époque and dominated its rival, the other city, Vienna. After the eclipse of the war years, Paris recaptured this international primacy in 1920, further reinforced by the prestige of victory, and exercised it until the great crisis of 1931."

As Anthony Sutcliffe also recalls (quoted by Marchand 1993: 206), "Paris had become the main centre of the bubbling international contacts that characterized the end of the nineteenth and the beginning of the twentieth century." Indeed, it was in Paris that the big artistic movements were born or developed: in painting, with impressionism, fauvism, cubism and then surrealism; in architecture and in the applied arts, with art deco and art nouveau; in literature; in theatre; etc. Paris thus became a place where artists from all over the world came together, with American writers such as Sinclair Lewis, John Dos Passos, Scott Fitzgerald and Ernest Hemingway, or painters such as Braque, Picasso, Soutine, Chagall. For Henry Miller, who settled in Paris in the *Années folles*, the 1920s, "the Vavin–Raspail–Montparnasse crossroads is the navel of the world" (quoted by Marchand 1993: 224). And, of course, the myth also told of Paris as the world capital of entertainment and pleasure, with its famous cabarets, as well as of fashion and luxury.

Paris built and maintained this international renown by staging the big events of the era. First, the universal exhibitions, with the French capital hosting no fewer than five between 1889 and 1939. The universal exhibition of 1889 coincided with the construction of the Eiffel Tower, which became the symbol of the city all around the world. The exhibition attracted more than 32 million visitors and exhibits from 35 countries. In 1900 Paris hosted a new exhibition, emblematic of the Belle Époque, centred on cinema, the automobile and radio. More than 50 million visitors flocked to the capital to visit 45 national pavilions, manned by 45,000 exhibitors of every nationality. It was already the flagship city for international events, hosting 87 per cent of international conferences (Higonnet 2005). In 1925 it was the turn of the International Exhibition of Modern Decorative and Industrial Arts, visited by 6 million people. It was followed in 1931 by the International Colonial Exhibition; more limited in its subject, it nevertheless attracted no fewer than 8 million visitors. Finally, in 1937 Paris hosted the International Exposition of Art and Technology in Modern Life, attended by some 31 million visitors.

In 1900 Paris hosted the second Olympic Games of the modern era, after the Athens games of 1896. They took place over five months in parallel with the Universal Exhibition, with 24 nations taking part. Then the French capital hosted the 1924 Olympic Games, after doughty competition with Barcelona, Lyon, Prague and Rome. More than 3,000 athletes participated, representing 44 nations.

On the eve of the Second World War Paris was undoubtedly one of the world's premier capitals in terms of culture (art, lifestyles, new ideas, etc.). She was "the queen of the world", to adopt Bernard Marchand's expression (Marchand 1993: 205), because the world came to her. Nonetheless, this international renown was attached almost exclusively to the city in particular, and Île-de-France was either ignored or equated with the capital itself.

## Paris Île-de-France: the birth of a global city region, 1945–2020

### *Social and demographic trends*

#### Dynamic demographics, especially in the suburbs

The different population forecasts for Île-de-France established in the two decades that followed the Second World War describe a region that was expected to house a population of between 12 and 16 million in 2000. Like many other countries at the time, France was over-optimistic in its predictions, since Île-de-France has only today reached the lower estimate of 12 million.

As shown in Table 2.2, the population of Île-de-France reached just over 12 million in 2019, but it nevertheless recorded very strong demographic

**Table 2.2** Population of France and Île-de-France, 1946–2019 (in millions)

| | France | Île-de-France | Idf/France (%) |
|---|---|---|---|
| 1946 | 40.5 | 6.6 | 16.3 |
| 1954 | 42.8 | 7.3 | 17.0 |
| 1962 | 46.2 | 8.5 | 18.4 |
| 1968 | 49.8 | 9.2 | 18.5 |
| 1975 | 52.6 | 9.9 | 18.8 |
| 1982 | 54.3 | 10.0 | 18.4 |
| 1990 | 56.7 | 10.7 | 18.9 |
| 1999 | 59.0 | 10.9 | 18.5 |
| 2008 | 62.1 | 11.7 | 18.8 |
| 2019 | 64.6 | 12.3 | 19.0 |

*Source*: INSEE, various censuses.

growth during the period, albeit with fluctuations. Above all, this was much greater growth than the French average, since, whereas France added some 24 million inhabitants between 1946 and 2019, an increase of almost 60 per cent, Île-de-France experienced an 86 per cent rise over the same period.

Île-de-France's demographic growth is explained to begin with by a positive migratory balance. It is a region of high immigration, and maintained a positive exchange with the provinces until the 1960s. Things changed after that, with the region losing population to the rest of France between 1960 and 2000. Thanks to foreign immigration, it remained stable until the 1970s, but it is the natural balance (births/deaths) that explains the continuance of its population growth. The birth rate in Île-de-France was higher than elsewhere in the country because its population was younger. Over the period from 1975 to 2018 the proportion of people aged over 60 in Île-de-France increased only from about 15 per cent to 20 per cent, whereas across the country it grew from about 17 per cent to 26 per cent.

Nonetheless, population growth in Île-de-France did not remain steady throughout the second half of the twentieth century. It was greatest between 1946 and 1962, when France as a whole gained 6 million inhabitants, but Île-de-France accrued 1.9 million – in other words, almost a third of the national volume – on its own. As a result, its share in the national population increases from 16.3 per cent in 1946 to 18.4 per cent in 1962. Since then, this percentage has remained virtually stable, despite a slight resumption of growth in the 1980s. In 2019 Île-de-France accounted for about one-fifth of the French population.

Île-de-France's demographic expansion has not, of course, been uniformly distributed across the region. Thus, the period from 1945 to 2000 saw the central city lose some of its importance in the regional population to the suburbs, in particular the more remote suburbs.

Between 1960 and 2000 most of the demographic growth took place in the outer ring. The inner ring, which had accrued population in the previous decades, increased very little (by 760,000 inhabitants over the period [IAU 2001] and increased by only 200,000 between 1968 and 1999, rising from 3.8 million to 4 million inhabitants), and Paris steadily lost population over the period. The population of the outer ring, by contrast, grew by 2.1 million to 4.9 million, an increase of 133 per cent. Since then there has been a reverse trend, with a stronger increase in the inner ring, from 1999 to 2019 (17 per cent), than in the outer ring (12 per cent).

Although the population of the central city has fallen substantially since the Second World War, there have nevertheless been many variations. It was in the 1920s that Paris's population was at its highest, with 2.9 million people. Between 1920 and 1960 Paris lost only 100,000 people or so, but the more profound decline began in the 1960s, with the capital losing 500,000 inhabitants between 1962 and 1975, almost 20 per cent of its population. Between 1975 and 1990 it fell by almost 200,000. This decline is explained by the abundance of accommodation in the suburbs and terrible housing conditions, combined with a rent increase, in Paris (see below). This led to an increase in commuting, since the capital increasingly became a central nucleus of jobs relative to its population, with an unemployment rate that rose from 1.3 in 1954 to 1.7 in 1975. This loss of population also signified a real decline in the importance of the city, at least demographically, in the region as a whole, however. The figures tell the tale: whereas Paris contained almost 41 per cent of the population of Île-de-France at the end of the war, by the end of the twentieth century it accounted for scarcely 20 per cent, and the figure is only about 17 per cent today (see Table 2.3).

**Table 2.3** Population of Paris, inner ring and outer ring, 1946–2019 (in millions)

| | Île-de-France | Paris | Inner ring (IR)* | Outer ring (OR)* | Paris/Île-de-France (%) |
|---|---|---|---|---|---|
| 1946 | 6.6 | 2.7 | – | – | 40.9 |
| 1954 | 7.3 | 2.8 | – | – | 38.3 |
| 1962 | 8.5 | 2.8 | – | – | 32.9 |
| 1968 | 9.2 | 2.6 | 3.8 | 2.8 | 28.3 |
| 1975 | 9.9 | 2.3 | 3.9 | 3.6 | 23.2 |
| 1982 | 10.0 | 2.2 | 3.9 | 4.0 | 22.0 |
| 1990 | 10.7 | 2.1 | 4.0 | 4.5 | 19.6 |
| 1999 | 10.9 | 2.1 | 4.0 | 4.9 | 19.3 |
| 2008 | 11.7 | 2.2 | 4.3 | 5.2 | 18.8 |
| 2019 | 12.3 | 2.1 | 4.7 | 5.5 | 17.1 |

*Note*: * No data, because the *départements* in the IR and OR were not created until 1964.

*Source*: INSEE, censuses.

Demographically, Île-de-France is a dynamic region, as its population was only just over 10 million in 1982. Since then its population has increased steadily, at a rate of around 0.5 per cent a year. Although most *départements* display a degree of dynamism, three (Seine-Saint-Denis, Essonne and Seine-et-Marne) have accounted for two-thirds of the region's demographic growth in the last decade or so. In contrast, the city of Paris – which had experienced slight population growth since the beginning of the 2000s – began a steady demographic decline in 2015, falling from around 2.2 million people to 2.15 million today, close to its 1990 level.

Population growth in Île-de-France is, essentially, attributable to its natural surplus. Although it has a negative annual migratory balance (e.g. a loss of 48,000 people in 2016), reducing its population by around 0.4 per cent every year, its natural balance is steadily positive, with an average rise of slightly more than 100,000 people per year (INSEE). This is explained by the fact that Île-de-France is a young region, with high fertility and the lowest mortality rate in the country. For example, in 2019 the 20–39 age group was over-represented (27.8 per cent, compared with 23.5 per cent nationally) and the over-60s under-represented (about 20 per cent, as compared with about 26 per cent for metropolitan France as a whole).[2]

Like many Western metropolises, Paris grew through immigration: Today about four immigrants in ten live in Île-de-France. As it has developed, the region has become more cosmopolitan, in terms both of the number of foreigners living there and of their geographical and cultural diversity. The data from the INSEE censuses indicate that about 18 per cent of the population of Île-de-France consisted of immigrants in 2015, reflecting a steady rise, since this figure stood at only 13 per cent at the beginning of the 1980s (INSEE Île-de-France 2017a).[3]

2. Metropolitan France is defined as French territory located within Europe – i.e. excluding French possessions outside Europe, such as New Caledonia and French Guyana.
3. One must be cautious when presenting data on immigration in France, since the considered population may vary according to sources. Immigrants may encompass different populations: immigrants, foreign and foreign-born. Immigrants may be both non-French and French citizens (foreign-born having acquired French citizenship). The foreign population is composed of immigrants who are not French citizens and of foreign people born in France. The total foreign-born population is composed of immigrants plus French citizens born in another country. In 2019 France counted 6.7 million immigrants (4.2 million non-French and 2.5 million French citizens), 4.9 million of foreign status (4.2 million non-French immigrants and 700,000 foreign people born in France) and 8.4 million foreign-born (6.7 million immigrants plus 1.7 million French citizens born in another country) (INSEE n.d.).

Indeed, Île-de-France has always been the main destination for the immigrant population in France. After the war, industrialization initially brought immigrants from southern Europe (Italy, Spain, Portugal) and from North Africa, who were employed in construction and public works, metal works and the car industry. In particular, there was a boom in the Algerian population, with "the Renault's OSs".[4] Subsequently, the region continued to attract immigrants from a wider range of origins, in equally large numbers. By way of example, in the early 1970s the Renault factory in Boulogne-Billancourt employed 4,000 Algerians, 2,000 Moroccans and 900 Tunisians (i.e. 21.6 per cent of its 32,000 employees) (Lillo *et al.* 2009). With the crisis of 1973, the government decided to suspend immigration, but families continued to arrive under the "family reunification" policy, in particular from Morocco and sub-Saharan Africa, most of whom settled in Île-de-France. In consequence, although France's foreign population fell by 3.6 per cent between 1982 and 1990, it grew by 2.8 per cent in the region (Lillo *et al.* 2009). In 1982 33 per cent of the immigrant population settled in Île-de-France, but by 1990 it was 36 per cent. In 1990 14 per cent of the population of Île-de-France was foreign; ten years later this figure had risen to almost 15 per cent (IAU 2013a). As of 2013 immigrants accounted for 18.5 per cent of the Île-de-France population, double the national percentage (INSEE Île-de-France 2017a).

Although the proportion of immigrants in Île-de-France's population has been growing continuously for the last 40 years, their geographical origin has altered significantly (see Table 2.4). There has been a net decline in the number of Europeans, relative stagnation in the number of people from Maghreb and a

**Table 2.4** Immigrant population in Île-de-France, 1975–2016 (total population and geographical origin)

| | Immigrants (%) | Europe (%) | Maghreb (%) | Africa (%) | Rest of the world (%) |
|---|---|---|---|---|---|
| 1975 | 12.2 | | | | |
| 1982 | 13.3 | 50.0 | | 7.6 | |
| 1999 | 14.7 | 34.7 | 29.2 | 14.9 | 21.1 |
| 2010 | 17.7 | 27.7 | 29.4 | 19.7 | 23.2 |
| 2013 | 18.5 | 27.0 | 29.0 | 20.3 | 23.7 |
| 2016* | 13.9 | 31.3 | 25.2 | 21.8 | 21.6 |

*Note*: * This figure includes the foreign population and does not include immigrants who have acquired French citizenship (see footnote 3).

*Source*: INSEE, various censuses.

4. OSs = *ouvriers spécialisés*: skilled workers.

sharp rise in the populations originating in sub-Saharan Africa. Other statistics confirm the stagnation in the proportion of the North African population, but also the increasing size of the Asian population in the "Rest of the world" category. Asians thus accounted for 10.9 per cent of the immigrant population in 1982, but 17.4 per cent in 2006 (IAU 2013a) and 18 per cent in 2013 (INSEE Île-de-France 2017a).

The immigrant population is not uniformly spread across the whole region. Here, again, there are significant differences in the distribution of the immigrant population between the region's *départements* (see Table 2.5). Whereas in 2013 Seine-Saint-Denis and Paris were, respectively, host to 20 per cent and 21 per cent of the immigrant population, Yvelines and Hauts-de-Seine accounted for only 8 per cent and 12 per cent. In 2013 20 municipalities were home to 30 per cent of the immigrant population, which was concentrated in Seine-Saint-Denis, in the north of Hauts-de-Seine and in a few municipalities in the outer ring (e.g. Les Mureaux, Mantes-la-Jolie).

In the 1950s and 1960s immigrants settled in the peripheral districts of eastern Paris and at the gates of the capital in shanty towns and slums, then in the social housing estates of peripheral municipalities such as Clichy and Sarcelles, or near the companies where they worked, in Argenteuil, Flins, Les Mureaux. From the mid-1970s North African immigrants began to move in large numbers into Île-de-France's social housing stock, which – given their location in the *départements* and towns to the north and east – contributed to social polarization. In 1999, for example, almost 22 per cent of the inhabitants of Seine-Saint-Denis's 1.4 million inhabitants were immigrants, much higher than the regional average of 15 per cent. Conversely, Hauts-de-Seine had only 14 per cent and Yvelines slightly over 10 per cent (IAU 2013a). In 2013 almost three out of ten inhabitants of Seine-Saint-Denis were immigrants, as against one out of five for Paris and Val-de-Marne and one out of eight for Yvelines and Seine-et-Marne (INSEE Île-de-France 2017a).

## Social polarization between the west and east of the region

One of the striking aspects of the period since the war has been the growing social and territorial polarization that occurred in Île-de-France. The better-off populations gradually settled in the centre-west of the region and the more modest in the north and east, which appears clearly in Table 2.6. Thus, Paris, Hauts-de-Seine and Yvelines are home to the highest-income populations. These *départements* saw a more sustained increase in their average incomes between 1984 and 2002 (Table 2.6). There is indeed a sharp contrast between the population of Paris and Hauts-de-Seine, whose average incomes respectively

**Table 2.5** Trends in the immigrant population by *département*, 1982–2013

| ***Département*** | **Number of immigrants** | | | | | **Share of immigrants in the population (%)** | | | | |
|---|---|---|---|---|---|---|---|---|---|---|
| | **1982** | **1990** | **1999** | **2009** | **2013** | **1982** | **1990** | **1999** | **2009** | **2013** |
| Paris | 400,184 | 399,433 | 386,398 | 453,364 | 455,486 | 18.4 | 18.6 | 18.2 | 20.3 | 20.4 |
| Hauts-de-Seine | 187,230 | 195,268 | 205,432 | 259,465 | 275,786 | 13.5 | 14.0 | 14.4 | 16.6 | 17.3 |
| Seine-Saint-Denis | 207,044 | 257,370 | 301,322 | 415,476 | 449,557 | 15.6 | 18.6 | 21.8 | 27.4 | 29.0 |
| Val-de-Marne | 155,368 | 171,804 | 187,946 | 248,680 | 270,442 | 12.9 | 14.1 | 15.3 | 18.9 | 20.0 |
| Seine-et-Marne | 76,436 | 98,212 | 115,878 | 152,188 | 171,790 | 8.6 | 9.1 | 9.7 | 11.6 | 12.6 |
| Yvelines | 120,952 | 133,552 | 141,017 | 170,313 | 184,478 | 10.1 | 10.2 | 10.4 | 12.1 | 13.0 |
| Essonne | 89,488 | 105,488 | 121,367 | 162,119 | 182,563 | 9.1 | 9.7 | 10.7 | 13.4 | 14.6 |
| Val-d'Oise | 101,252 | 127,665 | 151,648 | 197,487 | 216,071 | 11.0 | 12.2 | 13.7 | 16.9 | 18.1 |
| Île-de-France | 1,335,944 | 1,488,782 | 1,611,008 | 2,059,092 | 2,206,092 | 13.3 | 14.0 | 14.7 | 17.6 | 18.4 |
| France | 4,037,036 | 4,165,952 | 4,308,527 | 5,329,682 | 5,900,000 | 7.4 | 7.4 | 7.3 | 8.5 | 8.9 |

*Sources*: IAU (2013a); INSEE, census 2013; INSEE Île-de-France (2017a).

**Table 2.6** Trends in average income after taxes, 1984–2002 (€ 2002)

| | 1984 | 1990 | 1996 | 2002 |
|---|---|---|---|---|
| Paris | 15,493 | 18,693 | 18,454 | 21,113 |
| Seine-et-Marne | 15,043 | 15,936 | 15,442 | 16,703 |
| Yvelines | 17,273 | 19,163 | 19,026 | 21,211 |
| Essonne | 16,247 | 17,086 | 16,803 | 17,965 |
| Hauts-de-Seine | 16,160 | 18,518 | 18,522 | 20,992 |
| Seine-Saint-Denis | 13,359 | 13,498 | 12,742 | 13,052 |
| Val-de-Marne | 14,861 | 15,982 | 15,657 | 16,851 |
| Val-d'Oise | 15,319 | 16,126 | 15,726 | 16,551 |
| Île-de-France | 15,461 | 17,132 | 16,795 | 18,457 |

*Source*: IAU (2005).

increased by 36 per cent and 30 per cent between 1984 and 2002, by comparison with only 8 per cent for the Val-d'Oise and 0 per cent for Seine-Saint-Denis.

In fact, economic geography and social geography went hand in hand. Company headquarters and high-quality jobs moved into the west of the city of Paris and of Île-de-France, and the wealthy populations followed. The segregation processes continued after the 1970s crisis, with the result that the gaps between the municipalities where the wealthy classes live and those that are home to the less well-off have grown. As a result, some areas accumulated disadvantages: the housing crisis, deindustrialization and the associated rise in unemployment hit unskilled workers the hardest. Seine-Saint-Denis, which is home to the large majority of these social categories, was therefore the most severely affected and experienced growing impoverishment, along with other areas in the north and urban centres in the outer ring, such as Melun and Meaux.

These income differences are expressed differently across Île-de-France. The east of the region is, broadly speaking, poorer than the west. The *départements* of Paris and Hauts-de-Seine are thus the two richest in France, whereas Seine-Saint-Denis in the north-north-east of the region is the poorest in the country. The differences between the eight *départements* of Île-de-France had not diminished in 2017 (Table 2.7); Seine-Saint-Denis remained the poorest, with almost 28 per cent of its population living below the poverty line, almost double the regional average, whereas the western *départements* (Yvelines, Hauts-de-Seine, Paris) had, respectively, about 9 per cent, 12 per cent and 15 per cent in this situation (INSEE).

Social and territorial inequalities also find confirmation in the qualifications of the region's inhabitants. On the one hand, the population of Île-de-France is more "educated" (in terms of having a higher education degree) than the national average (see also Chapter 4): 41 per cent of its inhabitants have a

**Table 2.7** Trends in average incomes after taxes and poverty rates, 2017 (by *département*)

| | Average income (€) | Poverty rate (%) |
|---|---|---|
| Paris | 27,400 | 15.2 |
| Seine-et-Marne | 22,820 | 11.6 |
| Yvelines | 26,130 | 9.4 |
| Essonne | 23,360 | 12.7 |
| Hauts-de-Seine | 27,090 | 11.8 |
| Seine-Saint-Denis | 17,310 | 27.9 |
| Val-de-Marne | 22,290 | 16.3 |
| Val-d'Oise | 21,470 | 16.6 |
| Île-de-France | 24,190 | 15.3 |

*Source*: INSEE.

degree, rising to half the 25–34 age group, compared with 30 per cent in the rest of the population (IAU 2016a). In professional terms, executives and higher managerial positions represent 29 per cent of the region's working population, as compared with a national average of only 17 per cent. On the other hand, there are big differences within Île-de-France. Whereas in Paris, Hauts-de-Seine and Yvelines, respectively, 59 per cent, 51 per cent and 43 per cent of people aged 25 to 64 have a degree, this figure falls to 29 per cent and 25 per cent in Seine-et-Marne and in Seine-Saint-Denis.

The unemployment statistics confirm the description of a rich region containing very poor and very rich areas. In 2018 unemployment in Île-de-France stood at almost 8 per cent, compared with slightly over 9 per cent elsewhere. It was only 7 per cent in Yvelines and in Paris, however, compared with almost 12 per cent in Seine-Saint-Denis.

This rise in social polarization between zones was accompanied by a decline in social mix. Whereas until the 1960s Île-de-France could claim a relatively socially mixed population, this ceased to be the case. For example, the large housing estates (*grands ensembles*: see below), which were initially heterogeneous in their population, notably with a substantial minority of middle-class residents (a quarter of the large housing estates in Sarcelles were occupied by middle-class households), gradually saw these categories leave and be replaced by poorer populations. For instance, 81 per cent of the 28,000 new arrivals in Mantes-la-Jolie between 1961 and 1975 moved into social housing, much of which was in the large housing estates (IAU 2001). This shift was largely attributable to the increase in middle-class living standards and purchasing power. It enabled them to opt for more expensive, privately built housing, and so to leave the social housing, which therefore became increasingly "social". In the late 1960s and early 1970s, moreover, this housing was increasingly occupied by immigrant populations.

### *Anticipation and support policies: regional planning, housing and transport – the era of big public investment*

The period that began after the Second World War was one of intense urban growth. In response, central government embarked on a course of urban planning, first with the 1956 Paris region development plan (Plan d'aménagement de la région parisienne: PARP), which already prefigured the large housing estates and the future regional express network (RER), and then the Paris region development and general organization plan (Plan d'aménagement et d'organisation générale de la région parisienne: PADOG) of 1960. PADOG was based on Malthusian assumptions. Its aim was to stabilize the population of Île-de-France, to decentralize industry and slow down the tertiarization of the economy – in short, to limit the attractiveness of the capital region, in accordance with the dominant "graviériste" ideology of the time, which accused Paris of sucking the lifeblood of the provinces (see below and Chapter 3). From 1961, however, the government abandoned this impossible Malthusian approach that had inspired it for 30 years, and produced the Paris region urban master plan (Schéma directeur d'aménagement et d'urbanisme de la région parisienne: SDAURP), approved in 1965.

The planning horizon of the SDAURP was the year 2000 and its scope extended to the whole region – i.e. beyond the Paris conurbation alone. Acknowledging significant urban and economic growth in the decades to come, notably in the outer ring, it provided for the creation of eight new towns as new centres of growth intended to balance development, and the construction of several service industry hubs, starting with La Défense, where work had already begun. It retained the plan for the RER, added new railway lines and provided for the construction of expressways, in particular ring roads. It was therefore a pro-growth plan, representing a break with previous government choices.

The same principles would be maintained in the new urban development master plan (Schéma directeur d'aménagement et d'urbanisme de la région d'Île-de-France: SDAURIF) of 1976, which confirmed the general orientations of the SDAURP. Nonetheless, it removed three new towns and introduced green ribbon projects, the first environment-related ideas. In 1994 a new plan, the Île-de-France regional master plan, would be launched (see below).

Two major problems, housing and transport, drew on the cognitive, political and financial resources of the state and the authorities throughout this whole period. These problems remain equally salient today, as we will see in Chapters 5 and 6. From 1945 to 1960 infrastructure and housing problems grew worse. There were slums at the gates of Paris. The housing crisis was acute, reflected in ageing and overpopulated dwellings, estimated to represent a third of the housing stock in the early 1960s (IAU 2001). The eradication of the slums did not begin until 1965. In 1966 50,000 people were still living in 120 slums, and the last one – in Saint-Ouen – would not be cleared until the early 1970s.

The housing situation was a social and political issue that the state needed to tackle, notably following the call by Abbé Pierre in the winter of 1954.[5] It therefore embarked on a strong social policy for housing. In the 1950s and 1960s 80 per cent of new buildings were attributable to the state and public authorities, and would be subsidized housing. This began in particular with the emergency housing estate programme for the suburbs. In 1957 a bill for the construction of housing and public facilities was ratified. Between 1955 and 1958 around 200,000 homes were built, mainly in apartment blocks, some of them huge structures containing several thousand units. Between 1945 and 1966 a total of 800,000 dwellings were built, mainly in the suburbs. The rate of construction would be rapid, especially up to 1975, as shown in Table 2.8.

**Table 2.8** Number of buildings constructed per year, 1954–1980

| | |
|---|---|
| 1954–1962 | 70,000 |
| 1962–1968 | 85,000 |
| 1968–1975 | 105,000 |
| 1975–1980 | 75,000 |

*Source*: Merlin (1982).

This policy of intense construction took the form of "*grands ensembles*", massive apartment blocks containing at least 500 units, which would be built between the mid-1950s and the 1970s. The town of Sarcelles, which became home to one of the first such estates in 1954, is emblematic of this policy in terms of size, with 13,000 dwellings built in one go (see Photo 2.1).

To implement the policy, the government created zones à urbaniser en priorité (ZUPs: priority urbanization zones), an operational urban planning procedure that was used to create new neighbourhoods from scratch, not just with housing but also with services and public facilities. To this end, the government created a new body in 1962, the Paris region land and technical agency (Agence foncière et technique de la région parisienne: AFTRP). Twenty-two ZUPs were established in Île-de-France between 1958 and 1969.

Designed with the positive aspiration of regenerating old suburbs and built within a context of "resolute but concerned" humanism, the large housing

5. Following a particularly tough winter and the deaths of many homeless people, Abbé Pierre, founder of Emmaus in 1949, issued a call for the homeless to be supported. This campaign was a great success in terms of the funds collected.

**Photo 2.1** Sarcelles-95: construction of SCIC's (Société Centrale Immobilière Caisse des Dépôts) housing estates (architects Boileau and Labourdette)
*Source*: J. Bruchet/L'Institut Paris Region.

estates subsequently attracted sharp criticism, accused of having become dormitory suburbs because of their distance from centres of employment, their "concentration camp" appearance and their lack of public facilities and services, despite the initial intentions. Although there is a great deal of truth in many of these critiques, it is nevertheless the case that for a large proportion of their inhabitants, at least at the beginning, the large housing estates represented an improvement in housing conditions (more space, better sanitary conditions, etc.). Moreover, with 2.8 million units built, mainly before the mid-1980s, they represented a response, albeit partial, to the postwar housing crisis.

A not insignificant portion of the population of Île-de-France settled in the new towns, of which five were created by the government at the beginning

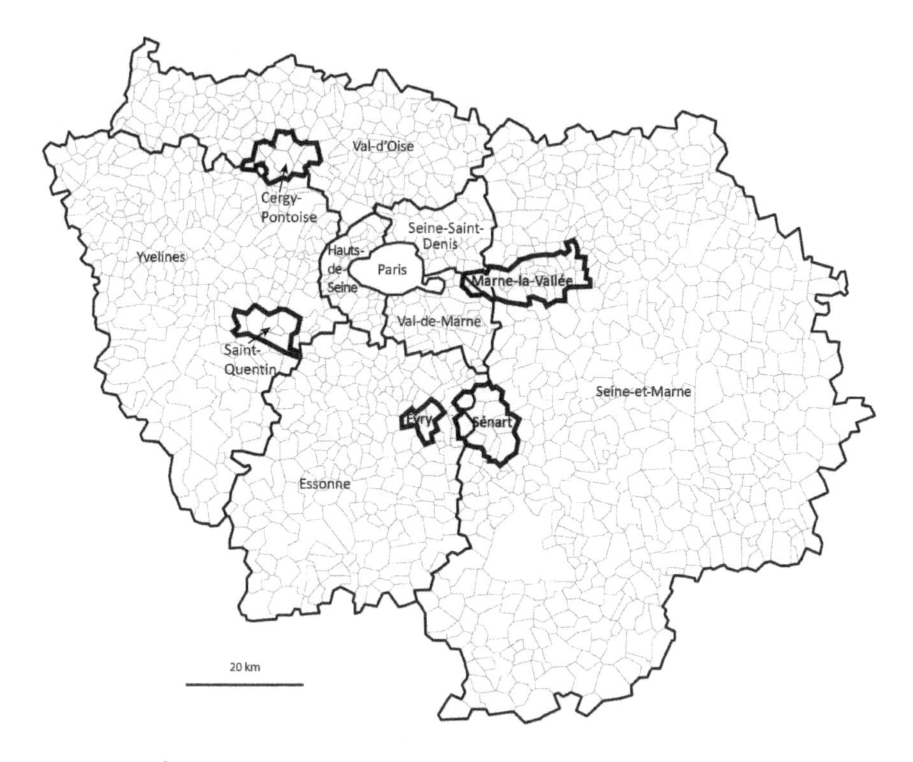


**Map 2.2** The Île-de-France new towns

in the 1970s: Evry in the south, Sénart in the south-east, Marne-la-Vallée in the east, Saint-Quentin in the west and Cergy-Pontoise in the north-west (Map 2.2). Their development was managed by the state through new government bodies, the établissements publics d'aménagement (EPAs: public development corporations), in concert with the local authorities. Between 1960 and 2000 the new towns accommodated 620,000 new inhabitants, essentially in the outer suburbs – i.e. 22 per cent of regional growth (IAU 2001) – and mainly over the period from 1975 to 2000, when they operated at full capacity. In 2000 the new towns were home to some 740,000 people, 7 per cent of the regional population; a significant accomplishment, but nevertheless only half the number forecast in the master plan.

After the abandonment of the large housing estates in the mid-1970s, a policy in favour of highly space-intensive detached housing came to the fore, which was to have serious repercussions for transport and travel provision. Until the early 1950s Île-de-France had possessed a relatively good public transport system, which played a driving role in the region's urban organization. Indeed, much of the urbanization took place along the axes served by the railway, and Paris's Metro network provided fine-grained coverage within the city (IAU 2001). On the other hand, the road network was very inadequate, frozen in the organization inherited from the eighteenth century. In the interwar period there was very little road or motorway construction, the only motorway built being the A13.

Between 1960 and 2000 travel demand increased by a factor of two and a half, and this would be accompanied by a very sharp increase in the number of cars in the region, which grew from 1.3 million in 1960 to 4.5 million in 2000 – i.e. by a factor of three and a half (IAU 2001). To tackle this situation, the state embarked on a policy of major projects that went much further than the transport systems alone, since between 1960 and 2000 Île-de-France saw the construction of the big airports (Orly and Roissy), the suburban universities, notably in the north and west (Nanterre and Villetaneuse), and the big national Rungis market in the south.

Until the early 1970s the emphasis was placed on creating a network of large-capacity infrastructure across the region, especially roads (expressways, motorways). The ambitious road-building programme in the PADOG, which had not been implemented, was carried over to the subsequent plans. Very sharp growth in car numbers justified the need to reduce congestion in the capital by means of radial expressways and ring roads. These big projects were accepted because there was general public support for the automobile (Flonneau 2003), which was also one of the industries that underpinned French economic growth and exports. This consent was expressed in the SDAURP, a pro-car document. It provided for the construction of no less than 1,400 km of new roads. Work began on five new motorways, and the Boulevard Périphérique and A86 ring roads were planned. As a result, the expressway on the right bank of the Seine was opened in 1967, and the Périphérique in 1973.

Nonetheless, public transport was not neglected. The Paris region district (see Chapter 3) launched the regional express network, opening the first line, the RER A, in 1969. New rail stations were built in the suburbs and extensions to the Metro were constructed. This policy would be further consolidated in the 1970s, when the first decline in support for the car emerged, notably following popular opposition to road construction and a reduction in the financial capacity of the state. The authorities began to realize that big road infrastructures, and, more generally, the car, could not resolve all mobility problems in a growing metropolis. The SDAURIF therefore put a stop to several motorways, some of which had been slated to extend into the centre of Paris, and instead provided for the construction of five new RER lines. The new emphasis on public transport was clearly expressed. The SDRIF of 1994 pursued the same priorities, further justified by the emergence of environmental issues that raised questions about the hegemony of the car. The contrat de plan État–région (CPER: state–region planning contract),[6] signed in 2000 and covering the period from 2000 to 2006, also emphasized the priority assigned to public transport.

Over some 40 years, therefore, Île-de-France substantially increased its transport provision, for cars and public transit alike. Whereas, in 1960, there had been only some 60 km of motorways running through the region, by 2000 this figure had increased to 850 km. With respect to public transport, the regional network (suburban trains plus RER) managed by the national rail company, SNCF, expanded to more than 1,300 km, including 465 km for the RER. The network managed by RATP (Régie autonome des transports parisiens), the public company that operates the Metro, the buses and one RER line, grew by 80 per cent for the Metro and RER (a total of 340 km) and 120 per cent for buses (a total of 2,730 km). This increase in provision was accompanied by a rise in the number of users, which grew slightly more quickly than population over the same period. Whereas Île-de-France had 2.5 million public transport users in 1960, it had 3.3 million in 2000 – i.e. 37 per cent more (IAU 2001). During the same period, car journeys increased by 150 per cent. Over the region as a whole, in 2000 the car accounted for 70 per cent of journeys, compared with only 30 per cent for public transport.

Nonetheless – and this is no surprise, in so far as Île-de-France follows the same trajectory as most big cities in the Global North – these colossal projects did not solve the recurring problem of mobility. At the end of the 1980s the RER A was already reaching saturation point, and the motorways were highly congested. Since then the situation has not improved, as we will see in Chapter 5.

## *Economic trends: industrialization, deindustrialization and tertiarization*

### From industrialization to deindustrialization

From the end of the war to the beginning of the 1970s Île-de-France underwent a period of sustained industrial growth. Sectors such as aeronautics, agri-food and automotive industries would develop, subsequently followed by light industries. In the 1960s the region accounted for 56 per cent of national employment in the automotive industry, 36 per cent of jobs in the machinery sector and 32 per cent in chemicals. In 1960 44 per cent of jobs were in industry, construction and public works (IAU 2001).

6. The state–region planning contract sets out the investments that the state and the region undertake to make over a six-year period.

Nevertheless, the geography of this industrialization changed. From the end of the 1950s industrial jobs began to decentralize, leaving Paris and moving to the west. Gradually they began to settle further and further away, in the outer ring. Whereas Paris accounted for 41 per cent of Île-de-France's industrial jobs in 1962, this figure had fallen to 27 per cent by 1986 (Guieysse 1986). At the same time, the proportion in the outer ring rose from 13 per cent to 28 per cent, while the inner ring remained stable at 45 per cent. This shift was all the more significant and spectacular in that industrial employment contracted during this period.

If we look closely at the figures, the period of deindustrialization began in the 1960s. It was initially very slow, since between 1960 and 1975 Île-de-France lost only 100,000 industrial jobs, with a fall from 1.4 million to 1.3 million in 15 years. Then the trend accelerated. Between 1975 and 1984 – i.e. in a decade – the region lost 300,000 jobs, 25 per cent of its industrial workers; between 1985 and 1994 the decline continued with an even sharper loss of 350,000 jobs. The momentum subsequently slowed, and by 2000 Île-de-France had lost "only" another 40,000 jobs. Between 1960 and 2000 overall, however, the haemorrhage was huge, with the region losing more than 50 per cent of its industrial jobs, a decline from 1.4 million (excluding the construction sector) to 660,000 (IAU 2001). The decline continued, with the loss of a further 60,000 industrial jobs between 2000 and 2018 (Institut Paris Région 2020a). Nonetheless, in 2000, and even today, Île-de-France remains France's premier industrial region (see Chapter 4).

Typically, as in so many other cities of the Global North, deindustrialization went hand in hand with a tertiarization of the economy. This has happened gradually. In 2000 80 per cent of jobs in the region were in the service sector – much more than the national average of 72 per cent – as compared with only 54 per cent in 1960. In 2019 about 88 per cent of jobs were in this sector (CCI Paris Île-de-France, Institut Paris Région & INSEE Île-de-France 2020). This tertiarization occurred through the development of business services, tourism, events (exhibitions and trade fairs), research and development (R&D) and, of course, finance. From the early 1990s the new economy (Internet, multimedia, biotechnologies, etc.) also brought its share of jobs, all of which took place against the background of the growing internationalization of the Île-de-France economy (see Chapter 4).

The development of the economy and jobs in Île-de-France after the war took the form of two geographical movements: a shift of jobs from Paris to the outer suburbs, and a reinforcement of the region's territorial polarization – in other words, a consolidation of what is a specificity of the economic and social geography of Île-de-France: a sharp imbalance between the east and the west of the region.

I have already mentioned demographic growth in the outer ring up until the end of the twentieth century, but this was accompanied by economic growth, as a growing share of regional jobs moved out. Nonetheless, despite this shift in employment, the phenomenon did not undermine the dominance of the central conurbation (Paris and the inner ring), not just in demographic terms but even more so in economic terms, even though the ascendancy was not so great. So, in 1998, 55.5 per cent of Île-de-France's population lived in the central conurbation, but accounted for 70 per cent of total employment. With regard to demographics, it was much less than 30 years earlier when about 70 per cent of the population lived in the central zone; in economic terms, however, the decline was modest, since, in 1968, 76 per cent of the region's jobs were located in the centre. As of 2015 the situation had stabilized, with about 67 per cent of regional jobs in the inner ring, Paris and Hauts-de-Seine capturing 50 per cent of total employment (see Table 2.9).

**Table 2.9** Geographical distribution of population and jobs, 1968–2019 (in %)

| | 1968 | | 1998 | | 2008 | | 2019 | |
|---|---|---|---|---|---|---|---|---|
| | **Population** | **Jobs** | **Population** | **Jobs** | **Population** | **Jobs** | **Population** | **Jobs*** |
| Paris | 28.3 | | 19.2 | | 18.8 | 31.3 | 17.7 | 31.2 |
| IR | 41.3 | | 36.3 | | 36.7 | 36.1 | 38.1 | 36.0 |
| Paris + IR | 69.6 | 76.0 | 55.5 | 70.0 | 55.4 | 67.4 | 55.8 | 67.2 |
| OR | 30.4 | 24.0 | 44.5 | 30.0 | 44.5 | 32.6 | 44.2 | 32.8 |

*Note*: * 2015 data.

*Sources*: IAU (2016b); DIRECCTE Île-de-France (2008), (2019), (2020).

As for the imbalance between the west and east of the territory, it is marked. For example, between 1961 and 1976 three-quarters of the region's jobs were created in the west. In 1975 75 per cent of researchers and industry were employed in the western half. In 1990 two-thirds of highly qualified jobs were located in inner Paris and in Hauts-de-Seine – in other words, in the west. Economic segregation grew and entrenched a situation in which the command functions were concentrated in the west of Paris and subordinate functions relegated to the north and east. Between 1960 and 2000 the centres of attraction in Île-de-France became specialized. The higher functions concentrated in the centre and west of Paris, especially La Défense (see below). Corporate management functions (workshops, laboratories, etc.) settled on the ring roads, notably to the north and south of the A86 motorway – in Vélizy, for example. Manufacturing and storage functions settled north of Hauts-de-Seine, in Gennevilliers, and in the outer suburbs, around the so-called "Francilienne" ring road. Finally, the warehousing and trade functions were established around big facilities such as the airports and the national market at Rungis.

Since 2000 the spatial organization of employment has stabilized (IAU 2016b), with the higher functions still in the centre and west of Paris, and logistics and industry mostly located in the outer ring.

## Economic development: the ambivalent policies of the state

The famous book by Jean-François Gravier,[7] *Paris et le désert français* (1947), called for an anti-Paris policy of territorial development, which would be rapidly implemented and would last in part until the end of the 1990s: "Paris is a trust that has colonized France and depopulated the countryside. Paris is a corporation that is paying and making France pay for the consequences of its hypertrophy. It is in deficit in every domain. It is devouring the people and riches of France" (Gravier 1947; quoted by Fourcaut *et al.* 2006: 271–2).

This Paris "trust", this Paris "corporation", are references to the demographic, industrial, commercial, financial, intellectual and artistic concentration in Île-de-France. According to Gravier, it was responsible simultaneously for the demographic decline of two-thirds of France's territory, for the disintegration of provincial life and the steady destruction of provincial elites, for the large difference in incomes between Paris and the provinces, for the shift in the industrial balance in favour of Paris and, finally, for monstrous urban overheads requiring large state subsidies.

This vision of Paris Île-de-France as a devourer of the nation would be adopted by government and translated into a policy of territorial development designed to correct the balance of the country by investing in the provinces, what Neil Brenner (2004) calls a "spatial Keynesianism". The "balancing metropolises" (*métropoles d'équilibre*) policy implemented by the national regional development agency (Délégation à l'aménagement du territoire et à l'action régionale: DATAR) from the 1960s was the spearhead of this effort. The aim was not only to invest in the provinces, however, but also to prevent Paris from growing, and to do this the region had to be punished. That would be the purpose of other public policies of relocation, of economic decentralization and of the authorization procedure,[8] which sought to relocate to the provinces activities that would otherwise naturally tend to settle in Île-de-France (see Chapter 3).

7. Jean François Gravier was a French geographer whose ideas profoundly influenced government policies in the postwar years.
8. Authorization is the procedure by which the state prevented firms from locating in the Paris region in order to encourage them to establish themselves in the provinces.

Nonetheless, it would be a mistake to believe that central government neglected the Île-de-France region throughout this whole "punitive" period. Aware of the region's importance to the national economy and society, the state would invest substantially in its infrastructures and facilities, as we have just seen. With respect to transport, it invested massively in roads and motorways (the Boulevard Périphérique inner ring road was inaugurated in 1973), but also in public transport with the opening of the RER in 1969 and in airports (Orly was opened in 1961 and Roissy in 1974). In the 1980s and 1990s there followed the "big presidential projects", which had already begun with Georges Pompidou (Musée Beaubourg) and Valéry Giscard d'Estaing (Orsay, La Villette), but gained momentum under François Mitterrand with the Louvre Pyramid, the National Library, the Arche de la Défense and Opéra Bastille.

The same was true in economic matters. First, at the end of the 1950s, the state mounted the project for a major business district, La Défense. In the early 1960s many big international French and foreign firms located their head offices there, such as Saint Gobain and IBM Europe. Several big shopping centres followed. At the start of the 1990s La Défense was already providing 11,000 jobs and claimed to be Europe's leading business centre. Pursuing this policy, the government developed the areas of Saclay in the south-west, Roissy in the north, around Charles de Gaulle Airport, and in the east around Euro-Disney, a project that began in 1987 and opened its doors in 1992.

The new towns were also the targets of economic policies designed to develop employment. The government began by locating public jobs there, notably in the two new *département* prefectures, Evry and Cergy-Pontoise. These new government administrations would also attract other public jobs, especially those in the big national companies (EDF, GDF, etc.). The government also created several specialist schools and universities. With regard to the private sector, the state encouraged companies to relocate in the new towns by granting tax advantages and by moderating the authorization policies (see Chapter 3). In 2000 they accounted for 7 per cent of Île-de-France's employment – i.e. as much as the percentage of the regional population living in them, although considerably below the most optimistic forecasts, which predicted twice the level.

The internationalization of the Île-de-France economy, which accelerated in the first two decades of the twenty-first century (see Chapter 4), along with the increasing competition between territories, would significantly change the national policies regarding Île-de-France, as we will see in Chapter 6.

What should we take away from this economic, social and spatial history of Paris and Île-de-France? First, the gradual establishment of a national economic capital, a real nerve centre of the nation. Second, the gradual construction of a world-ranking metropolis with significant demographic and economic growth in the second half of the twentieth century. Third, in social and geographical terms, the development of both a social and territorial polarization, with a rich and dynamic western zone, and a northern and eastern part where the areas in crisis were concentrated. Finally, an ambivalent attitude on the part of the state, combining a concern to tackle the problems and needs of a growing metropolis with the desire to encourage balanced development across the country.

# 3

# Political history of Île-de-France, 1789–2001

The political history of Île-de-France is a subject of debate, in particular because historical studies are still lacking or incomplete on a number of topics. According to many historians (Fourcaut *et al.* 2006), for example, there is a considerable imbalance between the number of historical studies on Paris, which are very numerous, and the much smaller number on its suburbs. This chapter takes no sides and forms no part of a debate between historians, since I have neither the legitimacy nor the desire to do so. The aim is rather, as a preliminary to the chapters that follow, to help readers understand the historical background to the system and political organization of Île-de-France and to identify the aspects that partly explain the main public policies pursued up to the present day (Chapter 6) and the problems of the relations between the actors concerned (Chapter 7). Three national factors and three factors specific to the situation of Île-de-France are worth noting in this respect.

First, France – and Île-de-France is no exception to the rule – has a political culture ruled by neocorporatism; in other words, a conception of the relations between actors in which the state appears dominant and in which it grants certain organizations a monopoly to represent the interests of social and economic forces. For example, the chambers of commerce and industry (CCIs) are entitled to represent the private economic sector, and in this capacity they are the primary interlocutors for government and local authorities in all public policies that affect companies. The outcome of this is the establishment of a comprehensive, highly institutionalized system of representational bodies, which plays an important role in territorial governance and in the governance of Île-de-France in particular.

Second, France's political and institutional system is largely based on state domination. It is historically well known that France is a highly centralized unitary nation in which the state possesses primary legitimacy and political authority, which it exercises across the country through a whole array of institutions and agencies under its control. Since this set-up is largely inherited from the Napoleonic era, it is what is usually called the Napoleonic system. At local level, however, the *commune* (municipality), the basic unit of political and administrative organization, enjoys a high degree of legitimacy, represented by the figure of the mayor. In this respect, it is a powerful institution. The relations between the state and the *communes* are an essential aspect of French territorial governance.

Finally, the links between the local political level and the national level are very strong. The accretion of local and national responsibilities is a feature of France's politico-institutional system, and this runs counter to a purportedly clear reading of the demarcation between local authority and state interests. Many *députés* (members of parliament) are also mayors or hold local offices. The Senate represents all the local authorities. Most ministers hold or have held important positions at local level. Under these circumstances, it is not surprising that local political functions are a springboard for national careers, and are perceived as such. This is especially the case in Île-de-France, and particularly in Paris.

This latter point leads us to three features specific to Île-de-France. The first is that Paris is not a local authority like any other, because it is both the most populous and richest municipality but, above all, the capital of France, and accordingly the headquarters of the state. The latter can therefore not but take an interest in the governance of this region. The second feature, which follows on from the first, is that the state has always been wary of its capital as a potential political rival, something that history has confirmed many times. The third feature, which ensues from this wariness and from the economic, cultural and social importance of Paris, is a political, administrative and institutional treatment that was initially specific to Paris, and then extended to Île-de-France, which thus distinguishes this region from the rest of the country.

This chapter is divided into three parts along historical lines. The first part covers the period from the Revolution to the fall of the Second Empire (1789–1871); the second part covers the whole of the Third Republic up to 1977; the final part considers the more contemporary period, and ends in 2001. These historical breaks are not an accident, but correspond to key events: 1789 marked the Revolution that shaped the foundations of the institutional system of Île-de-France; 1871 marked both the end of the Second Empire, the Commune and the start of the Third Republic; 1977 saw a partial return to ordinary legal status for Paris, with the election of a mayor and the beginnings of political regionalization, before the decentralization acts of the early 1980s; 2001 saw the left take power in the French capital, and therefore marked the end of the absolute dominance of the conservative forces that had reigned for a quarter of a century.

## The domination of the state, 1789–1871

After the abolition of the role of the *prévôt des marchands* at the end of the fourteenth century,[1] the whole of the administration of Paris fell into the hands of the monarchy. In fact, Paris retained only the appearance of a municipal existence, and, from the second half of the sixteenth century up to the French Revolution, the king succeeded in draining the commune of its political substance (Nivet 2004). The revolution would change this situation.

### *Political and administrative organization of Île-de-France under the Revolution*

In 1789 Paris once again became the official capital of the realm, in place of Versailles. In the following year the National Assembly established the administrative and territorial organization of France by creating 83 *départements*.

**BOX 3.1 MAJOR HISTORICAL EVENTS IN FRANCE AND PARIS, 1789–1871**

| | |
|---|---|
| 1789–95 | French Revolution |
| 1795–1804 | Directory, then the Consulate after the coup d'état of November 1799 (18 Brumaire) |
| 1804–15 | First Empire |
| 1815–30 | Restoration of the monarchy |
| 1830 | Riots |
| 1830–48 | The "July monarchy" ("monarchie de Juillet") |
| 1848 | Riots and Second Republic |
| 1851 | Coup d'état and birth of the Second Empire |
| 1852–70 | Second Empire |
| 1871 | The Paris Commune |
| 1871 | Third Republic (until 1940) |

1. The *prévôt des marchands* (provost of the merchants), elected head of the Corporation of Water Merchants, was the real head of the municipality, since he levied certain taxes and administered the city's revenues, its supplies of primary foodstuffs, the streets and the water supply. He represented a countervailing power to the provost of Paris, who was appointed by the king.

In the case of Île-de-France – although it would not officially take this name until the middle of the twentieth century – its territory was divided into three *départements*: Paris, Seine-et-Oise and Seine-et-Marne. The *département* of Paris grouped the present *départements* of Paris: Hauts-de-Seine, Seine-Saint-Denis and Val-de-Marne (see Map 1.1); and the Seine-et-Oise grouped the present *départements* of Val-d'Oise, Yvelines and Essonne.

This division is largely explained by the state's concern to contain the power of Paris by limiting its zone of influence to an administrative territory under state control (Bellanger 2010). The *département* of Paris – which was quickly renamed the *département* de la Seine – consisted of 81 *communes* (including Paris); at this time, it was a huge rural area with Paris at its centre, like an urban island. The second, mainly rural *département*, called Seine-et-Oise, contained almost 700 *communes*, with Versailles as its main town. At the time it had 420,000 inhabitants, and this figure had only grown to 560,000 by 1871. The third *département*, Seine-et-Marne, was entirely rural; it consisted of more than 500 *communes* and a population of some 300,000. Its population grew by only 40,000 in the period to 1871.

The *département* of Paris was divided into three districts (Paris, Saint-Denis and Bourg-la-Reine), but Paris enjoyed special status, while the other two districts were only administrative structures, with no political functions. Indeed, a law of 1789 granted Paris a special regime because of its huge population. The city had more than 500,000 inhabitants at the time, located within the "grant wall", the so-called wall of the Fermiers Généraux, which had just been built (see Map 2.1). The law that gave substance to this special regime was enacted in 1790. Obviously, it eliminated the administrative and political organization inherited from the ancien régime, and replaced it with a complex system consisting of an assembly, the General Council of the *commune* of Paris, a municipal council and a mayor, all elected. The General Council consisted of 144 prominent citizens, elected by selective suffrage. Within this assembly, 48 members – called municipal officers – held specific positions: 16 formed the municipal office, a sort of executive authority, and 32 formed the municipal council. For his part, the mayor was elected for two years, with the possibility of re-election for just one term. He presided over the municipal council.

Thanks to the Revolution, therefore, Paris acquired a special status that gave it a degree of autonomy and robust political legitimacy. Around the city, the Île-de-France region remained under the control of the state and appears to have been institutionally very fragmented, since it contained no fewer than 1,200 *communes*. This municipal fragmentation, established by the Revolution, is typical of French administrative organization and persists to this day, as we saw in Chapter 1.

### *Establishment of a centralized system: from the First to the Second Empire*

The Revolution was one of the few short periods in which the regime in Paris most closely resembled that of France's other *communes* (Nivet 2004). In fact, the state very quickly sought to regain control of its capital, a desire reinforced by the countervailing role played by the municipality during the Revolution.

After the fall of Robespierre in 1794, the new regime, the Directoire, voted for the elimination of the Paris General Council, and the creation in its place of 12 district councils directly administered by the *département* de la Seine. After the coup d'état of 18 Brumaire, the government introduced a law in 1800 that placed Paris under state supervision and assigned it a regime that would last for more than a century (Nivet 2004).

The act of 1800 created the post of prefect, the state's representative at local level. It placed all the *communes* in France under state supervision. Mayors were no longer elected but appointed, by the prefect in small *communes* and by the head of state (the first consul, then the emperor) in the largest ones. Within this framework, the administrative organization of Paris was particular. Although it remained part of the *département* de la Seine, it was under the supervision of two prefects: the prefect of police and the prefect of the Seine – a situation that persists to this day, since the two functions still exist. In this new political and administrative organization, the functions of the municipal council were taken over by the Seine General Council, in which the prefect held executive power. Its 24 members were appointed by the state.

The First Empire would thus seem to represent the most centralized point in French administrative history. For a while, the insurrection of 1830 loosened the grip of the state. Under the July monarchy, an act of 1831 re-established the election of the municipal councils by selective suffrage, with mayors being chosen from within the councils. In 1834 the act of 28 April "on the organization of the General Council and of the district councils of the Seine and the municipal organization of the city of Paris" established a new municipal council in which 36 members were elected by selected voters, while the remaining members consisted of citizens chosen for their capacities (retired officers, attorneys, notaries, teachers, etc.) (Nivet 2004).

Following the uprising of 1848, the government (the Second Empire) sought once again to take control and gave Paris a new special regime. The municipal council was abolished. At national level, mayors were once again appointed by the prefect. In Paris, it was the prefect Baron Haussmann who took command, believing that the state should intervene directly in Parisian affairs. This led notably to the forced annexation of the nearby suburbs (see Chapter 2), which had the effect of increasing the number of *arrondissements* (districts) to 20, as well as the number of municipal councillors – all state appointees.

The centralization imposed on Paris was not well received by the republican opposition, and at the end of the Second Empire several members of parliament called for a decentralization of the capital. Their efforts were to no avail, and in April 1871, following the fall of the Empire and the rise to power of a conservative-dominated republic (Adolphe Thiers was the first president of the Third Republic), a new act gave Paris a separate regime that clearly showed the state's mistrust of its capital. Although it maintained 20 *arrondissements*, each with a mayor and three deputies, all subordinate to the prefect and appointed by the state, it established two councils at city level: the municipal council of Paris, elected by citizens but with only minor functions; and the state-controlled Seine General Council. The law gave the municipal council a seat on the Seine General Council. Moreover, it eliminated the position of mayor of Paris, which would only be re-established in 1977, as we will see a little later.

May 1871 saw the start of the Paris uprising, better known as La Commune. It once again revealed the rebelliousness of Parisians to the conservative government and the threat that the city posed in its capacity to oppose the state, a lesson taken to heart by most of the political majorities of the Third Republic.

## Towards a conflicting political system, 1871–1977

### *State laissez-faire and the emergence of the red suburbs, 1871–1945*

The period covering the whole of the Third Republic was marked in the political arena by conflict between local authorities and the state in the governance of the Paris agglomeration, and by the rise of the left and in particular the Communist Party, with the establishment of the "*banlieue rouge*" (red suburbs).

#### Relations between Paris and its suburbs: conflicts and cooperation

The Thiers wall, boundary of the city of Paris, was a real wall that separated the capital from the surrounding *communes*. It was punctuated with dozens of gates and barriers that provided access to the capital. Running along its whole length was a 250 metre strip of wasteland, called the "zone". After the end of the nineteenth century this "zone" was very quickly overrun by slums, which further exacerbated the sense of exclusion felt in the suburbs. It was annexed by Paris in 1930. Within the city, the "grant wall", which would be eliminated only in 1943, reinforced this sense of a Paris under siege from the outside.

It was not surprising, therefore, that Paris was seen in the suburbs as a predator, first following the forced annexation of 1860, but also because of the policies of the capital, which relocated many infrastructures and facilities (cemeteries, landfills, etc.) necessary to its growth to suburban municipalities. In fact, in the 1880s suburban populations began to resist the encroachments of the central city, accusing it of using the suburbs as a dumping ground. This sense of being despised and dominated by Paris would leave deep marks in the imagination of suburban populations – traces that have remained to this day and that have left a sense of mistrust, even suspicion, towards the capital, which has heavily influenced the governance of Île-de-France (see Chapter 7) (Fourcaut *et al.* 2006; Subra 2012).

Nonetheless, many authors, such as Emmanuel Bellanger and Annie Fourcaut, without denying the bad relations between Paris and suburban *communes*, believe that those relations were "less conflictual than a succinct history of representations might suggest" (Fourcaut *et al.* 2006: 28). For all these authors, there is a stereotypical dichotomy in the perception of relations between the central city and the suburbs. Instead, they emphasize what they call "a forgotten solidarity", "a secular and radical republican sense of community, a solidarity arising from assistance and corrective interventions by the state and the local authorities" (Bellanger 2012: 55).

Indeed, there were obvious relations and cooperation between the central city and the suburbs, starting with those triggered in response to natural disasters such as the flooding of the Seine in 1910, which made politicians aware of the need for the protective policies at the right scale. Likewise, existing utilities and those under construction (canals, water, electricity, railways, gas, etc.) made it clear that measures were needed at a wider scale than municipal areas. And, then, there was also (see Chapter 2) the failure of the state to intervene in anarchic urban development, which required rationalization. In this respect, the Seine General Council would play a central regulatory and redistributive role, which would help to harmonize relations with local authorities. Its many policies and structures would make it an institution of political compromise, but also of equalization and coordination, or even urban cohesion. Moreover, although it continued to be controlled by Parisian councillors, who would always constitute a majority, the number of representatives from the suburbs gradually increased, rising from eight members in 1892 to 22 in 1908, 40 in 1925 and 50 just before the war, until it finally came to chair the council in 1936.

In fact, the Seine General Council was a powerful institution. It was responsible for important services such as roads, sewerage, water and energy, all politically sensitive sectors in a period dominated by social hygiene and public health concerns. It was through this institution that public policies began to be departmentalized (Bellanger 2008) with the creation of the Low-Cost Housing Office (social housing) in 1915 and the Social Hygiene Office in 1918, which would stimulate the construction of several garden cities, dispensaries and nurseries in many *communes*. In 1920 it established the Paris region public transport company (Société des transports en commun de la région parisienne: STCRP), and in 1933 it made the waste collection service a department.

Behind all these actions and policies there were certainly individuals, such as Henri Sellier, mayor of Suresnes and senator for the Seine, but also and above all a sense of a common destiny, which was also characteristic of Parisian politicians, since Paris was fully involved in the politics of its region. For example, it contributed three-quarters of the budget of the *département* de la Seine. Its elected officials, most of them aware of the need for cooperation, would "form alliances of convenience and of conviction with representatives from the suburbs, including communists. [...] The commitment of the capital's senior elected officials to the defence of Grand Paris is clear and runs counter to the reductive picture of a capital concerned solely with its own interests" (Bellanger 2012: 72). All these factors thus enhanced the legitimacy of the Seine General Council and meant that, on the eve of the war, parochialism and party political divisions were partially a thing of the past.

The cooperation between local authorities was not limited to the Seine General Council and its structures, however. Very early on, local authorities themselves began to initiate some actions. By the end of the nineteenth century *communes* were signing charters of intermunicipal cooperation. In 1909 the Union des maires de la Seine (UMS: Seine mayors union) was formed. It was thanks to this cross-party political organization that many intermunicipal joint authorities and organizations would come into existence. Between 1900 and 1930, for example, a dozen big joint authorities were formed in a wide range of domains. In 1903 55 municipalities established the Syndicat de gaz et de l'électricité de la banlieue de Paris (Paris suburbs gas and electricity syndicate); 1923 saw the foundation of the Syndicat des eaux des communes de la banlieue de Paris (Paris suburban municipalities water syndicate), with 66 municipalities; in 1924 it was the turn of the Syndicat intercommunal de la périphérie de Paris pour les énergies et les réseaux de communication (Paris periphery intermunicipal electricity and communication networks syndicate: SIPPEREC). In the same year the municipalities set up a loan bank to support municipalities in their efforts to upgrade failing housing estates (see Chapter 2). Most of these bodies still exist, and have been reinforced (see below).

As we can see, the history of the relationship between Paris and the suburbs is ambiguous: a mix of mistrust and solidarity. It is a history that would have a big influence in Île-de-France, and it is not possible to understand the present region's governance difficulties without reference to it.

Throughout this whole period the state maintained control over Île-de-France, but, by contrast with the postwar period, it was relatively inactive (see Chapter 2). Laissez-faire gave way to a few early interventionist ambitions, such as in 1928, with the creation of the Comité supérieur d'aménagement et d'organisation de la région parisienne (higher committee for the development and organization of the Paris region), which in 1934 proposed a development plan that never got off the ground. For the city of Paris, decree laws were published in 1939, just before the declaration of war, that further limited the powers of the municipal council. The end of the war was to result in a thorough reshuffling of the cards of governance for Paris and Île-de-France, however.

## Birth of the red suburbs

For historians, the red suburbs are both a reality and myth. The reality is that, roughly between 1920 and 1970, a significant segment of the Paris suburbs was controlled by the Communist Party. The myth is that of a capital encircled by a belt of communist bastions, a bourgeois and conservative central city surrounded by a more working-class periphery committed to the workers' movement (Fourcaut *et al.* 2006). The expression itself emerged in the wake of an article by Paul Vaillant-Couturier, "Paris encircled by the revolutionary proletariat", published in the communist newspaper *L'Humanité* after the elections of 1924 and 1925. A more precise definition describes it as "territorial bastions structured by a class-based parochial patriotism, led by a dense network of local groups organized around the French Communist Party (PCF), supported by the municipalities, which operate as welfare-towns (nurseries, holiday camps, social services)" (Fourcaut *et al.* 2006: 36).

In the 1924 general election the PCF won more than 26 per cent of the votes in Seine-banlieue (the suburban area of the *département* de la Seine) and over 24 per cent in Seine-et-Oise. It was a success that was in sharp contrast with the defeat of the left nationally a few years earlier. This rise of the PCF began in 1924 and at municipal level in 1925, with the party winning control of nine municipalities. It won two more in the 1929 election. In the 1935 election, 26 municipalities in Seine-banlieue and 29 in Seine-et-Oise fell into the party's hands. At national level, the PCF had 26 Members of Parliament in that year. In 1936 the Seine General Council was headed by a communist, Georges Maranne, who was also mayor of Ivry. Although the party was growing nationally, it was in Île-de-France that it was the strongest, with 35 per cent of members originating from the region. There was, in fact, a strong correlation between the rise of the communist vote and the industrialization of the region, and particularly with the size of the working-class population in the municipalities. In Ivry, for example, recently won by the party, 66 per cent of the population was working class in 1931. Communist success was also linked with the serious housing crisis that affected the suburbs in the 1920s and 1930s (see Chapter 2).

On the eve of the Second World War the party controlled the loops of the industrial Seine, the east, the north-east and the south-east. This power worried the right, and particularly the Gaullists, and that was why, even before the Liberation, the government in Algiers, led by General Charles de Gaulle, appointed a prefect of the Seine and a prefect of police from within its own ranks.

## *Strong state intervention and the building of political bastions, 1945–77*

The postwar period would see a rise in active state intervention, especially in the sphere of institutional reform. At the same time, there was a reinforcement of the political bastions between the right and the left. These two processes would combine to produce an increasingly conflictual political system.

### State management of the region: ambiguous objectives

From the 1950s onwards the government showed greater appetite for intervention in Île-de-France, as instanced by the creation of the public development corporation of La Défense (Établissement public d'aménagement de la Défense: EPAD). It also decided to establish a politico-administrative structure entirely under its own control, the District of the Paris region, responsible for directing numerous public policies within the Seine *département*. Facing a revolt by many local politicians, however, from both the right and the left, supported by the Union of Seine Mayors, who refused to sit on the district board, the government was forced to back off (Bellanger 2010). In 1961 a second district came into existence, the Paris region District, headed by a director-general, Paul Delouvrier, and reporting directly to the prime minister and the president of the Republic. Although local politicians were better represented on the district's board of directors, the latter was controlled by the state, which appointed half its members. Paul Delouvrier, prefect of the Seine, was accountable only to the highest offices of state.

The district's role was to plan and develop the Paris region over an area covering more or less the Île-de-France. From the prime minister's perspective, the task was to "put an end to the shameful anarchy which, for eighty years, has spread like leprosy across the Paris region" (quoted by Cottour 2008a: 75). The district's powers were in fact huge, since it could impose its decisions on local authorities, especially in matters of construction. The minister of the interior, Roger Frey, was very clear:

> The deliberative assemblies of the *départements* or *communes* cannot have such extensive powers as in the other *départements* [...] Local freedoms will be maintained insofar as they do not constitute an obstacle to the public interest [...] The general administrator may grant licences to the planning organizations in the event that the *communes* refuse. (quoted by Cottour 2008a: 75)

In order to perform its role, the district prevailed upon the government in 1961 to create the Institut d'aménagement et d'urbanisme de la région parisienne (IAURP: Paris Region Planning Institute) and in 1962 the Agence foncière et technique de la région parisienne (AFTRP: Paris region land and technical agency), a powerful design body and an agency responsible for managing land on behalf of the state (it could buy and sell and had a right of pre-emption). With the help of these structures, the new master plan was implemented in 1965, notably with the creation of new towns, developed by the state with its new public development corporations. In all the institutions and organizations, local elected officials – although present – were marginalized by government departments (Subra 2012; Cottour 2008a). It was therefore the state that planned and developed the region with the new town programmes in the 1960s and 1970s, and with the establishment of national interest operations (opérations d'intérêt national: OINs), which began with La Défense but subsequently proliferated. Specific public structures were set up for these OINs and the new towns, such as ÉPAD for La Défense in 1958, and the bodies created for Marne-la-Vallée in 1972 and Melun-Sénart in 1973.

However, the state's management of the region also entailed so-called sanction policies, designed to restrict the development of the Paris region, following in this respect the "*graviériste*" ideology (see Chapter 2) that was dominant within the state apparatus, and notably at the Délégation à l'aménagement du territoire et à l'action régionale (DATAR), set up in 1963 to develop the country's spatial planning. DATAR thus oversaw the introduction of so-called relocation policies and supported the authorization policy.

The relocation policy, designed to move public jobs away from the Paris region, was introduced in the 1960s with the creation of CITEP (Comité pour l'implantation territoriale des emplois publics: committee for the territorial location of public jobs), an organization charged with ensuring that public sector jobs did not stay concentrated in the capital. With this policy, thousands of jobs were relocated to the provinces from the 1960s onwards. The authorization policy, officially instituted in 1955, concerned the establishment of private and public companies in Île-de-France. Any company wanting to set up in Île-de-France had to apply for authorization from the administration. In parallel, the state began the decentralization of industries towards western France (Renault set up part of its production in Le Mans) and to southern cities (aeronautics in Toulouse, science parks on the Mediterranean coast, research and information technology in Grenoble). These relocation and authorization policies would have only minor effects on the development of Île-de-France, but they marked the state's ambivalent, not to say contradictory, attitude to the country's main region: to develop it while taking control but at the same time trying to put brakes on its development. This ambivalence would not be resolved until later, in the early 2000s.

## Changing political forces: reinforcement or creation of bastions

In 1945 the Communist Party, on its own or with the socialists of the Section française de l'internationale ouvrière (SFIO: French section of the Workers' International), won control of 60 of the 80 suburban municipalities; 50 of them elected a communist mayor. In the 1959 municipal elections it became the conurbation's leading political force: 1.4 million suburbanites had a communist mayor and Seine-Saint-Denis had 21 communist mayors and eight communist Members of Parliament out of the nine in the *département*.[2] The general election of 1973 accentuated this domination of the left, with the election of two more Members of Parliament in Val-de-Marne and one more in Val-d'Oise. The year 1977 was the high point of the PCF for municipal elections. Although it had already managed to get 46 mayors elected in 1971, in 1977 54 communist mayors became leaders of municipalities (see Box 3.2). In the parliamentary election of 1978 the PCF became the biggest political party in Île-de-France. All these successes explain the remarkable longevity of several communist mayors, such as Louis Peronnet, mayor of Bézons from 1926 to 1961, and Victor Dupouy, mayor of Argenteuil from 1935 to 1977.

For its part, the right triumphed in Paris. In 1947 the Gaullist candidates from the Rassemblement du peuple français party won an absolute majority of votes and seats (52 out of 90). From this point onwards Gaullism would seek to establish a stranglehold on the Paris region, relying on its new bastions in

2. See page 56 of this chapter for the regional reform that created eight new *départements* in 1967: Essonne, Yvelines, Seine-et-Marne, Val-d'Oise, Hauts-de-Seine, Seine-Saint-Denis, Val-de-Marne and Paris.

**BOX 3.2 THE FRENCH VOTING SYSTEM AT THE MUNICIPAL LEVEL**

Municipalities (*communes*) are governed by a municipal council. Councillors are elected on a proportional system with a majority bonus, in a two-round process. The winning list gets the majority of seats plus a bonus that represents the percentage of votes that the list received. For example, if a list gets 50 per cent of the votes in the first round, it wins and gets 50 per cent of the councillors plus 50 per cent of the remaining councillors. If no list gets more than 50 per cent of the votes in the first round, a second round takes place in which only the lists that got more than 10 per cent of the votes in the first round can compete. The list that comes first, whatever its result, gets 50 per cent of councillors plus the number of councillors based on the percentage of votes that the list received. For example, if a list gets 40 per cent of the votes, it gets 50 per cent of councillors plus 40 per cent of the remaining councillors. The mayor is elected by the municipal council. Generally speaking, (s)he is the leader of the winning list.

the central city and the western suburbs. In 1968 Yvelines elected conservative Members of Parliament and in the general election of 1973 Hauts-de-Seine and Yvelines were dominated by the right. It was the election of the mayor of Paris in 1977 that gave the right new momentum, however.

Following the institutional reform of the status of Paris (see below), the year 1977 saw the first election of a mayor of Paris since the abolition of the role in 1871, more than a century earlier. The mayor was appointed from within the municipal council, itself elected by direct universal suffrage. The Gaullist and liberal parties, rivals on the right, won an absolute majority of votes with 55 per cent and, as a result of the election, held 69 seats out of the 109 on the municipal council. The Gaullist Jacques Chirac was elected mayor of Paris. He thus became the de facto leader of the right-wing opposition in Île-de-France.

The end of the 1970s thus reveals an Île-de-France characterized by sharp political disparities, with communist and socialist bastions in the northern and north-eastern suburbs and in the southern suburbs, whereas the right was dominant in the central city and the western suburbs. The territorial cleavages were therefore strong and partly explain the conflictual nature of the politics of Île-de-France, which persists to this day. Nevertheless, as some historians have noted (Fourcaut *et al.* 2006: 37), "position in the geographical space of the conurbation sometimes proves more important than the right–left divide". This is what I will try to show in the chapters that follow.

## A territorial reorganization marked by hidden political agendas

Between 1920 and 1960 several institutional reform projects for the Paris region proposed by local politicians, and often cross-party in nature, clearly showed the need felt by some local elected officials for a change in the scale of government of this region (Fourcaut *et al.* 2006). It was in fact the government, however, that would implement this plan at the beginning of the 1960s.

It tackled Île-de-France as a whole by an administrative reform of the Seine *département*. Up to then, it will be recalled, the region was divided into three *départements*, Seine, Seine-et-Oise and Seine-et-Marne. From 1968 it was the eight *départements* that exist today that would become a reality, with the division of the Seine *département* into four smaller *départements* – Paris, Val-de-Marne, Seine-Saint-Denis, Hauts-de-Seine (the inner ring) – and the *département* of Seine-et-Oise into three new authorities: Val-d'Oise, Essonne and Yvelines, which, with Seine-et-Marne, formed the outer ring (see Map 3.1).

This new division was justified by the government as being more efficient. As Roger Frey, minister of the interior at the time, commented (quoted by Subra 2012): "A single authority [in the Paris region] is responsible for administering a population of 6 million, whereas in the rest of the country, there is an average of one prefect per 130,000 inhabitants [...] [T]he administration needs to be broken up to make it more human."

Behind this concern for humanization, however, was an important political motive: the boundary change had the effect of concentrating or containing the bulk of the communist voters in two *départements*, Val-de-Marne and Seine-Saint-Denis, and protecting the others, in particular Paris and Hauts-de-Seine, from a left-wing victory (Subra 2012). It also enabled the state to rid itself of a legitimate – elected – body, the Seine General Council, which might have acted as a counterweight to the government's newly created district, as

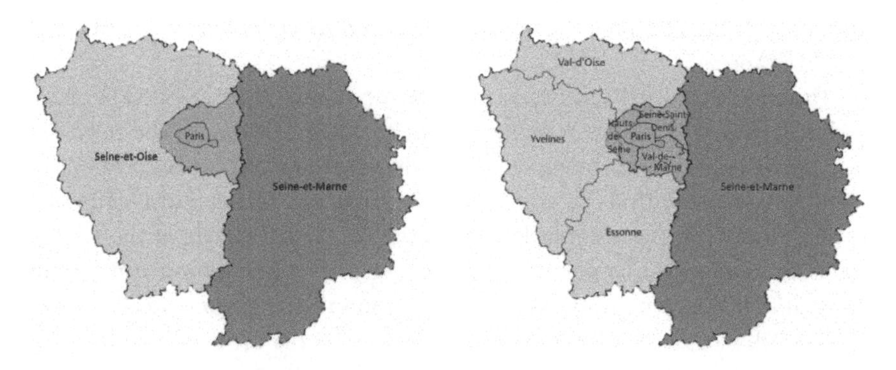


**Map 3.1** Île-de-France before and after the institutional reform

we saw earlier, especially as the Communist Party might have been sufficiently strong to achieve leadership of the council. The government therefore chose to fragment the red suburbs and to cede Seine-Saint-Denis and, to a lesser degree, Val-de-Marne to the communists.

This boundary change, undertaken without consultation and resolved by a small group headed by Charles de Gaulle in person (Bellanger 2010), aroused opposition from a large majority of the intermediate bodies, elected local officials of all political leanings who, rightly, saw it as a power grab by the state over the Paris region. The newly created district gave the government a free hand to take total control of the region, its public planning institutions and the prefectures of the new *départements*.[3]

In parallel with this territorial reorganization of Île-de-France, the state launched a process of regionalization at national level. The mid-1950s saw the establishment of the comités régionaux d'expansion (regional expansion committees) and 21 régions économiques de programme (programming economic regions). In 1959 these economic regions became circonscriptions d'action régionale (CARs: regional action districts), coordinated by a prefect. The regionalization process began to gain momentum in 1964 with the creation of the commissions de développement économique régional (CODERs: regional economic development committees), and with the regional prefects in 1966. The state apparatus was just beginning to equip itself with the beginnings of an administration covering the 21 regions. The CODERs were consultative assemblies representing the key players in the region (trade unions, employers, etc.). In 1972 this whole process led to the introduction of the établissements publics régionaux (EPRs: regional public corporations) through a merger of the CODERs and the CARs.

Île-de-France was only partially affected by the regionalization taking place at national level. To start with, it had an administration – the district – that to some extent already played the role of a regional institution, although it covered only the central part of Île-de-France (the Seine *département*). From the 1960s it also had a Comité consultatif économique et social (CCES: economic and social consultative committee), which somewhat resembled what the CODERs would become. Above all, however, it was excluded from the creation of the EPRs, which otherwise applied to the whole country. Île-de-France would partially return to ordinary status in 1976, when the district became the EPR de la région Île-de-France, endowed with new prerogatives such as transport and green areas. As with the EPRs elsewhere, however, this was not yet a

3. It should be remembered that at this time, before decentralization, the *départements* were headed by prefects, and the elected councils had few powers.

genuine authority, which would come into existence only after the decentralization laws of the early 1980s (see below) (Vadelorge 2012).

Over the period from 1945 to 1977 other territorial administrative changes took place. The year 1959 saw the creation of the Syndicat des transports parisiens (STP: Parisian transport syndicate), a body responsible for public transport and covering the areas possessing a public transport service – i.e. not only the Seine *département* but also part of Seine-et-Oise and Seine-et-Marne. The STP was headed by the state, but its board of directors included all the *départements* and the city of Paris. A second big technical institution, the Syndicat interdépartemental pour l'assainissement de l'agglomération parisienne (SIAAP), responsible for sanitation, covering the new *départements* in the inner suburbs, including Paris, was set up in 1970. It remained under state control.

Beyond this handful of structures, however, Île-de-France remained resistant to the process of intermunicipal cooperation that was developing elsewhere in the country. This is explained by the state's reluctance to see the establishment of strong intermunicipal institutions that could become counterweights to its authority, by the central city's hostility to being incorporated into such entities and, of course, by the suburban municipalities' mistrust of the capital. Moreover, the communists became advocates of municipal autonomy and had no real wish to delegate or share the powers of the *communes*, which would have been necessary in the case of intermunicipal cooperation. All this contributed to an extreme fragmentation of the institutional fabric, a fragmentation that has remained a feature of Île-de-France to this day.

Nonetheless, at the end of the 1970s, there occurred one big innovation, mentioned just above: a modification of the status of Paris. Back in 1963 Allain Griotteray (quoted by Fourcaut *et al.* 2006: 310–11), a Paris councillor and ferocious advocate of a return to normal for the French capital, had condemned the continuing special status of Paris, "conceived to deal with a nineteenth-century problem ... appropriate for defusing riots and revolutions, ... unsuitable to create a modern, dynamic and human organization of the city's urban life". He emphasized the international role of Paris, which needed a new status to pursue its mission: "The ambition of Paris should be to be a major European force [recapturing] the role that it previously played in France ... Paris must become the capital of Europe." Although the Paris Council gradually acquired more and more powers (Nivet 2004), it took almost 15 more years for the status of Paris to change and for the National Assembly to give it a mayor, by the 1975 act; the first election of the Paris executive by indirect universal suffrage thus took place in 1977.

In 1974 France had elected a new president, Valéry Giscard d'Estaing, who was a non-Gaullist and a liberal. With a score of close to 60 per cent in the presidential election in the capital, Paris seemed to be his. The idea began to gain ground that a mayor of Paris who was not a Gaullist and who would therefore be close to the new president was possible, and even probable. This was the political background to the 1975 act, which significantly reformed the status of Paris. This act was innovative in that it gave the capital a dual executive: the mayor of Paris, elected from among the municipal councillors, and the prefect of police; it also increased the size of the municipal council to 109 members. Paris was simultaneously a *commune* and a *département*, and the municipal councillors were therefore also departmental councillors.

The liberals saw their hopes dashed, since it was not one of their own who became mayor but the Gaullist Jacques Chirac. The battle of Paris was only beginning, however, as we will see in the next section.

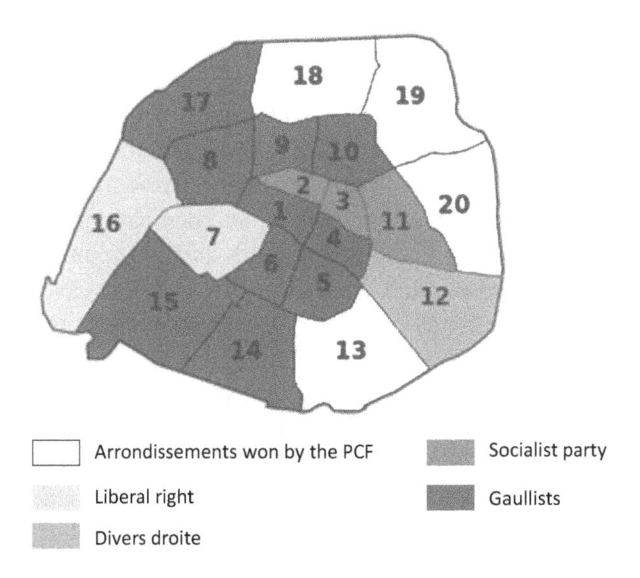


**Map 3.2** Results of the 1977 elections to the Paris municipal council
*Note*: White = *arrondissements* won by the PCF; grey = by the Socialist Party; dark grey = by the Gaullists; light grey = by the liberal right. The 12th is controlled by the "divers droite" – i.e. a neither Gaullist nor liberal right-wing alliance.

## Towards an unregulated political decentralization, 1977–2001

The period beginning in the late 1980s would be full of institutional and political changes. First of all, France would embark upon a process of decentralization that would permanently transform its institutional and administrative system, with continuing regionalization. Nonetheless, the state would remain an important player, especially in Île-de-France. Finally, the political contrasts would be further accentuated.

## *France begins to decentralize*

In 1981, for the first time since the birth of the Fifth Republic in 1958, the left won the presidential election. François Mitterrand, first secretary of the Socialist Party, was elected president. In the parliamentary election that followed almost immediately, the French chose a left-wing National Assembly, heavily dominated by the Socialist Party. Apart from representing a political landslide, this election would have major consequences for France's institutional and administrative landscape. During the electoral campaign the left-wing parties promised to begin a process of decentralization, a move in fact welcomed by a good many right-wing political groupings.

This became a reality in the following years, with the decentralization acts of 1982 and 1983. The intention was to effect a massive transfer of powers and financial and fiscal resources from the state to the local authorities. This transfer was to take place with no change in territorial organization, however – in other words, with no initial overhaul of the municipal map, notably by a regrouping of *communes*, as had previously been suggested. This meant that municipalities would be given significant powers and financial resources, despite the fact that most of them were both geographically and demographically small. This was especially the case for Île-de-France, with its 1,281 municipalities. With decentralization, *communes* and *départements* would have executives elected by universal suffrage, and state oversight, through the prefects, would be purely retrospective.

Decentralization established, at least on paper, the transfer of "blocks of competences". The *commune* thus became responsible for matters of urban planning, housing and economic development, while the law gave social affairs to the *département*. The state transferred significant financial resources through local taxation and through subsidies in the form of a block grant – i.e. money that local authorities could more or less freely use. *Communes* and *départements* would therefore enjoy quite significant autonomy, certainly far in excess of that they had exercised under the previous system. These powers and resources would be jealously guarded, a factor that would contribute to institutional fragmentation, especially in the big agglomerations such as Île-de-France; and this largely continues to this day, as will be analysed in Chapter 7.

The decentralization laws also established a new tier, however: the "region". Twenty-two regions, including Île-de-France within its historical boundaries (the former *département* of the Seine, Seine-et-Oise and Seine-et-Marne), were thus created in 1982. Initially, the regions were weak institutions, endowed with few financial resources and with no great powers. Like the other authorities, they had a council elected by direct universal suffrage, a deliberative body that elected the executive, the president and the vice-presidents. As they were newcomers, the first regional elections were not held until 1986.

For the 1986 regional elections, the voting method was proportional and limited to a single round. In Île-de-France the right won 45 per cent of the votes, the left 43 per cent and the National Front 12 per cent. Although the right was in a majority, it could not control the regional institution on its own, and the electoral method thus necessitated the establishment of coalitions, which prevented the emergence of a stable leadership. It was only in the early 2000s that the voting system would change to allow greater political stability. Weak in both responsibilities and resources, the regions were also politically weak, and Île-de-France was no exception.

With the arrival of the left in power, the battle of Paris would resume. Keen to take the capital, where it held power in some of the most populous *arrondissements*, in 1982 the leftist government launched a plan to reform the status of Paris. Under this plan, the 20 *arrondissements* would become municipalities in their own right – i.e. with mayors elected by the municipal council, as in every other *commune* in France, and endowed with the powers and resources that had been transferred by the decentralization acts. Once established, these 20 municipalities would be united in an urban federation, whose president would become mayor of Paris. The strategy was clear: the aim was to break the dominance of the right by fragmenting Paris and taking control of it by establishing an urban federation, a strategy that was all the more likely to succeed in that the *arrondissements* with left-wing majorities were the most populous, and therefore had proportionally the most municipal councillors.

This strategy failed, however, because, even though the National Assembly did indeed vote in 1982 for a new status for Paris, this in no way matched the wishes of the government. The act gave the *arrondissements* an elected mayor, but left them highly dependent on the municipality of Paris. Moreover, it increased the size of the municipal council to 163 members. The internal "decentralization" of the capital therefore did not happen, and the *arrondissements* remain to this day institutions with no great powers or resources.

### *A persistently strong state presence*

Decentralization did not lead to the state's withdrawal from Île-de-France – far from it – first of all because decentralization here was only partial, and, second, because the state would maintain its ambivalent attitude, fluctuating between measures and policies in favour of the development of the region and penalties designed to hinder such development.

With respect to decentralization, the state continued to maintain a powerful administration in Île-de-France around the regional prefecture (the Préfecture de la région Île-de-France: PRIF) and its numerous sectoral departments, among them the powerful Direction régionale de l'équipement d'Île-de-France (DREIF: regional infrastructure directorate), whose director held the rank of prefect. Then it controlled the prefectures of the seven *départements* (the prefect of the region was also the prefect of Paris) and, of course, the Paris Prefecture of Police, since the capital did not enjoy the same prerogatives as the other *communes*, particularly police powers (control of the roads, security, etc.).

In addition, however, the Île-de-France region was not given all the powers devolved to the other regions. This was the case for two responsibilities essential for territorial development: public transport and spatial planning. In the sphere of transport, the state already controlled the two main public transport operators, SNCF and RATP. But, whereas responsibility for public transport (transport policy, investment, price policy, etc.) was assigned to all the regions, in Île-de-France the state maintained control over the organizing authority, the Syndicat des transports parisiens. Although the local authorities were represented on the STP's board of directors, they were in a minority, and, moreover, the board was chaired by the prefect of Île-de-France, who held a casting vote. This state of affairs, strongly opposed by the local actors, would be the subject of a lengthy trial of strength with the state, which lasted until 2005. The compensation for state involvement in Île-de-France's transport policy was that the government financed investment and some of the operators' deficits. And, of course, it was DREIF that was in charge of all road and motorway policy.

With regard to spatial planning, the state kept control of general policy, and in particular the development and approval of the master plan, the SDRIF. This power was enormous, since the SDRIF was not just a planning document, setting the priorities for development and land use, but also had legal force, in so far as it was binding on all the public and private actors in the sense that it was "effective against third parties" (*opposable aux tiers*). The preparation of and vote on the SDRIF therefore led to a struggle between the government and the local authorities, the first skirmish in a recurring conflict that continues to this day.

From the early 1980s, and following the decentralization acts, the Île-de-France region asked the state to begin a procedure for the revision of the master plan, which dated from 1976 and already appeared obsolete. The government agreed, and the region decided to begin its own process of discussion on the master plan. In 1989, following the national, presidential and parliamentary elections, which strengthened the socialist government, the latter decided to take the matter in hand. It published a report titled *Réflexions préalables à l'actualisation du schéma directeur de la région de'Île-de-France* that set out the main priorities that it wished to see pursued in the planning and development of the region. The part that the government intended to play in this was clearly stated: "If the state does not perform its role, and in the absence of any overarching authority, the region's tendencies to 'Balkanization' will be exacerbated, with inevitable negative consequences for our economic dynamism and our European role ..." (Cottour 2008b: 117).

The region, supported by five *départements*, Paris and most of the municipalities, responded to the White Paper with a Blue Paper on Île-de-France entitled "Reflections on the White Paper". This Paper differed from that of the government and called for a greater role on the part of local authorities in drawing up the master plan. The government ignored it and in 1994 published a document called the SDRIF (Schéma directeur de la région Île-de-France), whose priorities conflicted with most of the wishes of the local actors. In this sense, the 1994 SDRIF was unquestionably government-imposed. It would remain in force until the early 2010s, when the new SDRIF was approved (see subsequent chapters). Moreover, the preface to the new master plan is clear on this point:

> The spatial organization of a region like Île-de-France, which has interregional and national influence, calls for ideas and choices that far exceeds the scope of intervention of the local authorities ... It is therefore incumbent [on these] authorities to incorporate the main choices and priorities of the Regional master plan into their own planning strategies. [...] It is not the task of the state to decide on the detailed content of urban plans, zone by zone, but it is its fundamental responsibility to set the main objectives ... and to establish the general rules that apply to each one.

In parallel, throughout this long period, the state would endeavour to develop the capital's cultural and touristic attractiveness by pursuing a policy of major projects that would culminate with what, under François Mitterrand, came to be called the "big Paris projects". The Centre Pompidou opened in 1977, followed by the Musée d'Orsay in 1986 and the Institut du monde arabe and La Villette park and centre in 1987; Opéra Bastille and the Grande Arche followed in 1989, for the bicentenary of the French Revolution; the Bibliothèque nationale de France followed in 1995, and then of course there was the massive Grand Louvre project, which began in 1981 and ended in 1999.

So, the state did not desert its capital in the two decades that followed the passing of the big decentralization acts. Nonetheless, the "*graviériste*" policy designed to check the development of Paris continued, conducted by DATAR. For example, 23,000 jobs were relocated out of Paris between 1960 and 1990, and a further 25,000 between 1991 and 2001. Institutions, some of them prestigious, left Île-de-France to set up shop in Strasbourg (École nationale d'administration), in Toulouse (Météo France), in Nantes (National Criminal Records and Pensions Department) or in Marseille (Institut de recherche pour le développement: IRD). In 2000 DATAR advocated an end to the relocatins, as Île-de-France was in demographic decline, but they nevertheless continued for a little longer (IRD was relocated in 2008).

As for the authorization procedure, this was relaxed to the point of becoming no more than an administrative formality, because refusals were rare, and it was seen as a failure (François-Poncet 2003). Moreover, by the end of the 1990s the state was no longer talking of "slowing down Parisian growth" but of "controlling the urban growth of Île-de-France". Île-de-France was also penalized by the state's refusal – via DATAR – to allocate European money and in particular money from European structural funds such as the European Regional Development Fund (ERDF). The reason given was the wealth of the region, and therefore its lack of need for European funds in order to develop. Until 1999, therefore, the region was declared ineligible for these funds, and particularly for the so-called "Objective 2" funds intended for industrial restructuring. The only European funds that Île-de-France obtained from the European Union came from the "Urban" programme, a European Commission initiative. The amounts involved were minimal, however, and carefully targeted at small urban areas (Aulnay-sous-Bois, Les Mureaux, etc.).

### *Exacerbation of political conflicts, 1977–2001*

The period that began after the 1977 municipal elections and the 1978 parliamentary election would bring significant political changes, both locally and nationally. It would see the collapse of the PCF and the near-disappearance of the red suburbs; the right would consolidate its territorial holdings and new political forces such as the National Front and the ecologists would emerge, leading to a partial reshuffle of the cards, notably on the left, where the Socialist Party would gradually replace the Communist Party as the leading political force.

#### Decline of the red suburbs

The Communist Party's stranglehold on a large section of the suburbs loosened fairly quickly following the presidential and parliamentary elections of 1981, and especially after the municipal elections of 1983. This sharp decline in the importance of the PCF was not confined to Île-de-France, since it was also apparent nationally, but the party's embeddedness in certain strongholds of Île-de-France further reinforced this decline, which came suddenly.

In June 1981 the Communist Party lost almost half its Members of Parliament, whose numbers fell from 86 in 1978 to 44. In Île-de-France, 11 consistencies controlled by the PCF shifted to other political groupings, mainly the PS. The slaughter continued with the next municipal elections. Between 1977 and 1989 the PCF lost 14 Île-de-France municipalities with populations in excess of 30,000. The first regional elections were no better: the party won only 11 per cent of the votes, largely outstripped by the PS, with 29 per cent. For the left, the pink tide was on the rise, and the PS gradually siphoned off part of the communist electorate.

Only Seine-Saint-Denis seemed to hold firm, at least until the 1995 general election. Indeed, in 1983, the first municipal elections of the party's decline, it nevertheless held its position in 19 out of 20 municipalities. This respite was short-lived, however, and in 2001 the PCF held only 13 municipalities in the Seine-Saint-Denis *département*. On the other hand, at *département* level, the results were a little better, since the party held onto Seine-Saint-Denis (which it would lose in 2008) and, in particular, Val-de-Marne, which it would lose in June 2021.

What was the cause of this sudden collapse of communist dominance in Île-de-France and more broadly across the country? Historians (Fourcaut *et al.* 2006) advance three explanations. First, the end of international communism and of "real socialism", which – although remote from communists in Île-de-France and in France generally – played a big role in structuring its working-class bases; second, deindustrialization and the concentration of foreign populations in municipalities headed by the PCF, which both reduced the working-class population in these areas and brought in a population that was not socialized into day-to-day communist ideology; and, finally, an incapacity on the part of elected politicians themselves to understand and adapt to changes in society (rejection of deindustrialization, rejection of social mixing, rejection of first-time homeownership, etc.). These three factors contributed to the withdrawal of the existing populations, which preferred either to abstain, or to join other political forces, on the left with the Socialist Party but also, in some cases, on the extreme right, with the National Front.

## Construction and reinforcement of strongholds by the right

Although the red suburbs collapsed and the socialists took advantage of the decline, the right-wing parties were not to be outdone in the institutions that they held.

The regional elections of 1986 confirmed that rightist parties were the main political force at this level. They were not in a majority, however, if one excludes the National Front. With 45 per cent of the votes but 43 per cent for the left – in other words, almost level pegging – they were obliged to accommodate other small parties, which prevented them from governing. The same situation arose with the next elections, in 1992. Although the right won again, it held only 40 per cent of the votes, which once again prevented it from governing. It was the new parties that saved the day for them: the National Front, which gained 18 per cent of the vote, and the ecologists with the same score. The left collapsed, with just 23 per cent of the vote. The regional council was therefore dominated by the right, but this grouping remained a minority in votes and in seats because of the almost perfectly proportional result of the election. Either it was forced to make one-off alliances with other parties, or it was paralysed.

It was, above all, at the level of the *départements* and certain municipalities in the west of the region (Neuilly-sur-Seine, Rueil-Malmaison, Rambouillet, Versailles, etc.) that the right was dominant. Yvelines, Hauts-de-Seine and Paris became strongholds. In Yvelines, the general council had been Gaullist since 1968 – in other words since the creation of the *département*. As for Hauts-de-Seine, it too was controlled by Gaullists with a high national profile, such as Charles Pasqua, minister of the interior in 1988 and then in 2004, or Nicolas Sarkozy, several times a minister and future president of the Republic. The other *départements* were either broadly centrist, such as Val-d'Oise, or fluctuated between right and left, such as Essonne and Seine-et-Marne.

It was in Paris, however, that the right would really thrive. Although conservative parties won the 1977 municipal elections hands down, they nevertheless lost some of the *arrondissements* in the east, in the centre and in the south to the left, and notably to the PCF, which controlled four of them with some of the largest populations (see Map 3.2 on page 59). In the 1983 elections the wind shifted, and the right won the grand slam, taking all 20 *arrondissements* in the capital (see Map 3.3). This triumph and the rout of the left was undoubtedly attributable to the collapse of the PCF, with Paris confirming the trend across the country and in Île-de-France, but also to the strong personality of Jacques Chirac; elected mayor in 1977, he had been several times a minister and then prime minister, and in 1981 became leader of the opposition to the left, which was in power nationally. Parties of the right repeated the grand slam in 1989. By the end of the 1980s the left had practically disappeared from Paris's municipal council. It was only with the elections of 1995 that it would make a reappearance, as we will see below.

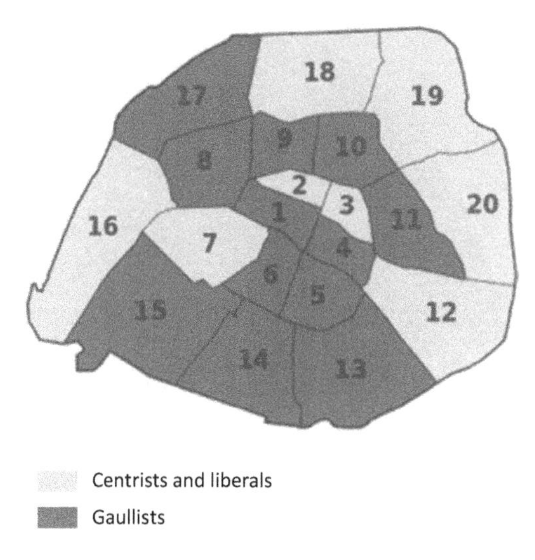


**Map 3.3** Results of the 1983 elections to the Paris municipal council
*Note*: Dark grey = the Gaullists; light grey = the centrists and liberals.

## Return of the left: the region and Paris

The collapse of the Communist Party was initially of benefit primarily to the Socialist Party, and subsequently to the ecologists as well. These two political forces, in which the PS was dominant, would also benefit from the internal squabbling of the right-wing parties, and in particular among the Gaullists, allowing them gradually to return to the front of the stage and to win significant political victories.

Winning the region and its capital was indeed a major objective of the Socialist Party, which, although victorious in the presidential and parliamentary elections of 1981 and 1988, was unable to establish a real presence in Île-de-France. The conflicts within the right would prove helpful, however. Chirac was no longer a player in Paris for the 1995 municipal elections, since he had won the presidential election a month earlier. His heir apparent, Jean Tibéri, former deputy mayor, was the Gaullist candidate. He lacked both the aura and charisma of his predecessor, not to mention his political capital. Moreover, he was selected by the Gaullists after an internal struggle that left its mark on the party. Despite this, he won the elections but lost six *arrondissements* (see Map 3.4).

Three years later the regional elections gave power to the left, called the "plural left" because several parties rallied around the PS, including the

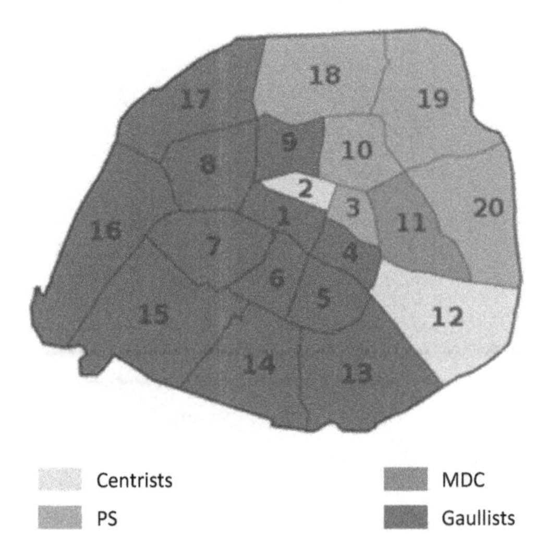


**Map 3.4** Results of the 1995 elections to the Paris municipal council
*Note*: Dark grey = the Gaullists; light grey (2nd and 12th districts) = the centrists; grey = the PS. The 11th district was controlled by the Mouvement des Citoyens (MDC), close to the PS.

ecologists. These elections confirmed the rise of the socialists in Île-de-France. The left and the right ran neck and neck. The left won more than 41 per cent of the votes, slightly ahead of the right. It held 86 seats out of the 209 on the regional council, the right 86, but the National Front won 36. It was therefore in a minority, but held the chair of the regional council. Like the right previously, it was obliged to engage in constant negotiation to win one-off majorities. This would change with the 2004 elections, in which a new voting system set the scene for more stable majorities, as we will see.

There are several reasons why the "plural left" captured the region, in particular the loss of support for a right that had little to show for its time in power, and the rise of the vote for the ecologists, which, combined with the votes of the other left-wing parties, expanded their electorate. This victory, which would be confirmed in subsequent elections, nevertheless marked a profound change in the balance of power between the parties and led to a relative levelling of the political system – a levelling that continued with the 2001 municipal elections.

In 2001 the left lost municipal elections. The Communist Party continued to decline and the PS lost 23 municipalities with populations in excess of 30,000. The Greens (the main ecologist party) emerged as winners in the electoral game. In Paris, thanks to a second-round agreement between the Socialist Party and the Greens, the left won 49.6 per cent of the votes and the right 50.4 per cent. Although this gave the latter a slight majority

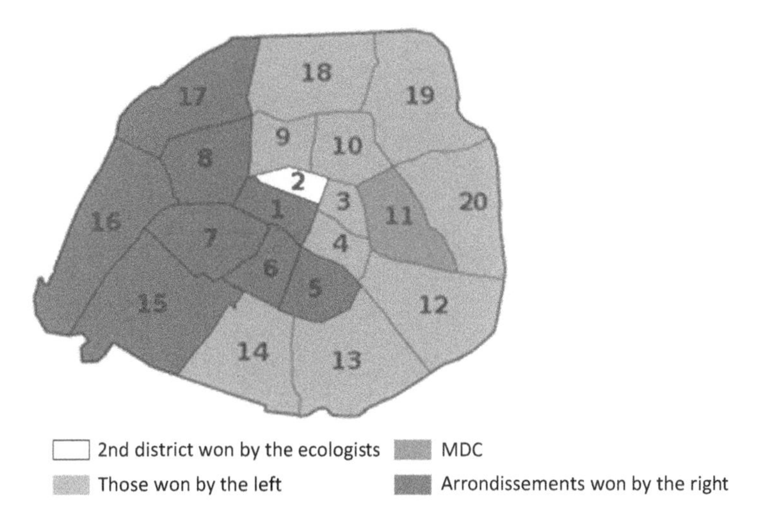


**Map 3.5** Results of the 2001 elections to the Paris municipal council
*Note*: Dark grey = the *arrondissements* won by the right; grey = those won by the left; white = the 2nd district, won by the ecologists. The 11th district was controlled by the MDC, close to the PS.

of votes, it was profoundly divided because of a breakaway group led by the former mayor, Jean Tibéri. This situation prevented it winning a number of *arrondissements* where the left came out ahead. In the final analysis, the left won 12 *arrondissements* (see Map 3.5), including those with the largest populations, giving it a clear majority on the municipal council. In June 2001 Paris elected its first socialist mayor, Bertrand Delanoë.

The picture that emerges from these almost 25 years of political life is that of a political system balanced between right and left. Real as this balance is, it is anything but peaceful. Instead, it is characterized by powerful conflicts between the parties, which are divided by different – not to say incompatible – visions of society and of Île-de-France in particular. These parties have been able to build now powerful territorial bastions, which they can use as resources to win power at other scales, local or national. What we see is, therefore, a highly conflictual political system, and one not predisposed to produce the public policies that citizens need to resolve the problems of Île-de-France, let alone to anticipate the challenges that lie ahead. This will be our subject in Chapters 5 and 6.

# 4

# The economy of Île-de-France: from national capital to global metropolis

The purpose of this chapter is to give an overview of the state of the Île-de-France economy at the beginning of the 2020s, to show its significance as a global metropolis and to shine a light on the specificities of the Paris region in comparison with cities of the same importance at the world level.

## From deindustrialization to internationalization: the birth of a global city region

With a GDP of €709 billion in 2018 (Choose Paris Region 2020), the Île-de-France region is one of the most powerful and one of the richest in the world (see Table 4.1). Yet its GDP growth is fairly low (averaging 1.3 per cent a year between 2000 and 2015), which distinguishes it from cities such as London (2.4 per cent) and New York (1.6 per cent), where GDP growth has been higher (Parilla, Marchio & Leal Trujillo 2016).

**Table 4.1** Île-de-France GDP in volume and per capita, 2002–2018

| GDP | 2002 | 2004 | 2010 | 2015 | 2018 |
|---|---|---|---|---|---|
| In volume (constant €) | 407,039 | 432,493 | 528,010 | 639,246 | 709,000 |
| Per capita (current €) | | 41,112 | 48,378 | 55,227 | 58,300 |

*Sources*: CCI Paris Île-de-France, Institut Paris Région & INSEE Île-de-France (various years); Choose Paris Region (2020).

### *From deindustrialization to tertiarization*

By and large, the recent economic history of the region is common to most cities of the Global North, moving from a period of deindustrialization, in parallel with a tertiarization movement, to a gradual internationalization.

Deindustrialization, which began in the 1960s, was initially slow, with the Île-de-France losing "only" 100,000 industrial jobs between 1960 and 1975. This trend accelerated in the following decade, with the region losing 300,000 jobs – i.e. 25 per cent of its industrial workers. Between 1985 and 1994 the decline continued, with an even sharper loss of 350,000 jobs. Then it slowed, but between 1960 and 2000 the haemorrhage of employment was huge, with the region losing more than 50 per cent of its industrial jobs. Since then this process has slowed down, with the region losing only about 100,000 industrial jobs between 2005 and 2018 (Institut Paris Région 2020a).

In parallel, the regional economy followed a tertiarization process. Since the mid-2000s around 87 per cent of added value has come from the service sector (see Table 4.2).

**Table 4.2** Added value per sector (percentage shares), 2002–2015

| | 2002 | 2005 | 2010 | 2015 |
|---|---|---|---|---|
| Agriculture | 0.1 | 0.2 | 0.3 | 0.1 |
| Industry | 12.4 | 8.3 | 8.1 | 9.2 |
| Construction | 3.6 | 4.0 | 4.4 | 4.0 |
| Tertiary – commercial | | 71.0 | 70.7 | 70.8 |
| Tertiary – non-commercial | | 16.6 | 16.6 | 15.9 |
| Tertiary total | 83.9 | 87.6 | 87.3 | 86.7 |
| Total | 100.0 | 100.0 | 100.0 | 100.0 |

*Sources*: CCI Paris Île-de-France, Institut Paris Région & INSEE Île-de-France (various years); Choose Paris Region (2020).

As for Île-de-France's working population, it has been incrementally but steadily increasing since 1999, and stood at more than 6.3 million in 2018, showing a net increase of almost 27 per cent, far above the population growth of 11.4 per cent over the same period (see Table 4.3).

**Table 4.3** Labour force and population (millions), 1999–2018

| | 1999 | 2005 | 2010 | 2015 | 2018 | 1999–2018 (% increase) |
|---|---|---|---|---|---|---|
| Employment | 5.04* | 5.42 | 5.58 | 6.11 | 6.39 | + 26.8 |
| Population | 10.95 | 11.47 | 11.79 | 12.08 | 12.2 | + 11.4 |

*Note*: * = urban area (aire urbaine).

*Source*: CCI Paris Île-de-France, Institut Paris Région & INSEE Île-de-France (various years).

**Table 4.4** Percentage of private jobs by economic sector, 1999–2018

| | 1999 | 2005 | 2010 | 2018 |
|---|---|---|---|---|
| Industry | 13.0 | 13.5 | 11.6 | 7.3 |
| Construction | 5.0 | 6.0 | 6.5 | 4.8 |
| Commerce | 13.0 | 17.8 | 16.9 | 25.3 |
| Services | 69.0 | 62.7 | 65.0 | 62.6 |
| Total | 100.0 | 100.0 | 100.0 | 100.0 |

*Sources*: IAU (2001); CCI Paris Île-de-France, Institut Paris Région & INSEE Île-de-France (various years).

Tertiarization has obviously marked this evolution. Although the service sector represented only 54 per cent of jobs in 1960, in 2000 it accounted for 80 per cent of jobs in the region, and almost 88 per cent in 2019, much more than the national average of 80 per cent (see Table 4.4). Consequently, although the number of farming jobs is today almost insignificant (0.3 per cent), industry accounts for only slightly more than 7 per cent of employment (CCI Paris Île-de-France, Institut Paris Région & INSEE Île-de-France 2020).

### *The birth of a global city region*

Over the last two decades the Île-de-France region has gradually developed and strengthened its relations with the rest of the world, in economic as well as political and cultural terms.

First and foremost, international exchanges (imports and exports) have increased considerably over the last 15 years, as shown in Table 4.5. As we can see, Île-de-France has been in continuous deficit with respect to the rest of the world, the balance between imports and exports being negative; whereas the volume of exchanges has significantly increased, however, the deficit has remained constant, and the ratio of imports to exports has significantly improved from about 65 per cent in 2005 to almost 70 per cent in 2019.

**Table 4.5** International exchanges between Île-de-France and the world (€ millions), 2005–2019

| | 2005 | 2010 | 2015 | 2019 |
|---|---|---|---|---|
| Imports | 102,289 | 119,111 | 136,601 | 150,337 |
| Exports | 66,165 | 67,555 | 83,228 | 104,232 |

*Sources*: CCI Paris Île-de-France, Institut Paris Région & INSEE Île-de-France (various years); Choose Paris Region (2020).

As a whole, the Paris region's main imports concern automobiles, oils and telecommunication equipment, while its main exports are in the sectors of automotive, space and aeronautics, luxury goods and pharmaceutical products. It principally deals with European countries (Germany, then Belgium, Italy and Spain), followed by the United States and China.

Regarding the finance economy, Île-de-France is a region that is internationally attractive. It drew slightly over $20 billion in greenfield investments (new subsidiaries created on foreign markets) between 2009 and 2015 (Parilla, Marchio & Leal Trujillo 2016), placing it in fourth position, close to New York ($26 billion), but a very long way behind London (almost $76 billion). Table 4.6 shows the increasing significance of foreign direct investment in the regional economy in terms of new sites and in the volume of jobs created. The investors are mainly European (from Germany and the United Kingdom), American and Chinese.

**Table 4.6** Foreign direct investment in the Paris region, 2005–2019

| | **2005** | **2010** | **2014** | **2019** |
|---|---|---|---|---|
| Sites | 217 | 243 | 368 | 415 |
| Created jobs | 9,001 | 8,415 | 5,032 | 9,660 |

*Sources*: CCI Paris Île-de-France, Institut Paris Région & INSEE Île-de-France (various years); Choose Paris Region (2020).

Today the number of jobs that depend on foreign companies has reached about 620,000 – i.e. one out of six private jobs. These companies belong to 90 countries, principally the United States, Germany and the United Kingdom. These jobs are first in the wholesale sector, then in industry, followed by scientific and technical activities and information and communication.

The international attractiveness and importance of the Île-de-France can also be seen in the number of headquarters of big companies located there. It is ranked second in the world as a location for the head offices of big companies, equal to New York, but behind London. As for the ranking established by the magazine *Fortune* of the headquarters location of the world's 500 biggest companies, Paris occupies third place behind Beijing and Tokyo, just ahead of London and New York (see Table 4.7), and this has been constant over the last decade.

The research and development sector has also internationalized. Numerous Parisian universities and higher education institutions are world-renowned, notably in mathematics, atmospheric science, business and fashion (Choose Paris Region 2020). Although 18.1 per cent of students were foreign-born in 2014 (Parilla, Marchio & Leal Trujillo 2016), this percentage had increased to 21 per cent in 2019, with about 120,000 foreign students in public and private universities and elite schools (Choose Paris Region 2020). They mostly came from Africa (about half), then from Europe, Asia and the Americas. More than 8,000 doctoral students are foreign – i.e. 34 per cent of the doctoral PhD students in the region. As a whole, the region hosts about 6,000 foreign researchers.

The internationalization of the region's economy can also be measured by the number of international trade shows that it hosts (see Table 4.8). With revenues of more than €6 billion and around 100,000 jobs in 2018, Paris is ranked first in the world for trade shows and congresses. In that year it hosted almost 1,200 such events. The number of foreigners accounted for 37 per cent of visitors and 28 per cent of exhibitors, but they were responsible for almost 70 per cent of the economic spin-offs (CCI Paris Île-de-France, Institut Paris Région & INSEE Île-de-France 2019). This has been made possible by the 22 big exhibition and conference venues, totalling 700,000 square metres, which is the most in the world. As a whole, in 2018 Paris attracted more than 9 million visitors to trade shows, congresses and conferences, and this has been a process of constant development for the last ten years.

**Table 4.7** Location of headquarters of Fortune 500 companies, 2007–2018

| | 2007 | 2012 | 2018 |
|---|---|---|---|
| Beijing | 18 | 44 | 56 |
| Tokyo | 50 | 48 | 36 |
| Paris | 26 | 31 | 28 |
| New York | 22 | 18 | 17 |
| London | 22 | 18 | 13 |

*Source*: Fortune Global 500 ranking (various years).

**Table 4.8** Trade shows, congresses and conferences, 2008–2019

| | 2008 | 2012 | 2016 | 2019 |
|---|---|---|---|---|
| Number of events | 863 | 1013 | 1088 | 1518 |
| Participants | 556,903 | 617,629 | 691,299 | 922,000 |

*Source*: CCI Paris Île-de-France, Institut Paris Région & INSEE Île-de-France (various years).

On the tourist front, Île-de-France is also very well placed. More than 19 million foreign tourists visited the French capital in 2019. Tourism generates some €15 billion in added value every year and the sector directly employs more than 260,000 people. The number of foreign tourists, based on

**Table 4.9** Evolution of tourism in the Paris region, 2007–2019[1]

| | 2006 | 2010 | 2015 | 2018 | 2019 |
|---|---|---|---|---|---|
| Arrivals (millions) | 31.1 | 31.8 | 32.4 | 35.0 | 35.4 |
| Percentage foreigners | 45.6 | 41.8 | 48.1 | 50.2 | 46.9 |

*Source*: CCI Paris Île-de-France, Institut Paris Région & INSEE Île-de-France (various years).

data from hotels and tourist residences, show a constant increase since the end of the 2000s (see Table 4.9).

The importance of tourism, and in particular tourism from other countries, is attributable to Paris's remarkable historical and cultural heritage, among the richest in the world. In particular, Parisian museums attract the most people, with the Louvre regularly leading the pack with more than 10 million visitors in 2018. Seventy-five per cent of the visitors are foreign, mainly American, Chinese or European. Apart from the Louvre, Île-de-France is home to many other remarkable sites, such as the Eiffel Tower and the Palace of Versailles, as well as world-ranking theme parks such as Disneyland Paris, which attracted more than 15 million visitors in 2018.

In addition to the international attraction brought by economic sectors such as research and tourism, the Paris region, and notably the city of Paris, has gained worldwide visibility with several scientific and cultural events and has a strong political presence.

Because of its history as the capital of a state that is keen to continue to play a significant global role, it is normal that Paris, and beyond it Île-de-France, should host such events. Paris has hosted no fewer than five great exhibitions, including several universal exhibitions, between 1889 and 1939; the Olympic Games of 1900 and of 1924. A century on, it will host the 2024 games. Other big sports competitions have taken place in Paris, such as the soccer World Cup in 1998, UEFA Euros in 2016, the Gay Games in 2018. Moreover, Paris regularly plays host to world-ranking sports events, such as the Roland Garros tennis tournament, one of the sport's four Grand Slam events, or its marathon, which attracts some 30,000 runners every year. In the scientific field, Paris has hosted several important scientific conferences, such as the conference on HIV science in July 2017 and the "Health Summit" in 2019.

1. The period from 2015 to 2019 was marked by several events that had a significant negative impact on foreign tourism: the terrorist attacks of 2015, strikes and *gilets jaunes* (yellow vests) demonstrations in 2018 and 2019.

In the international political arena, Paris is also one of the world's leading cities. It hosts several international organizations, including some of the most prestigious players, such as UNESCO and the Organisation for Economic Co-operation and Development (OECD). The French capital is also the headquarters of the European Space Agency, the World Organization for Animal Health (OIE) and the Organisation internationale de la francophonie. The Union of International Associations (UIA) ranks it second as a home for international organizations, both public and private, a position it has held for more than a decade, just behind Brussels and ahead of London and New York. Thus, according to the *Yearbook of International Organisations* published every year by the UIA, Paris was host to some 1,919 international organizations in 2005, although the number had fallen slightly by 2020 (1,863).

Regarding big political events, the national capital also plays a significant international role. For example, it has organized big conferences, such as those on peace in different parts of the world (e.g. the Conference for Peace in the Middle East, held in June 2016), the 2015 Climate Change Conference (COP 21) and UNESCO's annual conferences. More recently the One Planet Summit took place in Paris in December 2017, gathering heads of states, international organizations and NGOs. The fourth summit took place in January 2021, again in Paris.

Finally, the "worldliness" of the Paris region can be assessed by looking at the very many international rankings of cities that have been published in the last two decades. Although one needs to be cautious about these rankings, since they differ regarding the quality and comparability of their data, the number and types of cities analysed, the sector they focus on (culture, economic power, business, liveability, etc.), whether they emphasize the perception of the city by respondents or the reality of the city established by data, etc., they nevertheless offer a relatively adequate picture of the position of a city in the world and its evolution. In order to assess the "worldliness" of the Paris region, five such international rankings have been selected, which are among the most renowned:

1. The Globalization and World Cities Research Network (GaWC) ranking, directed by the British geographer Peter Taylor (see Table 4.10);
2. The Global Power City index, published yearly by the Japanese Mori Foundation;
3. The Global Cities Index of the international consultancy firm Kearney;
4. The Cities of Opportunity ranking established by PWC; and
5. The City brand index issued by the Anholt-Ipsos consortium (see Table 4.11).

All of them have been produced for more than a decade, and as such they can be used to assess not only Paris's position today but also its evolution.

**Table 4.10** GaWC ranking of cities, 2000–2020

| | 2000 | 2004 | 2008 | 2012 | 2016 | 2020 |
|---|---|---|---|---|---|---|
| London | 1 | 1 | 1 | 1 | 1 | 1 |
| New York | 2 | 2 | 2 | 2 | 2 | 2 |
| Hong Kong | 3 | 3 | 3 | 3 | 4 | 3 |
| Paris | 4 | 4 | 4 | 4 | 5 | 8 |

The Mori Foundation's Global Power City Index was first produced in 2008. Since then it has consistently placed Île-de-France third behind London and New York, and since 2016 fourth also behind Tokyo. This top position has been confirmed by the Kearney Global Cities Index, which has ranked Paris third every year since 2008, always behind New York and London, and ahead of Tokyo, Hong Kong and Los Angeles.

The Cities of Opportunity ranking, which since 2007 has analysed the performance of 35 world cities through ten indicators (technology readiness, intellectual capital, liveability, etc.) has positioned Paris fourth and sixth, depending on the year.

Finally, Île-de-France also holds an enviable position in the scientific and cultural spheres. Simon Anholt, who analyses a city's "brand" through six dimensions (pulse, quality of the place, reputation, potential, quality of the population and "prerequisites" [housing, schools, basis infrastructure, etc.]), has regularly ranked it at the head of the 50 world cities in his study.

**Table 4.11** Anholt ranking of cities, 2006–2020

| | 2006 | 2009 | 2013 | 2015 | 2020 |
|---|---|---|---|---|---|
| Paris | 3 | 1 | 3 | 1 | 3 |
| Sydney | 1 | 2 | 2 | 4 | 2 |
| London | 2 | 3 | 1 | 2 | 1 |
| New York | 5 | 5 | 4 | 3 | 4 |

As a whole, in spite of some annual changes, Paris has remained at the very top of the world ranking of cities over the last 15 years or so, confirming its economic and cultural power.

## The specificities of the Île-de-France economy

The economy of the Paris region thus demonstrates the importance of the Île-de-France as a powerful global territory. It holds this position for various reasons: first because of its place in the national economy, then because of its original economic model and finally because of its specificities. This second part of the chapter will develop these different dimensions.

### *A national capital with an original model of economic development*

#### The national economic capital

In terms of economic power, Île-de-France is France's leading region by far. With a GDP of almost €710 billion in 2018 (Choose Paris Region 2020), it accounts for almost a third (31.1 per cent) of national wealth. Its per capita GDP is €58,300, well above the French national average of €32,900. This domination has been constant over the decades, in spite of national public policies aiming at reducing the gap (see Chapter 2). With a stable share of population relative to the national population, it has slowly increased its economic weight over the last two decades (see Table 4.12), its GDP being far higher than its respective demographic importance.

**Table 4.12** The Île-de-France region in the national economy (percentage shares), 1999–2018

| | 1999 | 2006 | 2010 | 2016 | 2018 |
|---|---|---|---|---|---|
| Population | 19 | 19 | 19 | 19 | 18 |
| Jobs | 22 | 22 | 21 | 23 | 23 |
| GDP | 29 | 28 | 30 | 31 | 31 |
| R&D jobs | 42 | 39 | 40 | 40 | 40 |
| R&D expenditures | | 41 | 40 | 40 | 40 |

*Sources*: INSEE (2003); CCI Paris Île-de-France, Institut Paris Région & INSEE Île-de-France (various years).

Nationally, the region is dominant in a number of sectors (notably finance and the digital economy), but it is in research and development that Île-de-France stands out most sharply from the rest of the country. With its numerous universities, elite schools and research institutes and centres, it has no equivalent elsewhere in France. Île-de-France accounts for 40 per cent of national research and development expenditure, 42 per cent of patents filed and 35 per cent of scientific publications. It is home to 40 per cent of researchers based in France.

#### The Île-de-France economic model

In 2014 the Greater Paris Investment Agency (PICE) and the Île-de-France chamber of commerce published a study entitled *Compétitivité et attractivité: Le double défi des global cities: Comment réinventer le modèle économique de Paris*

*Île-de-France* (*Competitiveness and Attractiveness: The Twofold Challenge of Global Cities: How to Reinvent the Business Model of Paris Île-de-France*). In the study they identify four models of development, which can be observed in most global metropolises that are in competition with the Île-de-France.

The first model is the "generalist" model: a city that is a national or a continental capital, whose economic development is diversified. Tokyo, Los Angeles and Chicago are illustrations of this model. The second model is called "functional" and is represented by cities that possess a specialism and have a unique economic position, which allows them to concentrate their assets. Examples are San Francisco, Barcelona and Berlin. The third model is "multi-specialist". Cities belonging to this model possess a solid generalist base and have an active development of innovative sectors. This is the case with New York, London and Seoul. Finally, the "hub model" concerns cities that are logistic platforms and play a significant financial role at the world level, such as Singapore, Hong Kong and Dubai.

According to the study, Paris is positioned between the generalist and the multi-specialist models. Although this typology may be criticized, it highlights a significant feature of the Île-de-France economy: its diversity, in strong contrast with London and New York, for instance. Indeed, Île-de-France possesses a diversified economy, which may be explained by the long history of centralization of the economy by the state, which has boosted several economic sectors through many public policies, thus achieving a relative diversity, notably after the war during the so-called "*trente glorieuses*".[2] This has been the case in the automobile industry with the nationalization of Renault, aeronautics with the nationalization of Dassault, the energy sector with big national companies in gas and electricity and finance with banks such as Paribas. More recently it has been evident in the digital economy sector and telecommunications.

A diversified and generalist economy means that neither function nor sector is dominant, in industry as well as in the service sector. Although the region has gone through a deep deindustrialization process, this process has hit all the industrial branches, to the extent that, in 2010, 60 per cent of industrial employment was concentrated in no fewer than six areas: automotives, aeronautics, chemistry, pharmaceuticals, electronics and food processing. The same is true regarding services, with the bulk of the sector distributed between finance, media and telecommunications and tourism. According to Choose Paris Region, the regional agency in charge of promoting Île-de-France, "The Paris region is home to a truly diversified economy with industry

2. *Trente glorieuses*: the 30 postwar years of economic boom, from 1945 to 1975.

leaders, innovative start-ups ... It is renowned for its highly diversified economic landscape and sectors of excellence" (Choose Paris Region 2020). These are represented by key sectors such as business services, aerospace and defence, automotives, logistics and mobility, fashion, design and luxury goods, cleantech and energy, commerce and retail, creative industries, finance services and insurance, IT, health and life sciences, food industry, tourism, etc. (Choose Paris Region 2020).

This diversity can also be observed in the economic composition in terms of employment, which is relatively well distributed among enterprises of various sizes. In 2015 about 20 per cent of private jobs were in enterprises of fewer than ten employees, about 25 per cent in enterprises of between ten and 49 employees, about 25 per cent in companies with between 50 and 249 employees, about 20 per cent in firms of between 250 and 999 employees and a bit more than 11 per cent of firms with over 1,000 employees. This distribution has not significantly moved from a decade ago.

### *Specificities of the Île-de-France economy*

Positioned between the generalist and the multi-specialist models, the Île-de-France economy nevertheless offers some specificities that make it unique. The public sector is quite significant, retaining some important industrial subsectors, while several economic activities are among the top at the world level. It is relatively weak in finance, however.

#### Public economy

The public sector occupies a significant share of the Île-de-France regional employment. As of 2017 no fewer than 1.6 million jobs were in the public sector, which accounted for 27.5 per cent of total employment (CCI Paris Île-de-France, Institut Paris Région & INSEE Île-de-France 2020). This is almost 1 per cent more than ten years earlier, in 2007, which confirms the continuous importance of the public sector in the national capital for decades. Indeed, the main regional employers are public and dominate a variety of economic sectors, ranging from health to telecommunications and transport (see Table 4.13).

The significant weight of the public sector in the regional economy is largely explained by the strong presence of the state in the French economy, all the more so when it concerns the national capital. For instance, two of the main employers (AP-HP and RATP) are active only in the Paris region. AP-HP (Assistance publique–Hôpitaux de Paris) is the largest health care institution

**Table 4.13** The ten main regional employers in Île-de-France, 2005–2015

| | 2005 | 2015 | Sector | Status |
|---|---|---|---|---|
| AP-HP | 109,700 | 89,940 | Health | Public |
| Paris | 59,000 | 60,909 | Local government | Public |
| La Poste | 63,200 | 47,305 | Post and banking | Public |
| RATP | 43,800 | 45,653 | Mobility | Public |
| Air France | 49,000 | 40,657 | Air transport | Public |
| SNCF | 45,600 | 31,497 | Mobility | Public |
| Orange | | 31,497 | Telecommunications | Mixed* |
| Société Générale | 23,200 | 27,361 | Finance | Private |
| Paribas | 23,500 | 26,770 | Finance | Mixed* |
| PSA | 31,200 | 19,619 | Automobile | Private |

*Note*: * The French state is a shareholder.

*Source*: CCI Paris Île-de-France, Institut Paris Région & INSEE Île-de-France (2008), (2020).

of the region, with 39 hospitals and medical centres. RATP (Régie autonome des transports parisiens) is the main public transport operator of the region. The executives of both organizations are appointed by the council of ministers. The same is true for Air France, the national airline company, and SNCF, the national railways.

## Significant industrial sector

Despite reductions in the number of jobs in industry, the Paris region remains a significant industrial metropolis. In 2019 the industrial sector still employed 436,000 people and represented 7.4 per cent of regional employment and 9.2 per cent of regional GDP (CCI Paris Île-de-France, Institut Paris Région & INSEE Île-de-France 2020). With 14 per cent of national total employment, Île-de-France is the first French industrial region (Institut Paris Région 2020). The industrial sector has significantly changed, however, and has become more technological, requiring more highly qualified workers. Indeed, today 37 per cent of industrial workers occupy executive and highly qualified jobs (engineering and research). The dominant subsectors are the production of transport, automobile and aeronautical equipment (17.5 per cent of regional industrial jobs); the production of utilities, notably electricity and water (11 per cent of regional industrial jobs); the production of computers and electrical and optical products (11 per cent of regional industrial employment). Some of these industrial subsectors are growing, such as aerospace and the electricity production and pollution management industries.

## Weak financial sector

By contrast with some large global cities, such as London or New York, Île-de-France does not have a very powerful financial and real estate sector. With around 20 per cent of its GDP coming from the FIRE (finance, insurance, real estate) sector in 2015, and only around 7 per cent of this from finance as such, it cannot rival the powerful financial marketplaces of London and New York, which account for up to or in excess of 30 per cent of GDP for those sectors.

In terms of employment, the two sectors do not constitute more than 10 per cent of jobs, even though this has slowly increased over the last 15 years (see Table 4.14).

**Table 4.14** Jobs in the FIRE sector in Île-de-France (percentage shares of total private jobs), 2006–2018

| | 2006 | | 2015 | | 2018 | |
|---|---|---|---|---|---|---|
| | **Thousands** | **%** | **Thousands** | **%** | **Thousands** | **%** |
| Finance and insurance | 252 | 6.3 | 326 | 7.4 | 342 | 8.1 |
| Real estate | 45 | 1.1 | 77 | 1.7 | 79 | 1.9 |

*Sources*: CCI Paris Île-de-France, Institut Paris Région & INSEE Île-de-France (various years); DIRECCTE Île-de-France (2020).

Paris nevertheless holds some assets in this domain. It is home to several regional headquarters of international banks such as JP Morgan, HSBC, Citibank and BNP Paribas. It is also home to the Euronext headquarters, the largest stock exchange in Europe. Since 2017 the national government has launched several financial and fiscal reforms to improve the international competitiveness of the location. Nonetheless, Paris still falls short of not just the great financial hubs of London and New York, but also Tokyo, Frankfurt, Zurich, Shanghai and Hong Kong, largely because of the weak internationalization of its sector. The Global Financial Centres Index (GFCI) (Table 4.15)

**Table 4.15** Paris in the Global Financial Centres Index, 2009–2020

| | 2009 | 2015 | 2018 | 2020 |
|---|---|---|---|---|
| New York | 2 | 1 | 1 | 1 |
| London | 1 | 2 | 2 | 2 |
| Hong Kong | 3 | 3 | 3 | 5 |
| Singapore | 4 | 4 | 4 | 6 |
| Zurich | 6 | 5 | 9 | 10 |
| Tokyo | 9 | 6 | 6 | 4 |
| Frankfurt | 12 | 11 | 10 | 16 |
| Shanghai | 10 | 16 | 5 | 3 |
| Paris | 19 | 36 | 23 | 18 |

illustrates this situation. Although the ranking may change significantly each year, there is little fluctuation among the cities at the top and Paris, despite some progress remains far behind its major competing cities.

It is not yet clear whether Brexit will have any serious impact on Paris's situation in the finance sector. It is too soon to tell whether many jobs will leave the City of London, and Paris is not the only city that could benefit from Brexit. Other European competitors, such as Frankfurt, Zurich or even Milan, may also attract financial jobs, which would disperse the potential impact of Brexit across European financial centres.

## Île-de-France's strong economic sectors

Île-de-France is strong in six specific economic domains and subsectors, namely in aerospace and defence, luxury goods, health products and services, digital, research and development, and education and skills.

The aerospace, spatial and defence (ASD) sector is one of the most important economic sectors in the Île-de-France industry. With 100,000 workers in 2016, it represents about a quarter of total regional industrial employment (IAU 2018c). This sector is the domain of large firms, each grouping several thousands of employees, and includes world-leading firms such as Airbus, Ariane and Dassault in aeronautics and space, Safran and Thales in defence. Safran alone employs more than 20,000 people and Thales about 14,000. As a whole, more than 11,000 researchers work in these fields, accounting for 40 per cent of the nation's research in the sector.

The Île-de-France ASD sector is present over the whole set of activities, from research and development to the construction of products, supply and maintenance. This is because the region is home to the most important national research centres, such as the National Spatial Studies Centre (CNES), the Centre for Atomic Energy (CEA) and the laboratories of the National Scientific Research Centre (CNRS), and many constructors and suppliers. It is the first export sector of the region, and has been for decades.

France is the global leader in the luxury goods industry – that is, in the production of fashion, cosmetics, perfume, jewellery, leather goods, etc. – and Paris is the worlwide capital of luxury. Indeed, Paris-based firms such as LVMH (Moët Hennessy Louis Vuitton) and Kering are the two largest companies in the world for luxury goods. The luxury industry has become significantly concentrated in recent decades, with, for instance, LVMH now controlling no fewer than 70 world-famous brands, such as Christian Dior (perfume and cosmetics), Louis Vuitton (leather goods), Moët et Chandon (champagne),

Bulgari (jewellery) and Kenzo (fashion). Kering controls brands such as Gucci, Yves Saint Laurent and Balenciaga in the fashion sector.

In France, about 600,000 people work directly in the luxury goods sector, and indirectly 1 million jobs rely on the sector. About 30 per cent of such companies are located in Île-de-France, employing tens of thousands of people. The production of luxury goods is therefore an important asset for the regional economy. Eighty per cent of production is exported, making it the second largest export industry after aeronautics and defence.

Health is another sector of excellence of the regional economy. It has the highest concentration of firms in this sector in Europe. With more than 320,000 employees, and with 56,000 employed in the core of its activities (medical equipment, biotech), it is one of the largest employers in Île-de-France (Institut Paris Région 2019). The region is home to the largest research centres in the field, such as the Évry Genopole (genetics) or the Paris-Saclay University. These are among the top research facilities in biotech, genetics and medical imaging in the world. In addition, some of the most important international private firms, such as Sanofi, are located in Île-de-France with their headquarters and main research centres.

The health sector has gone through deep changes, partly as a result of the increasing use of artificial intelligence. Although the sector has increased its added value strongly because of this scientific transformation, it has had a negative impact on employment (4,500 job losses between 2007 and 2017) with the relocation of production abroad, notably to India and China. Over the same period, however, more than 2,000 skilled jobs in research and development have been added (Institut Paris Région 2019). The health sector is also one of the Paris region's international fields of competitiveness, with Medicen (see Chapter 6).

Île-de-France also has a strong digital sector, which is defined as all activities linked with information and telecommunications technology (software, telecommunication equipment, etc.). Indeed, 45 per cent of national employment in this sector is located in the region – that is, 620,000 jobs in 2015, representing 9 per cent of the total regional employment. There are around 20,000 firms in the digital industry, and some are top companies at the European level, such as ATOS, the European leader in cybersecurity and cloud computing (DIRECCTE Île-de-France 2019). A large number of these firms are very small, however, and in recent years the region – notably the city of Paris – has seen a proliferation of start-ups in this field; many business incubators have developed, such as "Station F", which is the largest start-up campus in the world (Institut Paris Région 2020). To support this economy, two clusters (see Chapter 6), Cap Digital and Systematic, have been set up and several enterprise networks have been formed, such as the French Tech and Optics Valley (Institut Paris Région 2020).

In research and development, Île-de-France occupies the top position in France, employing 40 per cent of all French public and private researchers. This is slightly more than 15 years ago, when "only" 35 per cent of French researchers were located in the region. This increase is largely attributable to the steady uptick in R&D expenditure, as shown in Table 4.16.

**Table 4.16** Expenditures and personnel in R&D in Île-de-France, 2006–2017

| | 2006 | 2010 | 2013 | 2017 | 2006–2017 |
|---|---|---|---|---|---|
| Expenditures (€ millions) | 15,512 | 17,441 | 18,664 | 20,281 | + 30.7% |
| % public expenditures | 33 | 35 | 32 | 31 | |
| Personnel | 137,272 | 146,213 | 155,135 | 165,547 | + 20.6% |
| % public personnel | 41 | 38 | 36 | 35 | |

*Source*: CCI Paris Île-de-France, Institut Paris Région & INSEE Île-de-France (various years).

This increase is essentially down to the private sector, however, which is responsible for almost all the growth in personnel, the public sector adding just over 2,000 researchers during this period compared to more than 25,000 by private firms. The quasi-stability of the number of public researchers in Île-de-France can partly be explained by the national policies to achieve a more even geographical distribution of R&D across France (see Chapter 2), as the rest of the country has experienced an increase of more than 20,000 public researchers. The bulk of expenditure on research, as well as on personnel, has been made by private firms, however, which account for more than two-thirds of total spending.

This financial and intellectual investment has enabled the region to be ranked supreme in Europe for spending on research and development, ahead of Stuttgart and Munich (IAU 2016a). This is also the case with the production of patents and scientific publications, for which Île-de-France was first in Europe until 2018, having recently been overtaken by Bavaria and Munich (Institut Paris Région 2020). In this field as well the region is by far the most important in France, with almost 60 per cent of patents (7,687) having been issued in 2018.

Another strong asset of the Île-de-France economy lies in its population, which is young and well educated by national and international standards. In 2018 25 per cent of people living in the region were below 19 years of age, 38 per cent were between 25 and 29 and 53 per cent were under 40. This is more than the rest of France, and for the 25–29 age range it is ahead of London, Lombardy, Andalucia and Catalonia (Institut Paris Région 2020a). Not only is this population young, it is also well educated, as Table 4.17 clearly illustrates.

**Table 4.17** Level of qualification of the Île-de-France labour force (percentage shares), 2008–2018

| | IdF | France | IdF | France | IdF | France |
|---|---|---|---|---|---|---|
| | **2008** | **2008** | **2010** | **2010** | **2018** | **2018** |
| No diploma | 16.7 | 17.1 | 16.8 | 16.5 | 13.2 | 10.6 |
| Baccalauréat* | 18.9 | 19.0 | 18.8 | 19.1 | 17.4 | 21.4 |
| Bac + 2** | 13.9 | 13.8 | 13.3 | 14.5 | 13.6 | 16.0 |
| 2nd and 3rd cycle*** | 26.9 | 13.4 | 28.8 | 14.6 | 37.8 | 21.4 |

*Notes*: * Baccalauréat = the final degree after high school. ** Bac + 2 = more or less equivalent to an American BA. *** 2nd cycle = masters level. 3rd cycle = PhD level.

*Source*: CCI Paris Île-de-France, Institut Paris Région & INSEE Île-de-France (various years).

Thus, almost twice as many people in the regional labour force hold a graduate degree (37.8 per cent) compared to 21.4 per cent in the rest of France. Forty-one per cent of the total population of the region holds a university degree, achieving at least an undergraduate degree. This level of education may be partly explained by the importance of the higher education system in Île-de-France in comparison with the rest of the country. Indeed, no fewer than 16 universities and 70 elite schools (*grandes écoles*) are located in the region. A significant number of the elite schools are in the fields of business, engineering and advanced technology. Among the business schools, three are top European schools, namely HEC Paris, Insead and Essec, respectively ranking first, fifth and seventh (Choose Paris Region 2020). As a whole Île-de-France contains about 40 per cent of all PhD students in France.

Tourism is also a strong and growing economic sector, as previously indicated. At the world level, Paris has reached top positions in the last decade, as illustrated in Table 4.18, which uses the Mastercard Global Destination Cities Index (GDCI). The Mastercard GDCI is based on international visitor arrivals, and the data are obviously very much dependent on specific events and situations. In the last ten years or so, however, there has clearly been stability in the top positions, Paris being in the top three and always ahead of New York and Tokyo. Indeed, as already indicated above, Paris's historical heritage and cultural renown is international. For instance, the Louvre is the most visited museum in the world. The economic importance of tourism can also be illustrated by the increasing revenues it brings to the regional economy and the many jobs it provides. In 2018 tourist consumption amounted to almost €22 billion (CCI Paris Île-de-France, Institut Paris Région & INSEE Île-de-France 2020), and it has risen constantly since 2015.

**Table 4.18** International ranking and number of tourists in the top ten cities, 2012–2019

| | 2012 | | 2015 | | 2019 | |
|---|---|---|---|---|---|---|
| | **Rank** | **Volume** | **Rank** | **Volume** | **Rank** | **Volume** |
| Paris | 2 | 16.9 | 3 | 16.06 | 2 | 19.10 |
| London | 1 | 16.9 | 1 | 18.82 | 3 | 19.09 |
| Bangkok | 3 | 12.2 | 2 | 18.24 | 1 | 22.78 |
| Dubai | 8 | 8.8 | 4 | 14.26 | 4 | 15.93 |
| Singapore | 4 | 11.8 | 7 | 11.88 | 5 | 14.67 |
| Kuala Lumpur | 10 | 8.1 | 8 | 11.12 | 6 | 13.79 |
| New York | 13 | 7.6 | 6 | 12.27 | 7 | 13.60 |
| Istanbul | 5 | 11.6 | 5 | 12.56 | 8 | 13.40 |
| Tokyo* | | | | | 9 | 12.93 |
| Antalya* | | | | | 10 | 12.41 |

*Note*: * Not in the top 20 in 2012 and 2015.

*Source*: Mastercard Global Destination Cities Index (various years).

## Small foreign population

Finally, another specificity of the Île-de-France economy and society is the relatively weak internationalization of its population, at least with respect to other comparable metropolitan areas in the world. True, as we have seen in the previous chapters, the municipality of Paris and the Île-de-France region have experienced a significant increase in their foreign-born population over recent years, but its importance in the total population is much less than in many other similar cities in the world, and the growth is slow compared to other urban areas (see Table 4.19).

**Table 4.19** Percentage of foreign-born population in urban areas, 2013

| **Urban area** | **Percentage** |
|---|---|
| Montreal | 23 |
| Paris | 25 |
| London | 37 |
| New York | 37 |
| Sydney | 39 |
| Los Angeles | 39 |
| Toronto | 46 |

*Source*: International Organization for Migration [IOM] (2015).

In conclusion, several significant points may be stressed, notably in comparative terms with its main rivals, London and New York. The Île-de-France economy is strong because it is at the same time the economy of a national capital and of a global metropolis. If the role of the public sector remains quite important for historical and political reasons, this nevertheless does not prevent the private sector acting as a powerful engine of economic growth, notably in several highly competitive areas internationally, such as ASD and health. Île-de-France is also home to several top firms in many sectors, such as infrastructure construction and urban utilities, whose activities play a role in making the Paris region a truly global metropolis.

# 5

# Problems and challenges

Île-de-France faces most of the problems that confront other big metropolitan regions in the West, and has to respond to largely similar challenges. The size of the metropolis, its density and its economic power mean that – as with London and New York – it is primarily attractive for economic rather than residential reasons. In this chapter, I propose to set out the main problems and challenges facing Île-de-France in terms of a fundamental tension between, on the one hand, an economic attractiveness and competitiveness that some consider to be in decline and, on the other hand, a rise in social and territorial inequalities that is perceived as a threat to the development of the metropolis. This choice is explained by the fact that these two problems and challenges are espoused by powerful coalitions of actors of roughly equal strength, which have long championed different views on what public policies to follow, on their territorialization and on reforms in the governance of Île-de-France, as we will see in the upcoming chapters.

More recently, the environmental question has become part of the debate, but that debate remains dominated by the dichotomy between competitiveness and rising inequalities, and it will also be presented in the light of that division. Unsurprisingly, it is questions of housing and transport that lie at the heart of the matter. In this sense, Île-de-France is no different from its big international rivals. These questions, which I will tackle in greater detail below, relate both to the doubts concerning the French capital's economic performance and to the emergence of an increasingly less inclusive city. They form a system.

For this reason, this chapter is divided into two parts. The first provides a summary of the main issues affecting the region today: housing, mobility, environment, socio-territorial inequalities, attractiveness and competitiveness are all covered, one by one. The second part shows how these problems generate challenges in terms of economic attractiveness and competitiveness, on the one hand, and the fight against inequalities, on the other. Questions such as air pollution, climate change and the region's resilience to different risks are tackled in the next chapter, which deals with the policies implemented to combat these problems and challenges.

## The main problems that Île-de-France faces: inventory

### *Housing: a matter of concern*

As with many big cities, Île-de-France has seen the emergence of a housing crisis, which primarily takes the form of housing shortages and prices that are too high for a large section of its population.

The last national housing survey (Enquête nationale logement: ENL), from which the main data here are drawn, dates back to 2013.[1] According to that survey, Île-de-France's housing stock consists of 5.1 million units, only a very slight increase on the 2006 figure of 4.9 million. Almost a quarter (1.2 million) are located within the city of Paris. Most of these dwellings are of fairly good quality, since the ENL identifies only 5 per cent as being substandard and notes that squalid living conditions have almost disappeared.

Half the households in the region are homeowners, the other half tenants. The period from 1998 to 2008 was favourable to first-time buyers, but the banking crisis of 2008, followed by a sharp economic slowdown, brought this trend to a halt, since the number of homeowners – which had been increasing steadily since 1998 – stagnated between 2006 and 2013. For the half of the population living in rented accommodation, 50 per cent are in social housing, 40 per cent are private tenants and 10 per cent live in hotels or have free accommodation. Île-de-France's social housing stock is therefore substantial. With 1.2 million units in 2014 and 1.3 million in 2017 (DRIEA 2020), it accounts for a quarter of France's total social housing stock. This capacity is not uniformly distributed across the region, however, with about 20 per cent in Paris, 46 per cent in the inner suburbs and 35 per cent in the outer suburbs. Worse, almost half the social housing capacity in Île-de-France is found in just 50 of the some 1,300 municipalities in the region: 32 in the inner ring, eight in the outer ring, with ten *arrondissements* in Paris, mainly in the north and east, completing the list. This distribution is not unconnected with the socio-territorial inequalities affecting the metropolis.

1. All data are drawn from the most recent national housing survey, carried out in 2013. The next one started in 2020, with the first results out by late 2021.

Nonetheless, this social housing provision is woefully inadequate for the demand. In 2017 2.3 million households were eligible for social housing – i.e. 45 per cent of the population of Île-de-France (IAU 2018b). But only half were in such housing, the rest being obliged to depend on the private rental market, which – as we will see later – entails much higher costs.

Moreover, although the quality of the housing is largely good, living conditions are less so. About 20 per cent of dwellings are overpopulated, and, in some areas such as Seine-Saint-Denis, or certain districts in northern and eastern Paris, this figure rises to 25 per cent, which indicates a mismatch between household size and dwelling size (see Table 5.1). By comparison, the national average is only 10 per cent. In addition, the ENL estimates that, in 2013, 9 per cent of the inhabitants of Île-de-France were experiencing poor housing conditions (squalid accommodation, insecure occupancy status, etc.).

**Table 5.1** Proportion of overpopulated dwellings (percentages), 2013

| | **Overpopulated (%)** |
|---|---|
| Paris | 27.1 |
| Inner ring | 22.0 |
| Outer ring | 14.0 |
| Île-de-France | 20.2 |
| France | 9.5 |

*Sources*: ENL (2013); IAU (2017b).

Another facet of the housing crisis is the growing number of rough sleepers or homeless people. Here, the statistics are fewer and are often a matter of dispute between the authorities and the organizations that support these populations. Nonetheless, the few official figures released by government (PRIF & DRIHL 2019) indicate that these numbers are on the rise. Whereas there were 78,000 in 2009, the number had risen to 105,000 in 2012. In 2017 103,000 individuals were using the administrative address system,[2] a figure that excludes migrant camps (around 7,000 people in 2016) and rough sleepers, for whom no official statistics exist (IAU & MGP 2018).

All these facts and figures reveal a serious crisis, fed partly by the continuing and increasingly steep rise in housing costs. First, housing is the number one spending item in household budgets, and this proportion has been growing in the region for the past several years (IAU 2018b). This is largely explained by

2. A system that enables a homeless person to be assigned an address with an official approved organization (Centre communal d'action sociale, for instance).

rising prices and the growing mismatch between this rise and the downward trends in household incomes. Thus, the price of older housing units increased by a factor of 3.7 in Paris between 1997 and 2017. In the inner ring they tripled, and in the outer ring they multiplied by 2.4. In Île-de-France as a whole, the price per square metre tripled while income only increased by 59 per cent over the same period. Taking 1996 as a base year (= 100), whereas the average income increased from 100 to 120, the average price per square metre grew from 100 to 222 in Île-de-France and from 100 to 268 in the municipality of Paris.

What is the reason for this explosion in prices? A joint report by the Institut d'aménagement et d'urbanisme de la région Île-de-France and the Métropole du Grand Paris (IAU & MGP 2018) identifies at least five structural causes: the growing concentration of population and activities in metropolitan regions, with Île-de-France at the top of the list (according to the ENL, rental accommodation in Île-de-France is on average more expensive and less spacious than in the rest of France); the revived attractiveness of urban centres; a fall in household sizes; the numerical domination of "baby boomers" on the housing market; and, finally, a fall in borrowing rates, which has led to increased housing demand.

Under these circumstances, it is logical that housing takes up a growing share of household budgets. This proportion varies greatly according to income and occupancy status, however (owner occupancy, tenancy, social housing, private rental). For example, private sector tenants spent 29 per cent of their income on housing in 2013, as compared with only 24 per cent for people in social housing. The reason for this is that rent levels in the private sector are on average much higher than in social housing (almost twice as expensive) (ENL 2013; IAU & MGP 2018). The situation is the same for first-time buyers, who, in 2013, were paying almost a quarter of their income to buy their home, as compared with only 21 per cent in 2006.

There is another – less structural – cause of the current housing crisis, however: the mismatch between construction rates and demand. The 2013 master plan (SDRIF: see Chapter 6) set a figure of 70,000 dwellings per year for the number of dwellings needed to be built by 2030 in order to absorb the shortfall, which has grown over the years, and to provide homes for the additional population anticipated by that time. Until 2015 the region was a long way short of the mark, with only some 50,000 dwellings built in 2005, 60,000 in 2010 and 69,000 in 2015 (DRIEA 2020). Since then construction has significantly accelerated, to a maximum of almost 100,000 in 2017, but this number fell again to 89,000 in 2018 and to 82,100 in 2019 (DRIEA 2020).

For all these reasons, both structural and cyclical, the housing situation in Île-de-France seems to be one of the main problems needing to be resolved.

*Travel and mobility: congestion on the networks and deteriorating transport conditions*

The statistical data on mobility in Île-de-France are abundant but disparate. For a general picture, we currently can use the various issues of the Enquête générale transport (EGT: comprehensive transport survey), which are conducted every ten years. Although the last one was carried out in 2010, we can also use the recent but partial results drawn from the ongoing EGT scheduled to end in 2022.

From the 2010 and 2018–22 surveys it emerges that the volume of trips in the region as a whole has stabilized. With 3.9 trips a day in 2010 and 3.8 in 2018, there was virtually no change over the period, the increase in total trips from 41 million in 2010 to 43 million in 2018 being attributable to the increase of population. What has changed, however, is the pattern of these trips, whether in terms of the purpose of travel, the modes of transport or the spatial distribution of traffic flows, for which there have been significant alterations over the past 20 years.

Regarding the purpose of travel, there has been a reduction in so-called "necessary" trips, in particular commuting (see Table 5.2). Accounting for 22 per cent of journeys in 2001, only 18 per cent in 2010 and 17 per cent in 2018, commuting has diminished as a share of total mobility. Nonetheless, if other "necessary" trips are added (education, transporting children, etc.), this category accounts for 29 per cent of the total in 2010 (compared with 32 per cent in 2001) and 30 per cent in 2018, but in particular it accounts for 41 per cent of travel time and 51 per cent of the distances covered (Table 5.3). Heavily concentrated in peak periods, it is these journeys that dictate the size of the transport networks (EGT 2010; OMNIL 2019).

**Table 5.2** Trip distribution by purpose (percentage shares), 2001–2018

| Trip purpose | 2001 | 2010 | 2018 |
|---|---|---|---|
| Home/work | 22 | 18 | 17 |
| Work-related | 10 | 11 | 13 |
| Home/studies | 14 | 11 | 11 |
| Home/shopping | 13 | 14 | 12 |
| Home/personal affairs | 8 | 6 | 6 |
| Home/escorting children | 11 | 12 | 11 |
| Home/leisure, visits | 13 | 16 | 17 |
| Secondary non-work-related | 9 | 12 | 13 |
| Total | 100 | 100 | 100 |

*Sources*: EGT, 2010; OMNIL (2019).

**Table 5.3** Distribution of distance and time spent in travelling by purpose (percentage shares), 2018

| Trip purpose | Time (%) | Distance (%) |
|---|---|---|
| Home/work | 28 | 38 |
| Work-related | 13 | 13 |
| Home/studies | 11 | 9 |
| Home/shopping | 8 | 7 |
| Home/personal affairs | 7 | 6 |
| Home/escort | 6 | 5 |
| Home/leisure, visits | 17 | 15 |
| Secondary non-work-related | 10 | 7 |
| Total | 100 | 100 |

*Source*: OMNIL (2019).

The primary modes of transport used for these trips by people in Île-de-France is walking (38.7 per cent in 2020 and 39.9 per cent in 2018). If we exclude walking, in 2018 57 per cent of trips were made by car (62 per cent in 2010) and 36 per cent by public transport (33 per cent in 2010) (see Table 5.4).

**Table 5.4** Total daily trips by mode (totals and percentage shares), 2010–2018

| Mode of transport | 2010 | | 2018 | |
|---|---|---|---|---|
| | Total | Percentage | Total | Percentage |
| Public transport | 8,290,000 | 20.2 | 9,420,000 | 21.9 |
| Bicycle | 650,000 | 1.6 | 840,000 | 1.9 |
| Walking | 15,900,000 | 38.7 | 17,170,000 | 39.9 |
| Motorized two-wheeler | 570,000 | 1.4 | 420,000 | 1.0 |
| Car | 15,530,000 | 37.8 | 14,800,000 | 34.4 |
| Others | 170,000 | 0.4 | 380,000 | 0.9 |
| Total trips | 41,000,000 | | 43,000,000 | |

*Source*: OMNIL (2019).

But, as we will see, the practices depend largely on household location. The large role played by the car is explained – as in every other city in the industrialized world – by the development of the automobile from the 1950s onwards. Its use began to decline in the 1980s, however. In 2010 the car ownership rate in Île-de-France was about 70 per cent, but it had declined to 66 per cent in 2017 (INSEE 2020), with significant variations according to place of residence (see Table 5.5). The 2010 data are confirmed by more recent data produced by INSEE in 2020. In 2017 the car ownership rate in Paris was only

**Table 5.5** Car ownership rate by household by *département* (percentages), 2010–2017

| | 2010 | | | 2017 | | |
|---|---|---|---|---|---|---|
| | **No car** | **1 car** | **2 cars or more** | **No car** | **1 car** | **2 cars or more** |
| Paris | 55 | 40 | 4 | 66 | 30 | 4 |
| Hauts-de-Seine | 27 | 54 | 20 | 35 | 50 | 15 |
| Seine-Saint-Denis | 34 | 50 | 16 | 38 | 47 | 15 |
| Val-de-Marne | 27 | 54 | 20 | 32 | 50 | 18 |
| Inner ring | *29* | *52* | *18* | *35* | *49* | *16* |
| Seine-et-Marne | 12 | 44 | 44 | 15 | 47 | 38 |
| Essonne | 13 | 46 | 41 | 16 | 49 | 35 |
| Yvelines | 10 | 49 | 41 | 16 | 49 | 35 |
| Val-d'Oise | 17 | 49 | 35 | 19 | 50 | 31 |
| Outer ring | *13* | *47* | *41* | *16* | *49* | *35* |
| Île-de-France | 29 | 47 | 23 | 34 | 45 | 21 |

*Sources*: EGT (2010); INSEE (2020).

about 34 per cent while in the inner ring it ranged from 62 per cent (Seine-Saint-Denis) to 68 per cent (Val-de-Marne), versus more than 80 per cent in the outer ring (80.7 per cent in Val-d'Oise but 85.3 per cent in Seine-et-Marne).

So, in 2017 a large majority of Parisian households did not own a car, whereas about a half of suburbanites had at least one car (Table 5.5). A downward trend began in the late 1990s, however, and car ownership is now decreasing even in the outer ring. Clearly therefore, trends in car ownership and car use have profoundly changed the modal distribution of travel. Motorized travel is now declining, and the use of public transport significantly increasing.

Another significant change that can be observed in most urban areas of the Western world is the increasing importance of trips that do not concern the central city. In 2018 trips that did not involve the municipality of Paris – i.e. those from suburb to suburb – represented some 70 per cent of the total. This trend has been observed consistently over the last 40 years.

This geography of movement largely explains the spatial distribution of mobility across modes. In 2018, out of the 9.4 million public transport trips in the region, about a quarter took place within Paris, one-third between Paris and the rest of Île-de-France and the remainder (about 42 per cent) across the region outside Paris. When it comes to the car, only 0.4 million of the daily 14.8 million automobile trips took place in the central city, 0.9 million between the central city and Île-de-France and the remainder – i.e. the great majority (13.2 million) – in the region outside Paris. The other transport modes – with the exception of walking – such as the bicycle, remained marginal in the region, although their development has been significant; the number of trips made by bicycle, for example, doubled between 2001 and 2010 then increased by a third between 2010 and 2018.

Although the total number of trips has scarcely increased, as we have seen, their distribution has been reorganized. This organization, both in space and time, has caused problems of congestion and overcrowding on the transport systems, roads and public transport alike. With regard to car traffic, although it largely remained static between 2000 and 2010, this stabilization occurred after sharp growth in the 1980s (3 per cent per year) and continuing but slower growth in the 1990s (1.4 per cent per year) (IAU 2013b). This situation led to overuse on the main road system, with traffic that scarcely diminishes between 6 a.m. and 9 p.m., resulting in congestion on certain routes. Île-de-France thus holds the European record for road traffic, with more than 240,000 car trips a day on five sections of expressway (A1, A4 and three sections of the Périphérique). Paris's Périphérique is in fact Europe's busiest artery, with 52 per cent congestion at peak hours (IAU 2013b). In 2017 and 2018, respectively, the system achieved the records of 562 and 588 km of traffic jams. At the same time, traffic within Paris fell by 5 per cent.

The situation is no better on the public transport front. Across all modes, traffic increased by 21 per cent between 2000 and 2010 (OMNIL 2010). More recent figures produced by OMNIL record an increase of more than 36 per cent between 2000 and 2018 (see Table 5.6). If we exclude the "Others" category, which has notably grown with the commissioning of several tram lines in the last few years, it is rail traffic (SNCF and RER) that has grown the most, at a rate of approximately 35 per cent since 2000, followed by the Metro and the bus, with an increase of some 25 per cent.

**Table 5.6** Public transport use (millions of annual trips per mode), 2000–2018

| | 2000 | 2005 | 2010 | 2015 | 2018 |
|---|---|---|---|---|---|
| All modes | 3,467 | 3,821 | 4,172 | 4,513 | 4,720 |
| Train | 1,045 | 1,192 | 1,277 | 1,359 | 1,409 |
| Metro | 1,248 | 1,373 | 1,505 | 1,520 | 1,560 |
| Bus | 1,150 | 1,209 | 1,281 | 1,367 | 1,436 |
| Others: tram, etc. | 24 | 47 | 109 | 267 | 315 |

*Source*: OMNIL.

As we will see in the next chapter, road and public transport traffic have both increased without the building of the infrastructures needed to absorb this surplus or adequate mobility policies. The consequence is a deterioration in travel conditions for users. On public transport, this deterioration is apparent in ageing equipment, longer travel times, overcrowded lines, diminishing punctuality and hence declining levels of comfort (STIF 2014). For RATP, overcrowding is the number one problem (Cour des comptes 2010). On the RER, many trains run late or not at all. Between 2004 and 2010 irregularity increased by between 12 and 37 per cent, depending on the branch (Cour des comptes 2010). With a volume of travellers in excess of 4 people per square metre at peak times on certain trains, overcrowding has reached the limits of tolerability.

### *The environment: contrasting conditions*

As in many big metropolitan regions across the world, it is not easy to characterize environmental conditions in Île-de-France, because the data are neither sufficient nor comprehensive, and do not cover periods long enough to reach a conclusion about environmental trends. The environment is a complex and multidimensional field (air, water, noise, etc.) that is difficult to gauge in its entirety. Nonetheless, recent studies (IAU 2017a; Institut Paris Région 2020a) have tried to characterize the global environmental conditions in which people live in Île-de-France.

According to these studies, 30 per cent of the region's inhabitants live in an "environmental green spot" – in other words, an area with a combination of positive amenities or containing at least three local green amenities (access to green spaces less than 200m away, presence of communal gardens, woodland, etc.). Conversely, 13 per cent live in "environmental black spots" or are exposed to at least three negative environmental factors (air, water or ground pollution, noise) – i.e. geographical areas in which several of these environmental problems combine.

A recent report produced by the Institut Paris Région (2020a) provides some interesting, albeit partial, information regarding the state of the environment in Île-de-France. Regarding greenhouse gas (GHG) emissions, it indicates that, although they declined by 7 per cent between 2005 and 2010 and by 15 per cent between 2010 and 2015, they increased by 0.7 per cent between 2015 and 2017. In any event, this reduction in GHG emissions is not sufficient to prevent a general increase in temperature in the next decades, the region having already experienced a 1.5 degree rise between 1959 and 2009.

On noise pollution, the same report indicates that in 2017 15 per cent of the regional population was exposed to levels above the official norms, mostly in the inner ring. A more recent report published in 2019 by Bruitparif, the public agency in charge of studies and evaluation regarding noise in Île-de-France, indicates that 90 per cent of the densest part of Île-de-France (i.e. over 9 million people) are exposed to levels of noise that are higher than the WHO recommended standards. For Bruitparif, noise is the second cause of death due to environmental risks behind air pollution (Bruitparif 2019).

On air quality, the publication *L'environnement en Île-de-France: Mémento 2015* published by the IAU is clear: it concludes that "air quality remains inadequate [and] that approximately 3.4 million people in Île-de-France are exposed to pollution levels above the regulatory thresholds" (IAU 2015: 198). More recent figures conclude that 1.4 million people were exposed to poor quality air in 2016 (Airparif 2018). Airparif, the agency responsible for monitoring and reporting on air quality in Île-de-France, measured levels significantly above the ceiling values for particulates and nitrogen dioxide ($NO_2$) in 2017. There were also numerous pollution episodes (18 days in 2016, 12 days in 2017, 14 days in 2018; Airparif 2019). In 2018 Airparif noted that 8 per cent of the regional population (mostly in the inner ring) were exposed to pollution level above the annual limit value for nitrogen dioxide. According to Santé Publique France, France's public health agency, air pollution was responsible for 48,000 excess deaths in France in 2015, including 6,600 in Île-de-France.

Nonetheless, although air quality is still bad, overall it has improved since the 1990s (MGP 2017; Institut Paris Région 2020). For pollutants – particulates ($PM_{10}$) and nitrogen dioxide ($NO_2$) – the figures are even impressive (see Table 5.7), with a fall of 98 per cent in $PM_{10}$ between 2007 and 2018, and 73 per cent in $NO_2$.

**Table 5.7** Number of kilometres of roads exceeding the daily ceiling value ($PM_{10}$ and $NO_2$) in Île-de-France, 2007–2018

| | 2007 | 2009 | 2011 | 2013 | 2015 | 2018 |
|---|---|---|---|---|---|---|
| $PM_{10}$ | 5,090 | 3,790 | 3,490 | 1,950 | 590 | 90 |
| $NO_2$ | 2,900 | 2,390 | 1,890 | 1,790 | 1,070 | 770 |

*Source*: Airparif.

When it comes to access to green space, which is perceived as an important measure of urban quality of life, the data are much less positive. Studies by the IAU (2017a) conclude that 9 per cent of people in Île-de-France live in areas without publicly accessible green spaces. Whereas the World Health Organization (WHO) sets the minimum desirable level at $10m^2$ of green space per person in inner-city areas and $25m^2$ per person in the suburbs, this threshold is not reached in the most built-up part of the region. So, although the availability of green space greatly improved between 1970 and 2001 (IAU 2015), increasing by more than 240 per cent over the period, it grew only from $2.62m^2$ per person to $8.6m^2$ – i.e. a figure well below the minimum WHO-recommended minimum. Since 2001, in fact, the area of green space per inhabitant has fallen in relative terms, in that it has increased more slowly than the population. In 2013 about 50 per cent of the regional population lived in places containing less than 10 square metres of green space per inhabitant (Institut Paris Région 2020).

As a whole, it is difficult to reach a general conclusion about the state of the environment in the region. This is evidenced by the *Mémento* (IAU 2015), which is careful not to arrive at a global conclusion in this domain. Nonetheless, however one sees the situation, it remains the case that the quality of the environment, and, notably, the quality of life in the region, has become an important societal and political issue (see also Chapters 6 and 7).

### *The rise of socio-territorial inequalities*

Between 2001 and 2015 the Île-de-France region substantially boosted its economic power with a 27 per cent growth in GDP, compared with no more than 18 per cent over the period in the rest of France. Nevertheless, this economic dynamism brought relatively few jobs, since employment grew by only 7 per cent over those 15 years (IAU 2019a). The unemployment figures partly reflect this situation: 6.4 per cent in 2001, 6.3 per cent in 2008, but 8.9 per cent in 2015 and 7.9 per cent in 2018. True, Île-de-France appears better off than the rest of France, but the level remains high, notably by comparison with other metropolitan regions such as London or New York.

The idea that socio-territorial inequalities are deepening is shared by almost all the experts and by Île-de-France's political class. This rise in inequalities has been extensively documented. A recent study (IAU 2019a) concludes that the region is steadily drifting towards an increasingly sharp polarization between wealthy and working-class neighbourhoods, although it also notes the existence of a large number of socially mixed areas. According to the study, the disparities between well-off and poor areas have grown, whereas peripheral areas have increasingly converged on an intermediate state. This rise in socio-territorial inequalities is seen as particularly sharp in the inner ring. According to this study, therefore, Île-de-France contains three types of areas.

1. "Wealthy" areas, where "well-off" households are over-represented and poor or modest households under-represented. 37 per cent of households in the region live in these areas; they are mostly located in Paris and in the west and south-west of the Île-de-France.
2. "Modest" areas, where "modest" or "poor" households are over-represented and "well-off" households under-represented. 32 per cent of households in Île-de-France live in such areas; the Seine-Saint-Denis (north and north-east of the region) and Val-de-Marne (south-east) *départements* are the best examples.

3. "Predominantly periurban" areas, in which extreme situations (wealthy or poor) are under-represented by comparison with intermediate conditions. 30 per cent of households live in these areas; they are mostly situated in the outer ring.

Observations of poverty in Île-de-France confirm this. For more than a decade the poverty rate has been rising. It stood at 13 per cent in 2006 and more than 15 per cent in 2017, above the French average of 14.5 per cent. Specialized data confirm the IAU study and highlight a contrast between the centre-west and the north-east that can be found in many other statistics, with a part of north-east Paris, in Seine-Saint-Denis, where poverty levels are particularly high (see Chapter 2).

A comparison of the main statistical data between the *départements* of Hauts-de-Seine (the second richest in France after Paris) and Seine-Saint-Denis (the poorest in France) is particularly enlightening (see Table 5.8).

**Table 5.8** Six key indicators about Seine-Saint-Denis and Hauts-de-Seine, 2016

| | **Seine-Saint-Denis** | **Hauts-de-Seine** | **Île-de-France** | **France métropolitaine** |
|---|---|---|---|---|
| Disposable median income by household (€) | 1,394 | 2,163 | 1,877 | 1,697 |
| Unemployment rate (%) | 12.7 | 7.5 | 8.7 | 9.7 |
| Poverty rate (%) | 28.6 | 12.2 | 15.6 | 14.7 |
| Poor single-parent households (%) | 34.1 | 20.0 | 23.9 | 29.9 |
| Households receiving minimum social benefits (%) | 23.5 | 9.6 | 12.7 | 13.6 |
| Population living in a QPV (%)* | 39 | 6 | 15 | 13 |

*Note*: * QPV = quartier prioritaire de la politique de la ville (see Chapter 6).

*Source*: Observatoire départemental des données sociales.

By comparing all these data, we can draw the following conclusions: Île-de-France is characterized by:

- sharp polarization between very wealthy areas (centre-west) and very poor areas (northern suburbs);
- a greater concentration of very rich households than very poor households;
- a low incidence of poverty in the outer suburbs; and
- a large number of mixed areas (mix of social categories with income profiles close to the regional average).

Although there is no doubt about the rise in social and territorial inequality, its scale has been extensively demonstrated for at least the past 15 years, which explains why it has become an important issue in public policy terms.

### *Economic attractiveness*

An alarmist report by the Paris Île-de-France Capitale Économique association and the Île-de-France Chamber of Commerce,[3] published in 2014, sets the tone. This report, also presented in Chapter 4 on the Paris region economic model, concludes that Île-de-France's attractiveness is in decline, despite many advantages. On this view, three factors are responsible for this situation: (1) inadequate adjustment to globalization, in particular high levels of taxation; (2) low levels of foreign direct investment (FDI), down 40 per cent over the period from 2008 to 2012, to the benefit of London and New York; and (3) failure to attract the headquarters of foreign companies, because of high taxes, complex bureaucracy, poor command of English and a lack of innovation (PICE & CCI Paris Île-de-France 2014).

Two other reports published in 2016 support and enrich this analysis. In a study entitled *The Trajectories of the Île-de-France Economy: Facts and Challenges*, the IAU recognizes that growth in the region generates few jobs, with a working-age population that grew more rapidly than employment between 1990 and 2012 (IAU 2016b). Moreover, in a comparative study with eight big cities around the world, the IAU and the Global Cities Initiative (GCI), a joint JP Morgan Chase and Brookings Institution project, finds growth in Île-de-France to be lagging behind other similarly ranked global metropolises (Parilla, Marchio & Leal Trujillo 2016). In terms of economic performance, for example, Île-de-France is found to have fallen from fifth to eighth place in the international rankings. Both organizations emphasize the region's deficit in innovation, particularly in terms of patents filed, weak linkages between industry and research, difficulties in attracting risk capital and an unemployment rate higher than in the other big metropolitan regions. Table 5.9 illustrates Île-de-France's position in relation to eight other competing regions.

What emerges from all these data and analyses is that there has been a relative decline in the region's competitiveness and attractiveness, to the point that some parties see resolving this situation as a public policy priority (see Chapters 6 and 7).

---

3. Paris Île-de-France Capitale Économique (PICE) is an association formed by the principal public and private companies in Île-de-France (see Chapter 1).

**Table 5.9** Performance indicators for Paris Île-de-France for five factors of competitiveness

| | Economic performance | International trade | Innovation | Talent | Infrastructure |
|---|---|---|---|---|---|
| Strong | London | London | San Francisco | San Francisco | Tokyo |
| | Los Angeles | Boston | Boston | London | London |
| | New York | San Francisco | London | Boston | **Paris** |
| | Boston | **Paris** | New York | Los Angeles | New York |
| | **Paris**, San Francisco | New York | Los Angeles | New York | Rotterdam–Amsterdam |
| Weak | Rotterdam–Amsterdam | Los Angeles | Chicago | **Paris** | Los Angeles |
| | Tokyo | Rotterdam–Amsterdam | Rotterdam–Amsterdam | Chicago | San Francisco |
| | | Tokyo | **Paris** | Rotterdam–Amsterdam | Boston |
| | Chicago | Chicago | Tokyo | Tokyo | Chicago |

*Source*: Parilla, Marchio & Leal Trujillo (2016).

## Île-de-France's problems in terms of the perception of the issues

The inventory above is, by definition, an overview of the main problems that the Île-de-France region faces, but it makes no assumptions about their importance to the different stakeholders and therefore about the public policy priorities. This is why, before tackling these policies in Chapter 6, in this second part I present the links between all these problems and the two main priorities identified by the stakeholders, whether public, private, economic, political or social: on the one hand, to increase the region's economic competitiveness – and, more broadly, its attractiveness; and, on the other hand, to tackle socio-territorial inequalities. These links largely explain the policies pursued.

### *Île-de-France's problems in terms of competitiveness and attractiveness*

Beyond the standard economic indicators of competitiveness mentioned above, there is one that clearly illustrates the Paris region's low level – or even lack – of attractiveness: its overall migratory deficit (with the rest of France and with the world). Whereas Paris continues to attract foreigners, this is not the case for the French population. Every year Île-de-France would seem to lose 76,000 people to the rest of the country (average figures over the period from

2008 to 2013) (IAU & MGP 2018). Although it attracts young adults, it fails to retain households with children and retired people. In this respect, it matches the pattern observed in cities such as Lille and Marseille, but differs from more dynamic cities such as Lyon, Nantes, Bordeaux and Toulouse, which gain inhabitants every year through a positive migratory balance. Île-de-France is therefore below the French average in this respect.

The reasons for this situation are relatively well known and relate primarily to a deterioration in living conditions. Île-de-France is not, in fact, the only big metropolitan region in the world where quality of life is a problem, although quality of life is of course difficult to assess, especially from a comparative perspective. For example, the international quality of living ranking published every year by Mercer invariably places mid-sized cities such as Auckland, Zurich, Vienna and Vancouver at the top, with the big cities far behind.

There are three main domains in which France's capital region fails the attractiveness test: housing, mobility and the environment as broadly construed (pollution, density, miscellaneous annoyances).

With regard to housing, it is primarily the difficulty of finding accommodation at an affordable price that makes the region unattractive. As we have seen, property prices have exploded in the Paris region, making access to housing more difficult. This means that growing households have to move into the outskirts, which leads to higher transport costs and longer travel times in worse conditions – a situation that is driving more and more households to leave the region. This increase in the cost of housing is presented as structural, an inevitable result of the metropolitanization process in what is still one of the world's leading regions (IAU & MGP 2018). For companies, it is increasingly hard to find executives who are prepared to move into the Paris region or, if they come, to retain them, since after a few years they prefer to try their luck in provincial cities where the quality of life is better and, above all, where accommodation is more affordable, cheaper and somewhat more spacious.

The same is true for a population that is particularly important to today's urban economy: students and researchers. Although Île-de-France remains the French region that attracts by far the most students and researchers, this is because of the high concentration of higher education and research institutions located there. Nevertheless, it is beginning to experience difficulties in attracting a student clientele whose incomes are often very modest and is therefore reluctant to "go to Paris", notably because of the high rents.

The link between the housing situation in Île-de-France and the region's attractiveness thus seems to be becoming increasingly problematic, as is well illustrated in the IAU/MGP study *Metropolitanization and Housing*, which has been cited several times:

> By adopting a broader and more inclusive vision of the overall functioning of metropolitan regions, one can understand how, by making the residential trajectories of a large proportion of Île-de-France's population difficult, the "housing crisis" caused by the increase in real estate prices could gradually bring metropolitan economic functioning to a halt. Indeed, it is open to question whether the current model is sustainable in the long run ... House price inflation might also force companies that wish to continue operating in the metropolis to offer inflated salaries in order to make themselves attractive to employees in relation to the housing costs that the latter face, etc. In the medium to long term ... excessively high housing costs and poor housing conditions could ultimately damage the general attractiveness of the metropolis, and even its image, both for temporary visitors like tourists, and also and above all for new incoming populations, and in particular for "key populations" (students, researchers, young executives, young engineers, entrepreneurs, etc.) who, without necessarily starting out with the financial resources needed to pay the rents charged in the Paris metropolitan region, are or will be the source of the innovations that will guarantee its future economic growth. (IAU & MGP 2018: 10)

With respect to transport and mobility, it is, first of all, deteriorating travel conditions that cause the economic stakeholders and certain political actors to worry about the competitiveness and attractiveness of Île-de-France. In terms of road travel, traffic conditions have been deteriorating almost continually for many years, as illustrated in Table 5.10.

Between 2007 and 2018, for example, congestion practically tripled on the region's main road network, and more than doubled on all roads. According to

**Table 5.10** Traffic congestion (thousands of km-hours per traffic lane), 2007–2018

| | **2007** | **2010** | **2013** | **2015** | **2018** |
|---|---|---|---|---|---|
| Île-de-France main network | 435 | 441 | 581 | 963 | 1,104 |
| Paris Boulevard Périphérique | 199 | 218 | 294 | 273 | 204 |
| Total Île-de-France | 634 | 659 | 874 | 1,225 | 1,308 |
| Rest of France main network | 444 | 440 | 602 | 663 | 570 |
| Total | 1,078 | 1,099 | 1,476 | 1,889 | 1,878 |

*Source*: Union routière de France [URF] (2019).

various statistical data, congestion has been rising consistently: by 2 per cent between 2010 and 2013, and by 11 per cent between 2016 and 2017, according to V-Traffic (n.d.). In 2016 every motorist spent the equivalent of 154 hours in traffic jams (*Journal du Dimanche* 2017).

On public transport, the situation is no better. Although transport provision has improved a little over the past 15 years, it has not kept pace with the increase in traffic. As we saw earlier, this has led to a big deterioration in travelling conditions, whether in terms of comfort or travel time. Old equipment, overcrowded routes, punctuality problems and line maintenance failures are the common lot of passengers in Île-de-France, and they are affecting the smooth running of the economy. Everywhere the blame is placed on a lack of investment, whether in improvements to the existing system or in the building of new infrastructures.

In this regard, the economic stakeholders – chambers of commerce, big companies, employer federations and local authorities – highlight glaring deficiencies that threaten the region's competitiveness. Two issues are particularly illustrative: transport links to the airports and to the main clusters and business centres. Île-de-France has two international airports, Orly and Roissy Charles de Gaulle, both of which are poorly served by public transport. There are no direct links, and plans to build them have either collapsed or have been on the drawing board in some cases for more than ten years, such as the Charles de Gaulle Express, which we will discuss in the chapters that follow. Clusters such as Saclay in the south-west of the region, touted by the government for more than 15 years as a world-ranking centre for scientific and technological research, with more than 16,000 scientists and PhD students, still has no direct or fast link to the centre of the metropolis. Access to La Défense, Europe's leading business district, whether by public transport or by car, is close to logjam. As for the clusters in the east of the region, around the new town of Marne-la-Vallée, public transport provision depends primarily on line A of the RER (regional express railway), one of the busiest in the world, which is also close to overload and is beset with delays and incidents.

The transport situation is a preoccupation for the authorities, as we will see in Chapter 6, and several improvement projects are in the pipeline, notably the Grand Paris Express (GPE), a massive automatic rail network designed to serve the airports and the main clusters and suburban towns. The difficulties – financial, technical and political – are colossal, however, which explains the slowness of the construction work and the continuous pushing back of deadlines.

Although the housing and transport situation has a negative impact on the attractiveness of Île-de-France, there are also other, newer, factors that exacerbate concerns about maintaining the French capital region at the summit of the world hierarchy of cities. In the past ten years or so environmental conditions and the quality of life in general have emerged as essential factors in making cities attractive – i.e. pleasant places to live. From this perspective – and even though there are many problems in defining what precisely is meant by the term "pleasant" – there is no way that big cities can compete with smaller population centres. Easier access to nature, better environmental conditions (air pollution, noise and other negative environmental factors), the density of the urban fabric, etc. do not operate in favour of very big cities. Although Île-de-France, and Paris in particular, offers its inhabitants unrivalled cultural resources, the same is not true of the other amenities discussed here, which reinforces the lack of attractiveness of France's premier region, not only for its population but also for a good number of its companies and scientific institutions. By way of information, an IPSOS poll conducted in 2018 with the whole population of France indicates that, if they had a choice, 43 per cent of the people polled would live in a mid-sized town (between 20,000 and 100,000 inhabitants), 35 per cent would prefer the countryside and only 22 per cent would choose the big city.[4]

### *Île-de-France's problems in terms of social and territorial inequalities*

As we saw above, social and territorial inequalities have been steadily increasing over at least the past 15 years. Income inequalities between municipalities and between neighbourhoods have therefore been on the rise since the early 2000s. Households have been getting poorer in the most modest suburban municipalities (northern Paris, east of Val-d'Oise, west of Val-de-Marne, north-east of Essonne). In addition, entire urban areas have become poorer in absolute terms. For example, in 44 of the poorest municipalities, the median income in constant euros fell between 2001 and 2015 (IAU 2019a). In parallel, there has been a marked improvement in Paris and the adjacent municipalities of Hauts-de-Seine, as well as in the loops of the Marne in Val-de-Marne, which are becoming gentrified. This is occurring in part because executives have a strong preference for the centrality of Paris, including municipalities close to Paris.

Housing issues run parallel, or even contribute, to this increase in inequalities. Rises in the cost of housing in particular have a big impact. For example, rental prices in old properties tripled across the region between 1999 and 2018, whereas incomes increased only 1.34 times over the same period (IAU 2019a).

4. The 2020/21 Covid-19 crisis has hit the Paris region more than any other part of France, and this is a result of the size and density of the area, considered in this case as a negative feature of big cities.

Accommodation accounts for a large percentage of spending in less well-off households, from 26 per cent for those in social housing to almost 40 per cent in the private sector. For the poorest households, housing difficulties thus contribute to socio-territorial inequalities, forcing people to move a long way from centres of employment. As pointed out once again by the IAU, "In the last 30 years, only executives have not moved out of the centre of Paris" (IAU 2016b: 23).

In addition, as the IAU (2016b) notes, "the housing crisis has also extended to the middle classes". The statistical data are clear: over ten years the price of property per square metre in Paris has doubled, forcing middle-class residents further and further out of the centre. The recent figures show that the increase in property prices extends well beyond the capital itself and has now reached the inner suburbs, notably as a result of the forthcoming arrival of the Grand Paris Express. For example, between 2013 and 2018 they rose by almost 40 per cent in Saint-Ouen in Seine-Saint Denis, and by some 20 per cent in Pantin and in Montreuil in the same *département*, driving out both poor and middle-class residents. It was the same in the adjacent municipalities in Hauts-de-Seine (Clichy: 22 per cent increase; Bagneux: 20 per cent; Montrouge: 17 per cent) and in Val-de-Marne (Villejuif: 19 per cent; Cachan: 17 per cent; Arcueil: 16 per cent) (Rey-Lefebvre 2019).

Île-de-France's transport networks are hard put to respond to this situation, which is driving large sections of the population ever further from the city centre, where many jobs are located, and, more generally, further from the other economic centres in the region. In fact, the transport system can even be said to indirectly contribute to the trend, both by helping to drive up rents and by failing to meet the travel needs of many residents, mainly the least well off.

The increase in housing costs around the future GPE stations is just one illustration – illustrative and localized – of the role of big transport infrastructures in generating social and territorial inequalities. But the inequalities are also expressed in differences in access to jobs, goods and services, caused by transport systems that are ill adapted to changes in mobility patterns and in the economic geography of Île-de-France. This is particularly true for public transport, which provides much less coverage at regional level, notably in the outer ring and, to a lesser degree, in the inner ring. Although more and more people are travelling within and between suburbs, and, as we have seen, such travel accounts for the great majority of trips, public transport primarily provides radial connections to the central city. This makes public transport less attractive in the areas close to Paris and elsewhere, where it is clearly inadequate, especially in the outer suburbs. For the populations living in these areas, therefore, there is no alternative but to resort to the car.

Yet car use is an additional factor of inequality for the populations concerned, first because it leads to high transport costs (notably because of the price of fuel) that many people find it hard to afford, as the "yellow vest crisis" of 2018/19 demonstrated,[5] and, second, because a significant number of households do not have their own car. In fact, as illustrated in Table 5.5, 35 per cent of households in the inner ring and 16 per cent of the outer ring Paris do not own a car. This percentage rises to 52 per cent for the poorest households. This results in what might be called a double whammy: on the one hand, the poorest households are driven into the outskirts, increasingly far from where the jobs are located; and, on the other hand, because of inadequate public transport, these households are forced to rely on the private car, yet more than half of them do not own one, with the result that their mobility is restricted.

Environmental problems further exacerbate the social and territorial inequalities. In the unambiguous title "Environmental and social inequalities are closely linked in Île-de-France", the IAU (2017a) signals that environmental disadvantages of all kinds primarily affect the poorest populations. Thus, low-income households are over-represented in more than half the environmental black spots (areas characterized by a combination of at least three environmental problems). Concomitantly, they are under-represented in areas with a large number of environmental amenities (three or above). The 2017 study thus concludes that "the most modest households are more heavily represented overall in environments with multiple exposure and a shortage of amenities" (IAU 2017a: 6).

In response to all these problems and challenges, different stakeholders in Île-de-France – starting, of course, with the public authorities – have reacted by developing specific measures and policies. This is what is discussed in the next chapter.

5. The yellow vest crisis is a crisis made up of social categories that feel threatened by a deterioration in their living conditions. It began following a government decision at the end of 2018 to increase fuel prices.

# 6

# The policies

National and local government have developed a multitude of policies to tackle all the problems and challenges that Île-de-France faces. As with the previous chapter, I have chosen to divide them into two: on the one hand, policies designed to combat social and territorial inequalities; on the other hand, those designed to enhance regional competitiveness and attractiveness. This dichotomy does not encompass all the measures that have been taken, however, particularly those relating to the environment. That is why these are tackled separately, as are a number of measures – notably in the spheres of housing and mobility – that were designed mainly as a response to emergency situations.

The previous chapters showed the importance of central government in the establishment of Île-de-France and in its development over the last few decades. It is therefore unsurprising that this importance is also reflected in the policies pursued. Central government is everywhere, and in many domains the main player. First, through its national policies, particularly in the fields of education, health, social affairs, economic development (e.g. industrial policy) and the environment. These nationwide measures do not specifically target Île-de-France but obviously have a big impact on the region. In addition, central government has developed policies that directly target the region and its specific problems, for example in transport, research and development and spatial planning.

As a general rule, public policies, whether national or local, are organized and implemented in most domains through plans and contracts. They can have a variety of names (plans, schemes, strategies, etc.) and may or may not be legally enforceable, depending on the case. One important example is the Île-de-France regional master plan (SDRIF), which we will be looking at in this chapter and the next.

The main plans cover the following areas: housing (local housing plan: PLH), climate (climate plans), mobility (urban travel plan), economic development (regional development scheme), etc. In the case of Île-de-France, they may be municipal, intermunicipal, departmental or regional, depending on the competences specific to the different levels of local government. They also cover different time frames, although they are generally between five and 20 years.

The plans, particularly their financial aspects, are generally implemented through contracts. These are documents that establish the framework for the policies and actions to be pursued. These contracts are agreements signed by the stakeholders, usually public entities and authorities, which jointly undertake to meet the objectives established in the plans through specific actions and over a set period.

Finally, it will be difficult for us to reach an assessment of the policies pursued. This is because, apart from the difficulty of isolating their impact in the light of the multiple variables that influence Île-de-France's economy and society, many policies have not been assessed, despite the fact that there exist provisions for evaluation to take place. With regard to the state–region plan contract (CPER; see PRIF & CRIF 2007) for 2007 to 2013, for example, a 2014 report by the Revenue Court (Cour des comptes 2014: 53) observes:

> The 2007–2013 CPER has not been assessed against its goals. The monitoring and evaluation bodies have not met. Performance indicators have been formulated, but not implemented. Therefore, although the Region claims significant results, it is impossible to know, on the basis of reliable indicators, whether the CPER has fulfilled the objectives that were assigned to it.

## Policies to combat social and territorial inequalities

There are significant social and territorial inequalities in Île-de-France and they have become deeper in recent years, as we saw in the previous chapter. This is the conclusion of an initial assessment of the SDRIF (IAU 2019b: 30), which states that "in 2018, despite a relative stabilization of inequalities after an increase between 2008 and 2011, disparities persist and poverty continues to rise ... The areas least richly endowed with resources are still concentrated in an arc that runs eastwards from the north of Hauts-de-Seine to the north of Essonne." Yet there have been numerous policies designed to reduce these inequalities, or even eliminate them, since the 1980s.

*"Comprehensive" policies: policy for cities, financial redistribution and territorial contracts*

**BOX 6.1 POLICY FOR CITIES (POLITIQUE DE LA VILLE)**

Policy for cities refers to a set of social and urban measures targeting areas that are characterized by a combination of social and economic problems defined according to specific criteria: unemployment levels, young people without skills, poverty levels, social housing levels, etc.

The policy was launched in the early 1980s and covers a variety of domains: employment and training, the living environment, culture, health, housing, education, economic development. Now targeting some 1,500 neighbourhoods, some of them defined as "priority areas" because of their economic and social situation, policy for cities has injected billions of euros into most of France's cities, particularly in Île-de-France. It has given rise to a complex system for allocating resources on the basis of criteria and zone divisions that have changed over time.

Policy for cities is a state strategy that has been embodied in several national plans, which have been rebooted with almost every new government. They are central and local government partnership policies that draw on national and local funding, as well as on EU structural funds. The measures and funding are packaged within contracts – city contracts – that have changed their name several times over the years.

In 2017 1.6 million people in Île-de-France were living in policy for cities (see Box 6.1) neighbourhoods, with more than a third living below the poverty line (INSEE 2017b). At the beginning of the millennium this situation – which also applied in many other French cities – gave rise to the City and Urban Renewal Steering and Planning Act (Loi d'orientation et de programmation pour la ville et le renouveau urbain), which created a financial instrument called the Plan national de rénovation urbaine (PNRU: national urban renewal plan) and a body to run it, the Agence nationale de rénovation urbaine (ANRU: national urban renewal agency). The goal of the PNRU is to reduce social disparities and gaps in development between urban areas, in particular by improving the buildings, refurbishing housing, and creating more good-quality public spaces. Île-de-France receives a significant share of PNRU funding because of the large number of policy for cities neighbourhoods in its territory, some of which are priority areas.

In the mid-2000s, for example, the government signed more than 100 urban social cohesion contracts (contrats urbains de cohésion sociale: CUCSs) with local authorities in Île-de-France, for the purpose of implementing the PNRU. It also created "urban free zones" (zones franches urbaines: ZFUs), similar to the United Kingdom's enterprise zones, to encourage companies to move into so-called priority neighbourhoods by offering tax exemptions.

In 2014 a new act, called the City and Urban Cohesion Programming Act (Loi de programmation pour la ville et la cohésion urbaine), came into being. It simplified the complex system introduced over the previous decades by creating a single zoning category – called priority policy for cities neighbourhoods (quartiers prioritaires de la politique de la ville: QPVs) – primarily defined by the residents' income level. Île-de-France contains 272 QPV.

What can we say about the results of policy for cities for Île-de-France? At national level, it is difficult, perhaps impossible, to assess: the results are inevitably uneven (Damon 2016). The same can be said for Île-de-France. The Paris city contract for the period from 2015 to 2020 made an initial evaluation of the results of the previous contract (2007–14). It recognized successes in improving certain parts of the capital, support for employment that has helped some 33,000 people; at the same time, however, it highlighted continuing gaps between the QPVs and the rest of the municipal area. The situation seems similar in Seine-Saint-Denis, which, by way of reminder, is France's poorest *département*. For this reason, the National Assembly's report on the effectiveness of the government's policies in that *département* (Assemblée Nationale 2018) blasts the state's mismanagement of its specific policy areas (justice, security, education). It reports that the priority education policies obtained "poor or limited results" (Assemblée Nationale 2018: 12) and failed to reduce the disparities in youth achievement. Likewise for security policies, the results of which are described as "disappointing" (Assemblée Nationale 2018: 16), showing no changes to the sense of insecurity. As for social and territorial inequalities, the data presented in the previous chapter show that they had not diminished, and had even deepened.

The government also embarked on a policy of financial redistribution across the whole country, but using a specific instrument in Île-de-France. At national level, it created the Dotation de solidarité urbaine (DSU: urban solidarity grant) in 1991, which in 2004 became the Dotation de solidarité urbaine et de cohésion sociale (DSUCS: urban solidarity and social cohesion grant). The purpose of this grant is to "contribute to the improvement of working conditions in urban municipalities that suffer from inadequate resources and high expenditures". The DSUCS is primarily aimed at municipalities with more than 10,000 inhabitants, and in 2019 amounted to some €2.3 billion for France as a whole. In Île-de-France, almost 170 municipalities receive the grant.

Alongside the creation of this grant, 1991 saw the introduction of the Île-de-France region solidarity fund (Fonds de solidarité de la région Île-de-France: FSRIF), a financial equalization instrument between municipalities in Île-de-France by correcting inequalities in the distribution of tax revenues and expenditures. Put simply, the richest municipalities are required to pay into a fund that is used to help the poorest. This fund, the level of which is set annually by government, has increased regularly to reach some €330 million in 2019; 140 municipalities contribute to it and 183 benefit from it.

In 2014, concluding that these redistributive instruments were not sufficient to reduce territorial inequalities, the *départements* of Île-de-France established a departmental solidarity fund of several tens of millions of euros, mainly financed by Paris, Hauts-de-Seine and Yvelines. Feeling the need to do more, in 2018 they decided to create a solidarity and investment fund. Endowed with some €150 million in 2019, this fund is intended to finance projects that benefit several *départements*, but it is a community effort in so far as each *département* contributes according to its means.

Finally, the effort to overcome social and territorial inequalities is also taken into account in the contractual policies. First, at regional level, by the state–region plan contracts (CPERs) signed between the government and the Île-de-France region. These CPERs are contractual documents signed between the government and each French region. In them, the signatories undertake to pursue shared objectives, which are broken down into actions that they will jointly finance. The CPERs run for a six-year term, drawing on national, regional and EU funds. Since 2000 three CPERs have been signed, for the following periods: 2000 to 2006, 2007 to 2013 and 2015 to 2020. Most of the finance from the CPERs goes into transport infrastructures and, to a lesser extent, into education and research. In Île-de-France, for example, half the funds from the 2007–13 CPER, a total of €5.5 billion, were allocated to transport and mobility. For the 2015–20 CPER, worth a total €7.4 billion, €5.3 billion went into transport and €1 billion into higher education and research. The region put in a little more than central government: €4.4 billion, as compared with only €3 billion (see PRIF & CRIF 2015).

Every CPER has a "territorial component" – i.e. a set of actions that are usually intended to support projects that foster cohesion and territorial equality across the whole region. Île-de-France's 2015–20 CPER thus had a territorial component with a budget of €600 million. One of the focal points was to "maintain territorial equality with support for periurban and rural areas, and neighbourhoods in difficulty". It had a clearly stated goal of reducing social and territorial inequalities, but also environmental disparities. Intended partly to contribute to policy for cities, it particularly funded actions intended to improve the living environment and to open up neighbourhoods, by creating better access to the surrounding areas and the rest of the region.

The Île-de-France region has also made its own contribution to combating inequalities through several of its regional strategies, and in particular its economic development strategies. So, in the first regional economic development scheme (Schéma régional de développement économique: SRDE; see CRIF 2007), which covered the period from 2007 to 2011, one of the goals of the employment growth strategy was "to reduce social and environmental imbalances as one of the drivers of a new dynamic". Emphasizing the deepening of territorial inequalities, it advocated support for the social and solidarity economy and introduced a regional policy to nurture economic development in deprived neighbourhoods: promotion of entrepreneurship, training, etc. The second SRDE (2011–14) pursued the same objective, with a focus on placing solidarity in territorial development at the heart of regional policies.

At infra-regional level, the territorial development contracts (Contrats de développement territorial: CDTs) also advance measures intended to reduce social and territorial inequalities. The CDTs were created by the 2010 Grand Paris Act. Signed by central government and local authorities, these documents concern sections of the regional territory, generally encompassing several municipalities and a few hundred thousand inhabitants. CDTs are planning and programming tools with a 15-year time horizon. Housing, culture, sport, social exclusion, the protection of farming and woodland areas and landscapes, transport, etc. are the main domains concerned. The CDTs foster economic, social and urban development in territories that are defined as strategic, and in particular those served by the Grand Paris public transport network (see below).

Every CDT is the product of a territorial project that is expressed through a territorial development strategy (schéma de développement du territoire: SDT), which sets out the objectives and the measures to be implemented, the funding method and the time frame. The CDTs cover a variety of themes and domains, because they depend on the economic, social and environmental situations of the areas concerned, but many of them highlight policies of solidarity and resistance to socio-territorial inequalities, the maintenance or expansion of the social housing stock, improvements to the living environment through housing refurbishment, the development of services and culture and, more generally, urban regeneration. This is notably the case for the CDTs of Plaine Commune and Est Ensemble (Seine-Saint-Denis intermunicipal authorities) or the Grandes Ardoines in Val-de-Marne.

In 2019 22 CDTs were signed. They covered 157 municipalities – i.e. 12 per cent of the municipalities in Île-de-France – and 4.4 million inhabitants (38 per cent of the regional population).

### *Reducing inequalities with housing policies*

In 2000, under the aegis of the communist minister Jean-Claude Gayssot, the PS government enacted the Solidarity and Urban Renewal Act (Loi de solidarité et renouvellement urbain: SRU), which, apart from reorganizing French urban planning, had a substantial social component. The SRU Act sought to "recreate a social equilibrium in every territory and to tackle the shortage of social housing" in towns. To this end, one of its provisions was that municipalities with more than 3,500 inhabitants belonging to a conurbation with more than 50,000 inhabitants must have at least 20 per cent social housing by 2025. In Île-de-France, this population threshold was reduced to 1,500 inhabitants. Municipalities that did not fulfil this obligation would be penalized financially. In 2013 a second act, called SRU 2, increased the percentage of social housing from 20 to 25 per cent.

On average, the SRU Act was applied well across the country. A 2015 report by the Revenue Court noted that the results in Île-de-France were uneven, however (Cour des comptes 2015). Over the period from 2002 to 2011 the proportion of social housing increased by 23 per cent in municipalities covered by the SRU Act, more than half (58 per cent) being built by the city of Paris. Certain rich towns, such as Neuilly and Nogent-sur-Marne, built slightly under half the required number of social housing units. In 2017, in France as a whole, out of some 1,200 municipalities subject to the act, a little over half had not met their obligations, as compared with only 387 in 2013. Most of these municipalities were located in the Provence-Alpes-Côte d'Azur region and in Île-de-France (Ministère de la cohésion des territoires 2017). In December 2018 there were some 66 municipalities in Île-de-France with a "shortfall" – i.e. they were penalized financially.

In the view of the Revenue Court and many observers, this situation is partly explained by the inadequacy of the legal penalties. For example, although municipalities pay a financial penalty if they do not achieve the social housing threshold, they can deduct certain expenses from the penalties, with the result that the latter are, ultimately, very small. In other words, it turns out that it costs municipalities more to obey the law than not to. In addition to this, there are structural factors, such as the shortage of land or excessive urban densities, that sometimes make it difficult to build social housing.

As we have just seen, therefore, the very poor housing situation in Île-de-France, especially for social housing, reveals the relative failure of the policies implemented and the legislative measures taken by the public authorities.

## Competitiveness and attractiveness policies

The beginning of the 2000s marked the end of the "*graviériste*" era (see Chapter 2), a period when one plank of government policy was to reduce the economic influence of Île-de-France in order to restore the balance of development across the country. Some of the actors, starting with central government, began shyly to hearken to the siren calls of globalization and to view the Île-de-France metropolitan region differently, not from a purely French perspective but within a European and global context. This shift began with the region becoming eligible for EU structural funds in 2000, but it was also expressed in official documents such as "The territorial exception: an asset for France" (François-Poncet 2003), a report presented to the Senate on behalf of DATAR. This document, which continued to adopt the *graviériste* stance but highlighted the relative failure of the spatial development policies implemented since the 1960s, emphasized the fact that "the metropolis is facing tough competition in the global arena" (François-Poncet 2003: 34). It therefore constituted a foretaste of a paradigm shift in the way government would approach the region's development policies.

The shift in the state's position would also become apparent in its choices for the location of big infrastructures, however, which would favour Île-de-France. The Soleil project is one example. An international project, the Soleil project is a third-generation synchrotron that was inaugurated in December 2006 by President Jacques Chirac. The decision to locate it on the Saclay plateau in Île-de-France was an undisguised attempt by the state to reinforce the competitiveness of the region. Out of the 11 regions eager to host this infrastructure, Île-de-France was the one finally selected, and the reasons for this choice clearly reveal the change in state policy in this domain. The minister of research at the time, Roger-Gérard Schwartzenberg, was unequivocal:

> Île-de-France has seen several scientific infrastructures that contributed to its strength moved to other regions for reasons of relocation. Locating the synchrotron elsewhere would risk further undermining the Île-de-France region's international reputation in research … Île-de-France is our primary research hub, one that is competitive at both European and international scale. We therefore need to prevent its relative decline continuing. (press conference, 11 September 2000)

From this time on, Île-de-France would become the focus for the implementation of a number of policies designed to improve the region's competitiveness and attractiveness in international competition. The policies would either target the region as a whole or be aimed at areas and specific infrastructures within the region.

### *National and regional policies: clusters, regional strategies and tourism*

The main policy for competitiveness, at least the one described as such, was the "competitiveness clusters" (*pôles de compétitivité*). Launched by the government in 2004 as part of its new industrial policy focusing on France's attractiveness and international visibility, its aim was to support the best R&D and innovation platform projects with special funding. To do this, the state earmarked "competitiveness clusters", defined as "grouping[s] of small, medium or large companies, research laboratories and training establishments, in a well-identified area and around a specific theme". The purpose of these clusters was to develop synergies in order to implement innovative economic development projects. This mechanism offered public subsidies and a special tax regime to companies belonging to these clusters. The aims were to make the economy more competitive, to create jobs and to bring together private and public research.

Following several calls for projects, the government selected 71 clusters across France as a whole. These clusters are classified into three categories, based on their potential for innovation: national, potentially global, global. The aim is primarily to reinforce the global clusters, and to nurture the development of the potentially global ones. Several billion euros in subsidies and tax reliefs have been allocated since the creation of the clusters. These subsidies make it possible to raise private funds.

Île-de-France has six competitiveness clusters, all either global or potentially global. Formed of big companies, small and medium-sized enterprises, start-ups, research centres and private and academic training bodies, as well as local authorities, they cover most of the region's main economic sectors, and are a driving force behind the launch and spread of innovative projects. They all have specific names.

The speciality of the so-called "Mov'éo" cluster is the design and development of forms of transport that are safer for people and the environment. The objective of "ASTech Paris region" cluster is to accentuate the leading European positions held by the region in air transport, aerospace, business aviation, propulsion and infrastructure. The ambition of the "Medicen Paris region" cluster lies in the field of human health (prevention, diagnosis, therapies, associated technologies), to facilitate the transfer of innovation to the industrial sector, to the market and to patients. The focus at the "Systematic Paris region" cluster is the design, production and management of complex systems. The "Finance innovation" cluster aspires to become the leading European platform for financial information and the European centre for financial training. And, finally, "Advancity" exists to develop any project that promotes sustainable cities and urban eco-technologies.

It is hard to evaluate the competitiveness clusters policy. In 2013 France stratégie, a national public agency that offers expertise and prospective studies on major economic and social issues, reporting to the prime minister, published an evaluation report for the period from 2007 to 2012 on all the competitiveness clusters in France. The general conclusion is favourable with respect to job creation and the volume of R&D produced by companies located in these clusters compared with those that are not. Nonetheless, the report emphasized that it is difficult to identify the impact of the policy of "competitiveness clusters" compared with other policies in the same domain (e.g. crédit impôt recherche).[1]

With regard to Île-de-France, no evaluation has yet been produced. The regional council launched an evaluation in 2018, the results of which are not yet available in 2020.

Policies on competitiveness and attractiveness would also play a leading part in most of the plans and contracts signed between central government and local authorities. For example, the 2007–14 CPER immediately made this objective one of the priorities of the contract, and it would in fact absorb most of the funds in the plan. In reference to the Lisbon strategy to which it was supposed to contribute,[2] the CPER would finance transport infrastructures and equipment, mainly in public transport, and inject several hundreds of millions of euros into research and development with the aim of increasing the region's international attractiveness. The objectives of the 2015–20 CPER were the same. More than €5 billion were allocated to transport, 84 per cent of this sum to public transport. It would contribute to the financing of the New Grand Paris programme (see below) with the construction of the Grand Paris Express and several metro extensions. In addition, €1 billion went into

1. Crédit impôt recherche (CIR): this tax credit for research is a measure created to support companies' R&D activities, with no restrictions regarding sector or size. Companies that spend on fundamental research and experimental development can receive CIR by deducting this expenditure from their taxes, subject to certain conditions.
2. Lisbon strategy: EU strategy decided by the European Council in Lisbon in 2000. Its objective was to make the European Union the world's most competitive and dynamic knowledge economy by 2010. It was founded on sustainable economic growth that was to go hand in hand with a quantitative and qualitative improvement in employment and greater social cohesion.

higher education and research, here to build university facilities and to provide research labs with access to very high-speed internet.

The regional council's own policies were not to be outdone. Although the first two regional economic development schemes, as we have seen, emphasized a change in the mode of development (ecological and social conversion) and focused heavily on questions of social and territorial inequalities, they nevertheless included a "competitiveness" component. Funding in this domain would therefore contribute to the establishment of some 30 business incubators and the labelling of more than 150 R&D projects by the competitiveness clusters.

Nevertheless, it is the SRDEII (Stratégie régionale de développement économique, d'innovation et d'internationalisation: regional strategy for economic development for internationalization and innovation), approved in 2016 and covering the period from 2017 to 2021, that clearly shifted the focus of regional policies to competitiveness and attractiveness (CRIF 2016). Although this strategy adopts the same principles as the previous SRDEs, by prioritizing Île-de-France's economic strengths, it emphasizes the region's negative migratory balance, a sign in its view that Île-de-France is falling behind its big competitors, such as London and New York. Proposing a profound revitalization of regional action, it made it a priority to create a favourable climate for business, in particular by focusing on the territory's international attractiveness. It declared that Île-de-France must become "Europe's leading smart region". To accomplish this, it concentrated on four main themes: investing in attractiveness; developing competitiveness; developing the spirit of entrepreneurship and innovation; and, finally, developing collective action in favour of companies and jobs. To implement this strategy, it created a body called Paris-region entreprises (PRE) with responsibility for coordinating the actions of the numerous actors of economic development and for developing the "Paris region" brand.

At the infra-regional level, the contractual policies between central and local government were on the same trail. For example, many CDTs include actions and measures designed to make their area more competitive and more attractive. Some, such as the Grand Paris Seine Ouest (GPSO) CDT, have banked on digital industries and, more broadly, the creative industries. The Orly CDT sought to take advantage of the presence of the international airport to increase its territory's international visibility and development. The Vallée scientifique de la Bièvre, an area located in the south of the region that encompasses 600,000 residents, 40,000 students and 10,000 researchers spread across 18 municipalities, wants to take advantage of the presence of big private corporations such as Sanofi, numerous CNRS research centres and the hospitals located on its territory to develop around the sector of health and biomedical innovations, etc.

Île-de-France is the metropolitan region that hosts the most trade shows and conferences, and regularly plays host to international events. It is one of the world's leading tourist destinations, perhaps the number one (see Chapter 4). Nonetheless, although Île-de-France remains a very attractive region in all these domains, many players – in particular the chambers of commerce and the tourist organizations – are warning that its attractiveness is under threat.

This situation explains the recent policies of attractiveness pursued in these domains by the public authorities, whether central government, the city of Paris or the regional council. In tourism, successive governments have made increasing tourist numbers a priority, with a particular focus on foreign visitors. The magic figure of 100 million foreign visitors a year for France as a whole has become a leitmotif. With 90 million tourists in 2018, the country is undoubtedly closing in on this target, but there is still much to do, especially in Île-de-France.

Paris and the Paris region are the leading French tourist destination. With 50 million total visitors in 2018, they account for more than a half of France's foreign tourists. This figure represents a slight increase on 2017 (48 million visitors) and on the previous years, which were notably marked by several terrorist attacks that had a negative impact on visitor numbers. In response to the goal of increasing the number of tourists in France, and therefore also in Île-de-France, and the fear in the tourist sector that this goal might be under threat, in 2017 the authorities – and in particular the regional council – launched a tourism development scheme set to run until 2021. The stated objective of this scheme is to maintain the attractiveness of Île-de-France, notably by comparison with London and New York. The actions planned under the scheme relate to improving the safety of people and places and access to the most popular sites such as the Eiffel Tower and the Palace of Versailles, notably by exploiting the benefits of digital technology.

Hosting big events is another goal that Île-de-France wants to prioritize, with the aim of raising its international profile and attractiveness. At the beginning of the 2000s the city of Paris experienced two successive failures, in its bids to host the Olympic Games in 2008 and 2012. Although the losing to Beijing for the 2008 Olympics has not left many traces, the loss of the 2012 Games to its European rival London proved demoralizing. As a result, Paris lacked the will to join the race for the 2016 and 2020 Olympic Games. In 2015, however, with the support of the regional council and central government, the city joined the race to host the 2024 Olympic Games, which it finally won after reaching an agreement with its rival, Los Angeles, which would host the 2028 games. This success prompted a number of entities, including the government, to propose that France should bid for the 2025 Universal Exhibition. The change of government in 2017 dealt a fatal blow to this application, since in 2018 the new government decided to withdraw the bid on financial grounds.

### *Targeted policies: La Défense, Saclay and the airports*

La Défense is Europe's premier business district. Created in 1950 by the government (see Chapter 2), subsequently established as an OIN (national interest operation) in the early 2000s, La Défense became a district of tower blocks and office buildings, structures that proliferated in particular between 2000 and 2005. By 2006 the district was home to 2,500 company headquarters and more than 3,000,000 square metres of offices, 150,000 jobs, 600,000 square metres of housing units with more than 20,000 residents, and 200,000 square metres of shops and services. Nonetheless, the competitiveness of La Défense seemed in decline. Of the ten big corporations located there in 1995, seven had left the district ten years later. Moreover, whereas London attracted a quarter of new company headquarters between 2000 and 2005, La Défense attracted only 5 per cent.

In response, the government decided to revitalize the district in 2005. To do this, it established a five-point La Défense renewal plan (Plan de renouveau de La Défense – 2006), consisting of the following actions:

1. Regenerating the old high-rise buildings, to create 350,000 square metres of offices;
2. Building new towers, by adding 300,000 square metres between 2007 and 2013 and locating the headquarters of the Ministry of Infrastructure in the district;
3. Increasing the residential offering, by creating 1,400 housing units over the same period;
4. Improving access to the site; and
5. Erecting taller towers, symbols of economic and technical power as well as wealth, in order to attract the biggest multinationals, a sector in which La Défense had fallen behind.

The renewal plan was set to end in 2015. It would never really be implemented, however, for several reasons. First of all, it attracted opposition from several local authorities (see Chapter 7), which would delay its implementation. Second, it was hit hard by the 2008 financial crisis. As a result, the construction of several new towers was either halted or cancelled, in particular the Signal tower, a building designed by the architect Jean Nouvel, for which the investors pulled out.

In 2010 construction resumed. In 2013 the Carpe Diem tower was completed, followed in 2014 by the Magenta tower. The operation seems to have been a success, at least in terms of building occupancy, since the vacancy rate fell from 13 per cent in 2014 to 5.4 per cent in 2018, despite the departure of a few big firms, such as SFR, which left the district in 2013.

To sum up, the development of La Défense, a district designed to reinforce the attractiveness and competitiveness of Île-de-France, was an entirely state-run project. Its implementation was hampered by unfavourable conditions, at least at the start, and significant opposition from the local authorities in areas close to the perimeter of the business district.

These implementation difficulties were not limited to La Défense, as we will see in the case of the government's other flagship project in this domain: Paris-Saclay. The objective of the Paris-Saclay project was to create a science and technology cluster some 30 km south-west of Paris, in a large area encompassing 27 municipalities. Launched by the government in 2006, its aim was to create a world-class centre of scientific excellence, comparable with Silicon Valley or the Cambridge area in Massachusetts.

The project was centred on an existing cluster of public and private research centres. These included several laboratories set up by the CNRS at the end of the Second World War. These were followed in the 1950s by the CEA (Atomic Energy Centre), a big national public institution, and Paris University. At the same time, several big firms – such as Peugeot-Citroen, Renault and Sanofi – located there. In the 1970s they were joined by certain elite academic institutions (Polytechnique, Télécom Paris). In 2000 the Soleil synchrotron (see above) was built there.

The objective of the project was to group all these public and private entities together to form a cluster, and to exploit the synergy that this cluster was expected to generate. The ultimate aim was for 20 to 25 per cent of France's entire research capacity to be located there. By 2019 the site was home to 45,000 research jobs (information and communication technologies, health and biology, future mobility, aerospace, smart energy management, etc.) and accounted for some 15 per cent of the country's public and private research.

Although the figures and volumes quoted above are impressive, the project is not progressing as rapidly as intended. In 2010 the government set up a new public entity, the Paris-Saclay Corporation (Établissement public Paris-Saclay: EPS), to manage the entire project. Nonetheless, it came up against numerous obstacles, starting with opposition to the project by environmentalist movements and some municipalities, which delayed its development. In addition, the multiple research institutions that were supposed to join forces are not finding it easy to generate the hoped-for synergy. Moreover, the big university, which was intended to combine 18 higher education and research institutions, has failed to come to fruition, because of conflicts between the institutional "partners". A 2017 report by the Revenue Court concluded that, despite public investment of more than €5 billion, the Paris-Saclay project had hit the buffers (Stromboni 2017). By way of explanation, the court pointed to the shortage of housing and transport, as well as the project's lack of a strategic vision, notably on the part of central government. With respect to transport, the future of the project relies heavily on good public transport provision. This should be achieved with line 18 of the future Grand Paris Express (see below), but that operation is running late. Initially planned for 2024, then 2025 for the opening of the Universal Exhibition, the opening has been postponed to 2027 at the earliest.

The attractiveness and competitiveness of a world-class metropolis necessarily demands good access to every corner of the planet. In this respect, the links between the city and its airports are fundamental. Île-de-France, like other big metropolitan areas such as London and New York, has poor airport transit services, however. Improvement plans have existed for many years, but for the moment none has come to fruition.

Service to Roissy Charles de Gaulle Airport, France's principal airport and the second in Europe behind London Heathrow, has been a bone of contention between central government and local authorities for many years (see Chapter 7). At the beginning of this century the government came up with a plan for the Charles de Gaulle Express, an express rail line linking Paris to the airport. It would offer a 20-minute journey time on a partly new line, at an estimated cost of €1.7 billion. The route would mostly follow the existing railway, but would require the construction of 8 km of new lines. The reasons advanced for this project were to increase the competitiveness and international attractiveness of Île-de-France, as the official website explains: "It is a critical priority for the economic competitiveness of Île-de-France [...] a major asset for our country's image and for the welcome given to tourists in France [...] an asset for Paris's bid for the 2024 Olympic Games."

After much shilly-shallying, Parliament approved the construction and funding of the project in December 2016, with the target of being operational for the 2024 Olympic Games. Yet the project has been blocked ever since, and in 2019 the government postponed the commissioning to 2025 at the earliest, mainly because the work deemed necessary was incompatible with the operation of line B of the RER (see Chapter 7).

The situation with transport to Orly, Île-de-France's second international airport, is the same. As part of the 2008 Grand Paris project (the Grand 8: see Chapter 7; see also Map 6.1), the plan is to extend line 14 of the metro southwards to link the airport to Paris city centre and to build a line that will serve it and the Paris-Saclay cluster. If the goal of the Grand 8 was to provide transport to the business district and economic hubs, as well as the two main airports of Orly and Roissy, in order to make Paris a "global city" able to hold its own in the international competition between the world's big cities, the difficulties encountered by the project, and the successive changes of government in 2012 and 2017, would significantly alter matters. Although the aim is still to improve transport links to the airports, the project is running late. It remains uncertain whether the 2024 target date for the extension to line 14, announced in 2014, will be met.

## Environmental policies

Rather than policies as such, what we see in Île-de-France is a set of actions carried out by the public authorities in which it is not easy to identify a coherent overall direction, or even coordination. Nevertheless, there have been multiple plans and strategies in the last decade at least, but they sometimes lack substance and, above all, follow-up and resources, particularly financial resources.

### *The environmental dimension of planning policies*

Many of the plans, schemes and strategies mentioned in the introduction to this chapter tackle the problems of the environment in Île-de-France, and in some of them the environment is a central focus. Although some, such as the SDRIF and the first SRDEs, are relatively old, others, such as the urban travel plan and the climate plans, are recent, and their implementation cannot yet be assessed.

In the SDRIF (Île-de-France regional master plan), published in 2008 and then revised in 2013 (CRIF 2013; see Chapter 7), the main objective is to promote the region's social, economic and environmental transition. The target is no less than "factor four" – i.e. a fourfold reduction in greenhouse gas emissions. In this respect, the SDRIF pursues a "Francilian model of sustainable development" based on the concept of a compact and energy-efficient city. To this end, the SDRIF places emphasis on the energy transition (developing renewable energies with the aim of gradually replacing fossil fuels), on the development of transit systems (to reduce car use) and on increasing urban density. An additional priority is "reducing the vulnerability of the city to risks, pollution and noise", with a particular emphasis on resilience to flooding, since 435,000 dwellings, 830,000 people and 750,000 jobs would be affected in the event of a once-in-a-century flood (IAU 2018a).

The SRDEs are the short- and medium-term economic component of the SDRIF. From this perspective, the stated objective of the first SRDE

(2007–11) was that Île-de-France should become Europe's first eco-region. It highlights three priorities – the development of eco-activities, respect for the environment and the development of high-quality agriculture – since 50 per cent of the land in the region is agricultural. The SRDEI (2011–14: CRIF 2011), more sensitive to environmental issues because of the global ecological crisis, maintains these objectives while emphasizing the need for an ecological switch in the economy, the new paradigm of growth in Île-de-France. This switch entails the introduction of new modes of production, and the production of high added value goods characterized by sustainability and shareability.

Similarly, most of the territorial development contracts highlight environmental priorities, although these vary in importance and content from one project to another. This is notably the case for the Grand Paris Seine Ouest CDT, which covers seven municipalities that are home to some 300,000 people in south-western Paris. In its title, "The digital, creative and sustainable city" (GPSO 2013), the CDT highlights the preservation of the ecological heritage of this territory (more than a third of it consists of green areas and woodland), which it defines as the "green lungs" of the city, as well as its policies for ecological improvement (construction of so-called "high environmental efficiency" dwellings and offices; the development of renewable energy, notably through district heating systems; etc.). Many development projects therefore prioritize public transit and "active modes" and protection of the environment. This entails the establishment of systems of green and blue corridors, a general and cross-cutting development tool that, according to the CDT, "will help to bring a global response to the different ambitions of GPSO: preserving the living environment, protecting natural resources and preventing natural risks, checking biodiversity loss and maintaining and increasing biodiversity, and combating climate change" (GPSO 2013: 23).

Published in 2014, the PDUIF (Île-de-France urban travel plan) also sets targets for sustainable mobility.[3] Over the period from 2000 to 2020, it set the goal of reducing GHG emissions by 20 per cent, in particular by increasing the use of public transport by 20 per cent and reducing car use by 2 per cent. To achieve this, it provided for a 25 per cent increase in public transport provision by 2020, through the reinforcement of existing lines and the creation of new ones. It also seeks to develop "active modes" (walking and cycling) within travel policies.

3. Urban travel plans (PDUs) are planning documents that determine the organization of passenger and goods transport, traffic movement and parking within an urban area. All modes of transport are therefore concerned. They are developed and approved by intermunicipal bodies and, in the case of Île-de-France, by the regional authority.

A mid-term assessment of the PDUIF conducted over the period from 2010 to 2015 by the Île-de-France transport syndicate (Syndicat des transports d'Île-de-France: STIF), the authority that organizes mobility across the region (STIF 2016), showed that these goals were on track to be met, with a 1.3 per cent increase in the use of public transport and a 0.5 per cent fall in car use over the period in question. Nonetheless, public transport provision had increased by only 9 per cent, below the stated target. Although this increase came from the opening of new tram lines, extensions to metro lines and the reinforcement of bus services, it fell short of the target because several infrastructure projects had been delayed as a result of funding problems. With respect to "active modes", the report noted a substantial investment in cycle paths with an increase in provision of more than 75 per cent – i.e. 2,400 km of cycle paths built between 2010 and 2015, a figure in line with the objectives set out in the PDUIF, which set a target of 4,400 km by 2020.

More recently, several local authorities (regions, intermunicipal authorities [EPCIs], *départements*) have drawn up climate plans, a new instrument designed to establish an environmental strategy and to schedule the implementation of future actions. For example, the Greater Paris metropolitan authority (MGP) approved its climate plan in 2018, as did the city of Paris. Under the title "climate, air, energy plan" (Plan climat, air et énergie: PCAE), the two authorities are pursuing the same objectives, albeit in different territories: the city of Paris within the Paris municipal area, MGP across its 131 municipalities (see Chapter 7). MGP's PCAE focuses on six priority strategic and operational objectives.

1. To achieve carbon neutrality – i.e. zero net emissions – by 2050, in line with the 2°C threshold set by the Paris Agreement and with the national climate plan.
2. To achieve factor four by 2050, in line with Île-de-France's 2012 regional climate air energy scheme and the Act on Energy Transition for Green Growth, passed on 17 August 2015.
3. To increase the metropolitan region's resilience to the effects of climate change.
4. To reduce concentrations of air pollution to levels that meet the thresholds set by the World Health Organization.
5. To massively reduce final energy consumption, notably in the residential and service sectors, as well as in transport, while taking new demand into account.
6. To achieve a diversified and zero-carbon energy mix, by means of renewable energies and energy recovery.

The city of Paris PCAE sets out the same objectives, with priority measures such as increasing the number of cycle paths within the city, increasing levels of greenery and eliminating diesel by 2024.

In many ways, there is a large rhetorical component to these plans. Although it is not possible to evaluate the results of all these schemes and strategies, the few assessments that have been carried out invite caution. For example, in a first assessment of the implementation of the SDRIF published in 2019 (IAU 2019b), the IAU concludes that "the environmental blackspots, i.e. sectors that are subject to at least three forms of damage and pollution [see Chapter 5], affected 13 per cent of the regional population in 2017, i.e. the same proportion as in 2012" (IAU 2019b: 77), indicating that the situation had not changed. Moreover, with regard to GHG emissions, although the report notes that regional emissions fell by 11 per cent between 2012 and 2015, largely because of improvements to the energy efficiency of buildings (a 6 per cent reduction in GHG emissions), emissions from road transport increased by 1.2 per cent over the same period.

### *Multiple and fragmented actions without real coordination*

Although central and local government have deployed a multitude of actions and measures to tackle the environmental problems affecting Île-de-France, unfortunately they fall short through fragmentation and lack of coordination. This is largely attributable to problems of governance, a question that I will tackle directly in Chapter 7. In this section, I simply mention the biggest – or, at least, the most significant – problems, in particular those that are most conflictual in that they typically oppose those who favour strong measures to resolve the environmental problems of the metropolis and those who are content with more gradual or less restrictive measures. Unsurprisingly, it is the issues of air pollution and car use that dominate the stage.

Although air pollution has on average fallen in Île-de-France (see Chapter 5), it nevertheless remains substantial. One of the typical symptoms of the persistence of this type of pollution is the peaks in pollution caused by particular climate conditions, dominated by fine particulates in winter and ozone in summer. The situation varies for different pollutants, but ozone pollution peaks have increased sharply recently, with ozone levels in 2018 exceeding the threshold the most times since 2003 (Airparif 2018). To tackle these episodes of pollution that seem politically urgent – in other words, that require immediate action by the authorities – numerous measures have been taken since the 2000s.

To tackle air pollution caused by car traffic, the state (which is responsible for this domain) initially established traffic alternation. In France, this measure has in fact been used just three times, in 1997, in 2014 and in 2015, and solely in Paris and the inner suburbs. It has tended to trigger power struggles between central and local government, with the latter – especially Paris – asking the government to take such a measure as quickly as possible, and the government either refusing or postponing implementation. Deemed fairly ineffective (a 20 per cent reduction in traffic for a mere 2 per cent reduction in pollution, according to the Île-de-France regional council (conseil régional d'Île-de-France: CRIF 2016), the traffic alternation measure was withdrawn. From 2016 a new way of restricting car use during pollution peaks was introduced: the air quality certificate (Certificat qualité de l'air), or "Crit'Air". Its aim was to differentiate between vehicles on the basis of pollution using a classification running from 1 (least-polluting vehicle) to 5 (most-polluting vehicle). Depending on the severity of the pollution event, vehicles are permitted to run depending on their pollution classification. This measure has been applied several times, with much reluctance on the part of government and little adherence from motorists, especially as the penalties for contravention are small.

Alongside these constraints, the Île-de-France transport syndicate, the authority that organizes public transport under the aegis of the regional council, decided that public transport should be provided free of charge across its territory during periods of high pollution. This free service was challenged in 2017 by the new president of the region, Valérie Pécresse, who favoured a one-off daily payment with a large discount. The reasons were financial, since free transport was costing STIF an average of €4 million a day.

Other, non-circumstantial measures were introduced to regulate car use, notably within the city of Paris. For example, "low emission zones" have been created, from which the most-polluting cars are excluded. This rule has been in force in Paris since 2017, where unclassified vehicles or vehicles with a Crit'Air classification of 5 are not admitted. Since 2019 those with a classification of 4 have also been excluded. Within the territory of MGP, several municipalities have applied this restriction since 1 July 2019.

As we can see, measures and actions relating to the environment are plentiful and varied, but they singularly lack coordination. This is partly explained by the fact that powers to act in the environmental sphere are divided between central and local government and that there are no coordinating structures between them. In addition, the importance attributed to environmental issues varies between authorities, which do not necessarily agree with each other – a fact that does not favour cooperation on this issue.

## Emergency response: housing and mobility policies

The two big emergencies on the political agenda are transport and housing.

When it comes to transport, it is the situation of public transport that seems the more critical, especially as this is seen as the mode that needs to be developed, both for reasons specific to the sector (reducing urban congestion by encouraging a modal shift from the car to public transport) and for its positive impact on pollution and the environment.

It is mainly through supply-side policies – i.e. improvements to existing networks and the construction of new lines, especially tramlines and metro extensions – that the question of mobility in Île-de-France has been tackled. As we have seen, despite an increase in provision, the situation has hardly improved. True, public transport uptake has increased, in part – according to the IAU (2019b) – because of this increase in supply, but it has not been sufficient to meet demand and has not happened quickly enough to deal with the crisis. For example, numerous metro extensions have fallen behind, the most significant being the northwards extension to line 14, which was supposed to be finished in 2017 but will probably not be fully ready before 2024, although a small portion opened in December 2020.

It is the construction of the Grand Paris Express, however, that is highlighted as the ultimate solution to mobility problems. This is a colossal piece of infrastructure that is presented as the only possible solution for the congestion on Île-de-France's public transport system. What is it?

In 2008 the secretary of state for the development of the capital region, Christian Blanc (see Chapter 7), unveiled a project to build a 200-km-long automatic metro line primarily to serve the main clusters of economic development (the areas around the airports, Saclay, La Défense, the east of Île-de-France) along with central Paris. This project was very quickly baptised the "Grand 8" because its route forms a figure-of-eight through the densest part of the region. After a major conflict between central and local government (see Chapter 7), this Grand 8 was replaced by a new project, the New Grand Paris, which combines the construction of the Grand Paris Express (a modified Grand 8) with a transport recovery plan. The GPE is an automatic double orbital metro that serves 68 stations. It consists of four new lines and an extension to line 14 to the north and south of the capital (see Map 6.1).

The whole GPE – or, at least, a big part of it – was initially scheduled to be commissioned for the 2024 Olympic Games. The first estimates set the costs at some €22 billion, but these were very quickly judged to be over-optimistic. In 2012 the Auzannet Report, submitted to the minister of territorial equality and housing, reckoned the eventual cost to be in the region of €30 billion

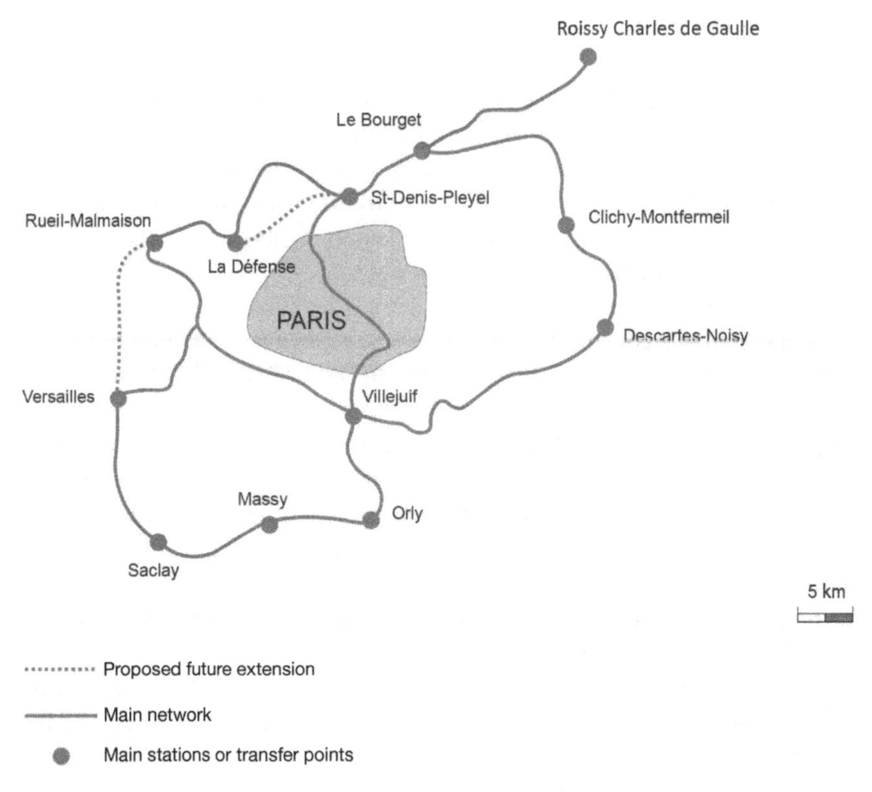


**Map 6.1** The Grand Paris Express

(Auzannet 2012). In 2017 the Revenue Court assessed the cost of the project at €35 billion (Cour des comptes 2017). In parallel, the completion date was pushed back, with a good number of lines and extensions not set to open now before 2030. Spiralling costs, funding problems, postponements: the rollout of the GPE was proving chaotic. Nonetheless, work began in 2015, and in 2019 the tunnel-boring operations began. The project is definitely under way, and the lines are opening progressively (part of line 14 opened in January 2021) – between 2024 and 2030 for the four new lines.

In parallel, other operations scheduled under the transport recovery plan are under way: reinforcement of line A of the RER, modernization of lines B and C of the RER, extension of line E (Eole) westwards towards Mantes-la-Jolie, extension of line 1 eastwards towards Val-de-Fontenay, etc. Once again, the costs are significant and have risen sharply. In its December 2017 report, the Revenue Court assessed the cost of this revitalization plan at more than €3 billion.

The question that remains is whether – despite these colossal investments – the new infrastructures that will come online in the next ten years will be sufficient to halt the current congestion on public transport systems, or whether they themselves will not be overwhelmed the moment they open.

On the housing front, the situation is equally tight. The target set out in the 2013 master plan is to build 70,000 dwellings a year between 2010 and 2030. Hitting this target is the only way the current crisis can be lastingly resolved. Under the SDRIF, the objective is to build 38,000 dwellings a year to cover demographic growth, 12,000 to avoid increasing the current deficit and to absorb it, 17,000 to offset lost housing and 3,000 to maintain market fluidity. Of these 70,000 dwellings, 30 per cent will need to be social housing. In addition to the construction of new housing, the existing stock needs to be upgraded.

As we have seen, however, although construction rates have markedly increased in recent years, this is not sufficient to meet the need. A report on the implementation of the SDRIF states: "In 2018, despite a sharp uptick in housing construction, difficulties remain in access to homeownership and in the living conditions of households in Île-de-France" (IAU 2019b: 12). The report also concludes that the situation of the housing stock has not improved, because, "in addition to insufficient production of social housing, there is a growing problem of household impoverishment within the existing stock" (IAU 2019b: 12). With regard to old housing, the report states that "recent years have confirmed the growing deterioration of a large proportion of old dwellings, which no longer meet current quality requirements. Since 2013, there has been an increase in the phenomenon of multiple occupancy in housing" (IAU 2019b: 12).

With regard to housing costs, we have seen that the gap between incomes and prices has continued to widen. In response, local authorities have resorted to a number of measures, the most dramatic being rent controls. Introduced in 2015, especially in Paris, these controls were overturned by the courts in 2017. The ELAN Act (Loi d'évolution du logement, de l'aménagement et du numérique: Development of Housing, Spatial Planning and Digital Technology Act) of 2018 once again made rent controls legal, and Paris decided to resume them in 2019, citing the stability in rents observed between 2015 and 2017.

This act also turned the spotlight on new players in the housing market, digital platforms such as Homelidays and Airbnb, which were accused of contributing to the housing crisis. The city of Paris considered these platforms to be partly responsible for the rise in rents between 2012 and 2017. It complained that 26 per cent of the dwellings in the capital's four central districts were no longer used to house Parisians, as landlords preferred to convert them into tourist accommodation. To combat what was seen as aggressive action on the part of these platforms, the city of Paris appealed to the government to give it the resources to regulate them. In fact, according to Airbnb itself (2015), Paris is the "world capital of peer-to-peer rentals on Airbnb". Yet the city of Paris broadly welcomed the platform in 2015, judging that it would increase the attractiveness of the city. The situation quickly turned conflictual, however.

In 2015 Paris implemented the first measures against Airbnb to prevent speculation. It restricted the rental period to 120 days a year (Aguilera, Artioli & Colomb 2019). In 2016 the Digital Republic Act introduced a requirement to register this type of rental activity. These measures had little effect, however. The ELAN Act added a further obligation to provide local authorities with data relating to this kind of rental, but only once a year, a measure that the municipalities deemed inadequate and ineffective. The conflict continued in 2019, when Airbnb notably referred the dispute to the European Court of Justice.

Faced with a housing crisis, municipalities seem to have few means of responding, and the handful of measures just described do not seem capable of providing a solution. This is explicitly recognized in the SDRIF report produced in 2019, which states that "the proliferation of Airbnb properties in the heart of the city and the very rapid increase in requirements for emergency housing are raising new problems over regional capacity to meet needs" (IAU 2019b: 12). The same is true with respect to two phenomena that are growing in importance in the capital: rising numbers of homeless people and hosting migrants.

With regard to the homeless, the authorities have significantly reinforced emergency provision, in particular since 2015. They have increased the number of shelters, and facilitated access to health care and to work integration schemes. For 2019, 7,000 places were made available for the homeless, part by central government, the rest by local authorities – a doubling of provision, according to the Île-de-France prefecture. Nonetheless, these arrangements remain globally inadequate. In 2019 the number of homeless people every day in winter was estimated at 1,600. At least 300 people were sleeping in the metro. Although the statistics are uncertain, this is a long way from the estimate of 50 or so cited by the minister for territorial cohesion in an interview on public radio in January 2018. The INSEE data for 2012, the date of the last survey on homelessness, estimated the number of homeless people in France at 140,000. If this figure is related to the population of Île-de-France, it can be assumed that the region has some 20,000 homeless people. For the city of Paris alone, the last count carried out, in January 2020, in a *maraude* (prowl) conducted by the municipality and civil society organizations, found no fewer than 3,550 people sleeping in the capital's streets. The promise made in 2017 by Emmanuel Macron, then a candidate and now president of France – that, "[b]y the end of the year, no one should be sleeping outside, in the streets, in the woods" – has not been kept, by the government's own admission. Obviously, the measures and resources applied have not been equal to the phenomenon.

The same is true for the handling of migrants. Every year Île-de-France is thought to handle some 40 per cent of the asylum requests made in France. In legal terms, dealing with migrants is a matter for central government. The first policy pursued by government was to increase the number of places in the reception centres – an action that has proved radically insufficient, with the result that migrants have settled in camps on the outskirts of Paris and in suburban towns. The second policy was the regular dismantling of these camps, which almost invariably re-form afterwards. A recent dismantling, which took place in January 2020, affected some 1,400 people, who were temporarily rehoused. That was the 60th evacuation since 2015, suggesting that this kind of measure may be less than effective!

The local authorities (in particular the city of Paris) and central government have been passing each other the buck in this matter. The city of Paris believes that government is not doing its job, while the government claims to be increasing resources. It is clear that demand far outstrips supply, and, although the city of Paris and other local authorities are doing their bit (for example, the city created two humanitarian reception centres in the north of the capital), the subsidies provided by the authorities are not equal to the scale of the problem.

The different actors in the region, whether central government or local authorities, have developed and implemented a multiplicity of policies, whether to combat social and territorial inequalities or to make the region more attractive. Moreover, they have developed responses to emergency situations. Although it is difficult – and perhaps impossible – to reach a global assessment of all these measures and policies, it can only be concluded that they are inadequate to resolve the cyclical and structural problems that the region has been facing for several decades. Beyond the difficulties inherent to the nature of these problems, one of the explanations for this situation – perhaps the main explanation – lies in the incapacity of the different actors in Île-de-France to coordinate and cooperate together, which reveals a system of governance that is failing; this is the matter of the next chapter.

# 7

# A blocked system of governance

On the eve of the 2000s Île-de-France's system of governance was beset with conflict, as we saw in Chapter 3. This level of conflict was in part the consequence of struggles between still highly ideological political parties, espousing different if not antagonistic visions of society in general and of Île-de-France in particular.

We have seen that the divergences between the political forces were nothing new, but had been constructed not only over time but also in space. This construction took place in two ways. On the one hand, the parties tried – with a degree of success – to anchor their dominance territorially by forging institutional bastions: broadly, the western *départements*, the city of Paris and the region for the conservatives, the northern, eastern and, partly, the southern *départements* for the forces of the left.

On the other hand, they formed more or less lasting alliances, the Gaullist parties with the liberals and centrists, the communists with the Socialist Party, and the latter with the green movements. These political alliances in part maintained the pre-existing territorial configurations. The picture that emerges from this is one of a political system with a balance of forces between right and left.

The situation was to change significantly in the early 2000s, notably with the city of Paris (in 2001) and the region (in 1998) shifting to the left of the political chessboard. That is where these victories on the progressive side came to a halt, however. Although Paris remained within the orbit of the left, the region fell into the hands of the right in 2015 and again in 2021. Gradually, communist and socialist municipalities and certain left-wing *départements*, such as Val-d'Oise, joined the conservative camp, which began to pitch its tents in the former red suburbs. As we will see, the political – and party-political – squabbles, which would be exacerbated throughout the period at numerous elections, were to dominate the governance of Île-de-France, to the great displeasure of the business community and elements of civil society.

Central government would prove incapable of regulating – let alone controlling – these conflicts, first because decentralization removed some of its resources for doing so and, second, because the state either chose sides and thereby intensified the conflicts, or let the local actors get on with things, having neither a specific vision or strategy with respect to Île-de-France.

I will tackle the question of the governance of Île-de-France in three stages. First, I show how the system has become more conflictual between 2000 and the present day, and explain how this potential for conflict has led to logjam. Next, I look at the unsuccessful attempts by certain actors to gain leadership over the metropolis and thereby to try to steer its development. Finally, I describe the recent institutional reforms and show how they have produced an institutional imbroglio that resolves neither the conflictuality nor the logjam in the system.

## A system of governance with growing potential for conflict

All the ingredients for reinforcing the conflictual nature of the system of governance were present at the beginning of the 2000s. Decentralization was taking place with no one really in charge (Béhar & Estèbe 2007), elections had become substitutes for negotiation between Île-de-France's actors, and the sources of conflict were proliferating (Pouvoirs locaux 2007).

### *Unregulated decentralization*

The political logic that moulded the decentralization process in France built conflict into the institutional system. This was not specific to Île-de-France but had an impact there as elsewhere. Decentralization in France is structured by two constitutional principles with a propensity to generate conflict: the principle of the general competence clause of local authorities and the principle of non-hierarchy between those authorities.

The general competence clause means that any local authority (municipality, *département*, region) can, if it deems it in its interest, intervene in all areas of public action. As a result, every local authority can exercise the powers assigned to each of them by the decentralization laws, with the consequence that conflict can arise between authorities. It was only recently, with the passing of the New Territorial Organization of the Republic Act (the so-called NOTRe Act) in August 2015, that the general competence clause was removed for *départements* and regions, although it was retained for municipalities.

The principle of non-hierarchy between local authorities means that no institutional level has authority over another. This means that the region cannot impose anything on a *département* or on a municipality, and vice versa. Only central government has this power. So, if conflict arises between local authorities, it can be resolved only in the courts. This principle of non-hierarchy between local authorities is invariably reiterated in every piece of decentralization legislation, and many politicians and parties call regularly for its elimination, asking the government to make a choice by prioritizing one institutional tier; this it has never done, however.

The application of these two principles means that in areas where local authority levels sit side by side and where powers overlap, such as metropolitan regions, there are many potential conflicts, and resolving them is more difficult, notably because these two principles grant each institutional level a great degree of autonomy.

This situation is exacerbated by the transfer of competences from central government, which divides responsibilities and resources fairly equally between institutional levels. Thus, all the decentralization laws that have been introduced since the 1980s (see Box 7.1) distribute the new powers to all local authority levels. Although the legislation of 2003 and 2004 grants new responsibilities to the regions, notably in the spheres of rail transport, secondary school management and vocational education, others, such as social housing and roads, are assigned to the *départements*. Although the regions acquired powers in 2015, especially over economic development and support for business, the *départements* were given greater powers over spatial planning and roads. The government's refusal to prioritize one level and its insistence on an even sprinkling in the transfer of powers have therefore led to the emergence of a local politico-institutional system in which rivalries, and the desire to protect newly acquired autonomy, became the framework for relations between local authorities.

---

### BOX 7.1 DECENTRALIZATION LEGISLATION: 1982–2015 (SIMPLIFIED VERSION)

The different legislative moves are generally divided into three periods, called "actes".

#### "Acte I" of decentralization: the 1982 and 1983 legislation

These texts created the regions as new local authorities, assigned several government prerogatives to municipalities, *départements* and regions and transferred local executives, previously run by the prefects, to the elected assemblies.

**"Acte II" of decentralization: the 2003 and 2004 legislation**

These texts established the principle of financial autonomy for local authorities, transferred new powers to the regions and *départements* and granted the regions – experimentally and on a voluntary basis – the possibility of departing from the legal provisions regulating their powers. In addition, the 2004 legislation authorized local referendums.

**"Acte III" of decentralization: the 2014 and 2015 legislation**

These texts created new structures of public intermunicipal cooperation (EPCIs), the metropolises, in a dozen metropolitan regions, including three with special status in the Paris, Lyon and Marseille areas. They redivided the regions, reducing their number from 22 to 13, but Île-de-France was not affected. They redistributed powers between the regions and the *départements* and increased the powers transferred to the regions, especially regarding economic development.

(www.collectivites-locales.gouv.fr)

---

In this new institutional framework, Île-de-France nevertheless retained a special status, for two main reasons. The first was the reinforcement of the regional level, the second the development of intermunicipal cooperation.

The first decentralization measures in the 1980s deprived the Île-de-France region of powers and resources granted to the other regions: spatial planning and public transport. With the reforms of the early 2000s, Île-de-France came back under common law. As a result, it was granted the competence of "spatial planning" and given responsibility for drawing up the master plan (SDRIF), albeit in association with central government. It took advantage of this change to initiate a revision of this plan in 2004 (see below). Likewise, under a 2004 law it obtained powers over public transport, chairing the board of the transport organizing authority, STIF, from which government quite simply disappeared. This was a major change, in that public transport became the primary responsibility of the regional council, which thus acquired the capacity to act across the whole of Île-de-France, and therefore also over the other tiers of local government. As we will see later, the planning and public transport powers granted to the region were to lead to serious conflicts with central government and some local authorities.

Although the strengthening of the respective powers of the local institutions would enable them to maintain their autonomy, this did not mean that there was no cooperation between them. We saw in Chapter 3 that cooperative structures such as the intermunicipal joint authorities (EPCIs) developed throughout the twentieth century, although most of them did not cover the entire regional area and some did not include important players, such as the city of Paris. The situation would change substantially in the early 2000s, but in a slightly paradoxical way, in so far as the new cooperative instruments that were introduced on the one hand reinforced this cooperation, but on the other hand increased the institutional fragmentation of the Île-de-France metropolitan region, because they applied to limited parts of the territory.

---

**BOX 7.2 THE MAIN INSTITUTIONS OF PUBLIC INTERMUNICIPAL COOPERATION (EPCIs) (SIMPLIFIED VERSION)**

The EPCIs differ from local authorities in two specific respects: a principle of speciality, which means that an EPCI can act only within the limits of the responsibilities transferred to it by the municipalities or by the law; and a democratic principle, which means that the boards of the EPCI are not elected by direct universal suffrage but are made up of representatives from the member municipalities. The most powerful EPCIs in terms of powers and resources are those that have their own tax-raising powers. In 2020 they were classified as follows.

The *métropoles* (metropolises), created by a 2010 act, amended by further legislation in 2014 and 2015: these affect the most populous urban areas, with more than 650,000 inhabitants. Under the law, they compulsorily acquire a very large number of competences (planning, environment, public transport, economic development, waste management, culture, policy for cities, etc.). As of 2020 there were 21 metropolises.

The *communautés urbaines* (urban communities), created by legislation in 1966, amended several times subsequently: they cover urban areas with populations in excess of 250,000. The legislation gives them a very large number of competences, similar in this respect to the metropolises. As of 2020 there were 14 of these urban communities.

The *communautés d'agglomération* (agglomeration communities), created by the 1999 legislation: they affect urban areas with more than 50,000 inhabitants. They acquired a number of competences through the legislation, but fewer than the urban communities and the metropolises. As of 2020 there were 222 of these structures.

The *communautés de communes* (communities of *communes*), created by the 1999 act: they affect population centres with more than 15,000 inhabitants. They have a few powers transferred by the municipalities, but are much less powerful than the other forms of EPCI. In 2020 there were 997 across the country.

---

Until the early 1980s Île-de-France was seen as the black sheep of French intermunicipal cooperation. In fact, whereas most of the other big urban areas had institutions of intermunicipal cooperation (some, such as the urban communities of Bordeaux, Lyon and Lille, with significant responsibilities and resources), there was nothing like this in Île-de-France. There, intermunicipal joint authorities were essentially technical and mono-sectoral structures. In 1999 new legislation on intermunicipal cooperation was introduced. It proposed the creation of integrated intermunicipal authorities – i.e. structures with numerous competences (transport, water, environment, waste, planning, economic development, etc.) and adequate resources, in particular tax revenues, in areas with populations above a certain level (see Box 7.2).

The regional prefecture took the view that this law should not apply to Île-de-France because it was an agglomeration in its own right that already had a regional authority. It argued that the creation of integrated intermunicipal cooperative entities in Île-de-France, with their own tax-raising powers, could break up the regional territory into multiple structures, thereby further exacerbating the region's significant institutional fragmentation. Central government did not agree, however, and the legislation was applied to Île-de-France.

In the years that followed, therefore, the 1999 law would lead to the establishment of more than 100 EPCIs, with their own tax arrangements, covering varying population sizes, some of which – such as Plaine Commune in Seine-Saint-Denis – would prove very powerful. Most of these new EPCIs were added to the existing bunch, contributing to yet further institutional fragmentation in Île-de-France.

As a result, Île-de-France has grown increasingly politico-institutionally fragmented over the last two decades. In parallel, the different decentralization laws strengthened all the local authorities, giving each of them additional means of protecting their autonomy. Under these circumstances, cooperation is difficult and conflict more likely. This makes regulation of the system of governance essential. Central government was the only player with the legitimacy to do this, but, as we will see, it showed itself incapable of so doing, leaving the way open to conflicts that would prove sterile.

### *Resolving conflicts by electoral battle rather than by negotiation*

There are multiple reasons for the conflicts between institutional entities in Île-de-France. First, there are differences, profound ideological divergences, which the globalization process has amplified. On one side we find actors for whom globalization primarily means competition between big cities – competition that needs to be won and that therefore requires the prioritization of economic competitiveness and attractiveness policies. These are essentially the right-wing, richer authorities, such as the western *départements*, Hauts-de-Seine and Yvelines, and central government when conservative and liberal parties are in charge. As a general rule, the business community – the big employer federations and the chambers of commerce – support this position.

On the other side, globalization is, above all, seen as responsible for the rise in social and territorial inequalities, and the emphasis must therefore be placed on fighting such disparities. It is primarily the progressive forces associated with the Socialist Party that argue for this position. They are found on Paris municipal council, in the region up to 2015, in the poorest *départements* in the north and east (Seine-Saint-Denis and Val-de-Marne) and, to a lesser extent, in central government when it was led by the left between 2012 and 2017.

This apparent dichotomy does not mean that the right is not sensitive to inequalities or that the left is not interested in competitiveness, but the stated priorities are different and lead to divergent public policy orientations.

In the early 2000s the issue of the environment was added to the ideological mix, and somewhat altered the balance. Although most of the parties now recognize that the environment needs to be included in public policies, here again they differ in their view of the level of priority accorded to it. So the forces on the left would be more inclined to explore – or even move towards – a new, alternative model of growth, even though members of this current, such as the Communist Party, are still hesitant, afraid that green growth could destroy more jobs than it creates and hence exacerbate lingering unemployment. For the conservative parties and the business community, the opposite is largely true, because they sometimes see the policies propagated by the left (see Chapter 6) as "too green" and detrimental to economic growth.

Second, the conflicts are fuelled by territorial interests that also differ. The city of Paris upholds its dominant position within Île-de-France, given its demographic importance and, above all, its economic predominance, and the needs and constraints that these create. Any hint of change in the tiers of power in this respect, any attempt at reform when this is not initiated by the city itself, is eyed with mistrust. As for the region, it takes a dim view of the rising power of other tiers of authority, such as the intermunicipal structures and in particular, as we will see later, the metropolitan tier. It will therefore oppose any change in the institutional organization of Île-de-France. The same is true of the *départements*, which are equally wary of any territorial political reorganization that might challenge their very existence. This is particularly the case for the *départements* in the inner ring, which fear that they could disappear if a metropolitan authority were to be created for the so-called "dense zone" of the region. For their part, the municipalities are afraid of losing some of their prerogatives and resources as the intermunicipal structures become increasingly powerful. These territorial interests are in conflict, and are not necessarily party political. For example, the city of Paris and the region, which were in the same political camp between 2001 and 2015, were often opposed over many issues because of differences in interests.

Finally, one should not underestimate the impact of personal conflicts, arising either from rivalries for leadership within a single political party or from individual enmities. It was well known, for example, that the mayor of Paris and the president of the region had little fondness for each other (Mansat & Lefèvre 2021). Such conflicts are inevitably greater in Île-de-France, because the political leaders are also often national leaders and may pursue strategies to gain power over political structures and institutions that could further their aspirations to higher positions. Before becoming president of the Republic, Nicolas Sarkozy was president of the Hauts-de-Seine *département*, several times a minister and leader of the Conservative Party. The mayor of Paris, Bertrand Delanoë, sought control of the Socialist Party as a potential springboard for a shot at the presidency. The current president of the region is a former minister and a big hitter in the conservative camp. The current mayor of Paris, Anne Hidalgo, is speaking openly of being a candidate in the 2022 presidential election.

It is therefore not surprising under the circumstances that the numerous elections that took place between 2000 and 2021 invariably crystallized conflicts (see Box 7.3). The stakes are undoubtedly high. Given the balance between conservative and progressive forces at regional level, every election challenges that equilibrium and can shift the advantage to one side or another. Winning a local election, whether municipal, departmental or regional, can sometimes have fundamental repercussions for the whole of the political system and a big influence on policy orientations. This is particularly true of elections involving crucial institutional actors such as the mayor of Paris, the Île-de-France region, certain *départements* and, of course, central government.

Public actors, backed according to circumstances by the business community or certain civil society organizations, will therefore tend to favour institutional conquest over negotiation, because, if the institution is captured, the conflict is resolved without the need for compromise. Negotiation takes place only subsequently, depending on the result of the election. A few examples help to illustrate the process.

In 2008 the municipal elections in Paris were won by the left, which increased its majority. The mayor of Paris could therefore pursue his metropolitan strategy in opposition to central government (see below), which would not have been possible if the right had won, because the municipality would have fallen into line. In 2010 there were multiple and serious conflicts between

**BOX 7.3 NATIONAL AND LOCAL ELECTIONS, 2001–20**

| | |
|---|---|
| 2001 | Municipal elections: the "plural left" majority (Socialist Party, Communist Party, ecologists, etc.) takes control of the city of Paris. |
| 2001 | Departmental elections: the right wins in four *départements* out of seven. |
| 2002 | Presidential and parliamentary elections: a win for the right. |
| 2004 | Regional elections: the "plural left" wins the elections but does not obtain an absolute majority on the regional council. |
| 2004 | Departmental elections: the left wins in four *départements* out of seven. |
| 2007 | Presidential and parliamentary elections: a win for the right. |
| 2008 | Municipal elections: Paris stays on the left. |
| 2008 | Departmental elections: the left wins in five *départements* out of seven. |
| 2010 | Regional elections: the region remains on the left and reinforces its positions. |
| 2011 | Departmental elections: the left wins in four *départements* out of seven. |
| 2012 | Presidential and parliamentary elections: a win for the left. |
| 2014 | Municipal elections: Paris stays on the left. |
| 2015 | Regional elections: a win for the right. |
| 2015 | Departmental elections: the right wins in five *départements* out of seven. |
| 2017 | Presidential and parliamentary elections: a "centrist" president and assembly are elected. |
| 2020 | Municipal elections: Paris stays on the left. |
| 2021 | Regional elections: the regional council stays on the right |
| 2021 | Departmental elections: the right wins in six *départements* out of seven. |

the regional council, headed by the left, and central government, in the hands of the right. If the right had won the regional elections, the conflicts would have faded, because once again the region would have fallen into line. In the event, the left came out on top, so central government had no choice but to resort to negotiation.

Beyond general considerations such as these, however, the conflicts are an expression of tangible and important issues and policies, to which we now turn our attention.

### *Issues that crystallize conflicts, block versus block*

Three domains in particular – transport, spatial planning and economic development – feed the conflicts between the different players.

In the transport sphere, the first dispute relates to the Charles de Gaulle Express (CDG Express), the plan for a direct public transport line linking the airport to the Gare de l'Est railway station in 20 minutes, at an estimated cost of some €1.7 billion (see Chapter 6). The route would mostly follow the existing railway, but would require the construction of eight km of new lines. As we saw in the previous chapter, the reason given for the project is that it will make Île-de-France more internationally competitive and attractive.

A conflict very quickly emerged between those in favour of the project for this reason and those opposed to it on the grounds that there are greater priorities, in particular improvements to the existing network. Among the supporters of the CDG Express are central government, the business community represented by the Paris-Île-de-France chamber of commerce, MEDEF Île-de-France, Paris Île-de-France Capitale Économique (PICE) and, since 2016, the Île-de-France region. After long opposition to the project, the city of Paris acquiesced in 2016, because "the project is indispensable to the development of the Paris metropolis" (*Le Parisien* 2016).

The opponents took issue with a luxury service that would enjoy preferential pricing and would be run by a private operator, a choice justified by insecurity in Seine-Saint-Denis, which it would cross without stopping, and by the fear of strikes affecting SNCF or RATP. They denounced the scheme as a "VIP project" and argued that improvements to the RER B line would be sufficient. For the left-wing *départements* and the region, the cost of the infrastructure could have been put to better use by improving the RER B line, used by some 870,000 passengers daily, compared to the expected 50,000 riders of the CDG Express, mostly tourists and business travellers. The city of Paris was opposed until 2016 because of the line's environmental impact on the capital.

Since 2017 the positions have changed somewhat. First, parliament approved the construction and funding of the CDG Express, which is to be managed by a company comprising Paris Aéroport, Caisse des dépôts and SNCF – i.e. a public operator. Second, although the region gave its backing to the project following the change in the majority on the regional executive in December 2015, its position has altered since, as has that of the mayor of Paris. In 2018, in fact, the two authorities asked the government to postpone the construction of the CDG Express on the grounds that this would entail major works that would undermine the operation of line B of the RER, which was already struggling. This change of stance is largely explained by the fear of a major malfunction of the system with a serious impact on the service provided to RER users.

The second focus of conflict is the future automatic metro system. In 2007 the region, dominated by the left, proposed a new infrastructure, Arc Express, which would enhance inter-suburban links and improve the relations with existing lines. In 2008, however, the new secretary of state for the capital region proposed the Grand Paris scheme, a plan for a "Grand 8" (G8) figure-of-eight network consisting of three new automatic metro lines running across the region (see Chapter 6). In April 2009 President Sarkozy officially announced the construction of such an infrastructure, with the stated objective of serving business districts and economic hubs, as well as the two main airports, Orly and Roissy, with the aim of making Paris a "world city". Through the Grand Paris Act of June 2010 (see below), the government instituted the G8 and created the Société du Grand Paris (SGP), a public company in charge of building the infrastructure and of developing the land around the many stations on the new network.

Arc Express and Grand Paris (G8) were immediately seen as competing projects. Time to choose! As we have seen, Grand Paris was supported not just by the government but also by the business community, starting with MEDEF Île-de-France and PICE, and by the main political leaders on the right. For example, Valérie Pécresse, right-wing candidate for the regional elections in 2010, declared: "Arc Express, designed for the next 20 years, is obsolete before it starts." In a similar vein, MEDEF Île-de-France argued that "Arc Express is a response to short- and medium-term needs, whereas the G8 meets long-term needs [...] and better meets the objectives of strong economic growth (3 to 4 per cent) and the control of urban sprawl" (MEDEF Île-de-France 2010: 1). Without really taking sides, PICE and the Paris Chamber of Commerce (CCIP) nevertheless argued in favour of "a network that links together the key hubs" (PICE 2010: 1). They were joined by the Hauts-de-Seine general council, which adduced the same arguments in favour of G8.

Opposition to G8 and support for the Arc Express of course came primarily from the region, followed by the left-wing *départements* in Île-de-France and the city of Paris. The regional vice-president responsible for transport and mobility, Jean-Vincent Placé, declared: "G8 is an authoritarian and productivist project primarily aimed at a business class that shuttles between clusters and airports" (Forray 2007). The conference of the presidents of the eight regions in the Paris Basin objected to this project "both in its content and in its method", claiming that "the vision of development that the government is promoting through the Grand Paris transport network is in contradiction with the development strategy supported by the regions in the Paris Basin" (Conférence des présidents des 8 régions du basin parisien 2011: 4).

Because the conflict had reached gridlock, other entities (such as CESER, Paris Métropole [see below] and CRCI Île-de-France) spoke out in favour of compromise. This became possible when the government and the right lost the regional elections in 2010. Following a public debate that continued between September 2010 and January 2011, the government and the region finally reached an agreement on a scheme called Grand Paris Express (GPE) (see Map 6.1), a combination of the two projects. The conflict had lasted three years.

With regard to spatial planning and economic development, the conflicts concerned interlinked issues: the development of La Défense; the new master plan (SDRIF) proposed by the regional council; and the region's first development strategies.

Although all the players recognize the importance to Île-de-France's economic dynamism of La Défense, they do not all agree on its development. As we saw in the previous chapter, in 2005 Nicolas Sarkozy, chairman of the general council of Hauts-de-Seine, president of EPAD and minister of the interior and of spatial planning, launched the La Défense renewal plan because of the urgency of the need to react to competition from London and other international financial centres. In 2006, against the advice of the region and Nanterre municipality, the government proposed an extension to the OIN (national interest operation; see Chapter 6). In 2007 the Paris chamber of commerce and industry backed the project, arguing that, "overtaken by Greater London, with Catalonia in hot pursuit, Île-de-France needs to reinforce its position in the competition between metropolitan regions to attract the headquarters and decision-making centres of international corporations" (CCIP 2007: 3).

The government forced through the project in August 2007 with the publication of a decree for the extension of La Défense. In 2010 it enforced the creation of a new public development corporation covering the extended area, the Établissement public d'aménagement de la Défense Seine Arche (ÉPADESA) to "build a financial hub as provided for in the Grand Paris project". The Hauts-de-Seine general council approved all these decisions, saying that the region had ignored the specific character of La Défense, failing to appreciate that it was a regional and national engine of job creation, innovation and international influence.

Several local authorities took up positions in opposition to these players. For example, the regional council was critical of the undermining of the SDRIF and its decision to rebalance the development of Île-de-France in an easterly direction. It took the view that La Défense was already congested and that the business district should stay as it was.

The conflict around La Défense should in fact be seen as part of a more general struggle over the master plan, the SDRIF, which the region had started revising in 2005, under the Spatial Planning and Development Act of 1995, which granted it powers in this domain in association with central government. The SDRIF project as envisaged by the regional council provided for economic growth of 2 per cent, the creation of 28,000 jobs and the building of 60,000 homes every year over the period in question (up to 2030). It expressed an ecological choice in favour of a dense and compact city and sought to make Île-de-France Europe's leading eco-region. Equity between territories was one of its major priorities, with a rebalancing of economic development towards the east. The SDRIF therefore challenged the renewal plan for La Défense. This regional authority project was backed by the city of Paris and Île-de-France's left-wing *départements*, and was approved in September 2008 by the regional council.

The opening salvo was fired by Nicolas Sarkozy, soon after his election as president of the Republic. In June 2007 he declared in a speech: "France will not be strong and ambitious if Île-de-France withdraws into itself, if it gives up building Europe's tallest structures, if it gives up trying to attract the world's best researchers, if it gives up its ambition to be a leading financial marketplace … I do not want to see a new SDRIF adopted before these questions are fully explored" (Sarkozy 2007).

This position was supported by the big economic players (chambers of commerce, notably), which gave an unfavourable official notice (*avis*) to the master plan: "The planning orientations for the implementation of the SDRIF […] do not provide the conditions needed for a dynamic of lasting economic development and job creation" (*La Tribune* 2007).

For its part, the government felt that the SDRIF lacked ambition because, in its view, the target should be annual growth of at least 4 per cent, 60,000 jobs and between 70,000 and 75,000 homes a year. In a letter to the socialist president of the region, Jean-Paul Huchon, in July 2007, the prime minister, François Fillon, argued: "[There is a] need for ambitious targets for growth and economic excellence in order to consolidate Île-de-France's position … among the world's leading economic and scientific regions … The revised SDRIF project is manifestly not compatible with such an ambition" (Fillon, quoted in *Les Echos* 2007).

The westerly local authorities were not to be outdone. While Yvelines general council declared itself opposed to an easterly shift, its counterpart in Hauts-de-Seine expressed its disagreement, notably on the subject of La Défense. Both these two *départements* thus took a negative view of the draft master plan.

In September 2008 the government refused to submit the region's plan to the Council of State. It demanded that the project should be placed under revision and include the G8 scheme. The regional council gave way, agreeing to restart the revision process, but continued to emphasize the urgent need for a change of development model with the social, economic and environmental transition ("The goal of the 2030 SDRIF is to commit the Île-de-France region to the process of undertaking a new development model in which territorial solidarity should be the primary value": SDRIF, "Exposé des motifs") and maintained its target of creating only 28,000 jobs.

In 2013 the regional council submitted a new project to all the parties concerned, to a mixed reception. At national level, however, there had been a change to a left-wing government, which was more inclined to negotiation. Since the project still had the backing of the leftist *départements* and the city of Paris, and the government was prepared to go along, the regional chamber of commerce and CESER approved it, albeit with numerous reservations, highlighting in particular its "lack of economic ambition with respect to the challenges that the capital region faces in the twenty-first century" (CESER 2013). MEDEF Île-de-France was again opposed, judging it to be "strongly coloured green", and declared: "On analysing this document, one might wonder about the project's desire and ambition to help support the global competition in which Île-de-France is engaged" ("Avis sur le SDRIF", September 2012). The three *départements* with right-wing majorities (78, 92 and 95) once again expressed their disapproval. The Hauts-de-Seine general council declared: "The SDRIF should be modified to refer clearly to the need to complete the La Défense renewal plan. La Défense must continue to receive investment so that it can remain attractive and competitive on the world stage" ("Avis du 92 sur le SDRIF").

Nonetheless, the new SDRIF was adopted by the regional council in September 2013 and approved by a decree of the Council of State in December of the same year. Although the hatchet seemed to have been buried, antagonistic positions remained and would undoubtedly re-emerge at every new electoral deadline.

The question of Île-de-France's economic development strategies was the third bone of contention between the region's stakeholders. The conflicts on this issue were less violent and less well publicized, since, until 2016, the region's strategic documents had no prescriptive dimension and therefore placed no demands on the different protagonists.

The first regional economic development plan (SRDE), for the period from 2006 to 2010, described itself as "committed to human and integrated development for the construction of an eco-region". With respect to this goal, the economic players, in particular MEDEF Île-de-France and the chambers of commerce, proved somewhat circumspect. The chambers of commerce took the view that "the region's approach would gain from being perceived more in terms of its attractiveness to business" ("Avis des CCI sur le SRDE", 8 September 2006).

The regional economic development and innovation strategy (SRDEI) for the period from 2011 to 2014 pursued the objectives of the regional council, disregarding the business community's views. The region maintained its plan for an ecological and social transition, and received the same response from the representatives of businesses and the economic and corporate players. CESER noted that "the project lacks an objective for economic growth" and called for "real ambition in order to pull Île-de-France upwards, [to] consolidate and reinforce its role and position in Europe and in the world" (CESER 2011: 4). MEDEF Île-de-France once again condemned "a project entirely coloured green".

After the regional elections of 2015 the new regional council – now conservative – found itself in charge of producing a regional economic development, innovation and internationalization plan (SRDEII), covering the period from 2017 to 2021, which became enforceable following the NOTRe Act of August 2015. Published in December 2016, this plan was entitled *Regional Strategy for Growth, Employment and Innovation*. It set out three main priorities: (1) the region's international attractiveness, (2) making the region an "international innovation hub" and (3) the development of an entrepreneurial mindset. The questions of ecological, economic and social transition, along with the idea of a new development model, were discarded in favour of the target of "once again becoming a region that is favourable to business, rich in jobs, and offers a climate of confidence to entrepreneurs and international investors". Although the aim was indeed to "found the development of Île-de-France on the exploitation of environmental opportunities" (CRIF 2016: 10), the regional executive's change of direction in this respect was clear and the business community was well aware of it. CESER and MEDEF Île-de-France approved the new strategy.

## The impossibility of territorial leadership: abortive attempts

Three entities can claim leadership of the Île-de-France metropolis for different reasons: the city of Paris, for its economic and political power; the region, for its geographical perimeter; and, finally, central government, for its political and financial importance and its constitutional legitimacy. In consequence, each of them would try to take leadership by very different means, and each of them would fail in the attempt.

### *Paris's try: from Metropolitan Conference to Paris Métropole*

Following the 2001 municipal elections, the new socialist mayor, Bertrand Delanoë, decided to create a position of deputy for territorial cooperation, to which he appointed Pierre Mansat, a member of the French Communist Party. This decision was based on the mayor's observations that the core of the conurbation was not working well, and that public policies were needed at this scale. A broader perspective was needed in order to stretch Paris beyond its inner orbital road, the "Périphérique". In September 2002 the mayor explained the reasons for this "new scale of action for Paris" as follows: "Parisians, like all inhabitants of Île-de-France, currently experience their city at the scale of the entire metropolitan region. Transport, mobility, safety, housing, environment, solidarity, economic growth ... The more together a metropolis is, the better it works" (*Extramuros*, September 2002).

Between 2001 and 2006 Mansat took up his pilgrim's staff and gradually managed to form bonds with several suburban municipalities and *départements* by signing charters of cooperation with them. This process led to the idea of shifting up a gear by launching a Metropolitan Conference for the Paris conurbation, a discussion forum open to all local authorities of Île-de-France. This became a reality in July 2006 with the first of these conferences, held in Vanves in the southern suburbs. The letter of invitation clearly explained the purpose of the event: "Meeting to share our experiences and compare our ways of dealing with issues that are largely common to all of us." Although the pitch remained very general, it nevertheless emphasized the fact that "fractures and inequalities persist and oblige us to undertake a productive dialogue and develop collective action to meet the needs of a global metropolis". It was also specified that the Metropolitan Conference would do its work in parallel with the preparation of the SDRIF, which was then in progress.

This body worked on a "one authority, one vote" principle, with the result that all the authorities were on a level playing field regardless of population size, be it the mayor of Paris, the president of the region or the mayor of a municipality with a few hundred inhabitants. The purpose of this principle was to avoid any one authority (in practice, the city of Paris) dominating this process of cooperation. Nonetheless, the work of the Metropolitan Conference was in fact sustained by the Atelier parisien d'urbanisme (APUR: Parisian urban planning workshop), a Paris municipal agency, which produces studies, statistics and maps on the core of the region. In logistical and administrative terms, it was also the city of Paris that acted as the secretariat of the Conference.

Between July 2006 and December 2007 the Metropolitan Conference met seven times in different suburban areas (Vanves, Vincennes, Montreuil, etc.) and in Paris. The meetings dealt with questions of housing, transport, economic development and, finally, "the future of metropolitan governance".

Initially boycotted by many authorities on the political right, the Metropolitan Conference gradually brought them on board. In June 2008, just after the municipal elections won by the left, particularly in Paris, where Delanoë was comfortably re-elected, the "meeting of the agglomeration" was held. It was attended by more than 200 elected officials, and central government was present in the person of the newly appointed secretary of state for the capital region, Christian Blanc. This conference decided to set up a joint authority, federation of local governments, christened Paris Métropole, which replaced and gave more institutional form to the Metropolitan Conference.

Paris Métropole was officially created in June 2009. The preamble to its statutes specifies that "economic development requires a considerable reinforcement of territorial solidarities, notably through financial and fiscal tools". Three objectives were set for the new authority: to identify partnerships for metropolitan projects; to examine and produce proposals on financial solidarity; and to examine and produce proposals on the governance of the metropolis. Article 3 of the statutes thus states: "For the general purpose of durably reducing inequalities of development within territories, of contributing to the ecological adaptation of the metropolis and to foster economic flourishing across the metropolitan area, the objective of the syndicate will be to conduct metropolitan scale studies." The priorities were therefore clear; but they did not satisfy everyone, in particular right-wing local authorities. The Hauts-de-Seine general council refused to join Paris Métropole because it did not want Paris Métropole to become a "weapon of war" against the global Grand Paris project, backed at the time by the government.

In 2010 things changed, notably with the amendment of the statutes of Paris Métropole to introduce rules for balance and political alternation in the management structures, which gave the authority neutrality in party-political terms. In this climate of relative peace, the Hauts-de-Seine general council, as well as many municipalities in the *département* and the Yvelines general council, joined Paris Métropole.

From this point, Paris Métropole was able to continue on its merry way. Nonetheless, it was not able to become anything more than a study structure, without decision-making powers, and in particular found it hard to take a stand on the question of governance, as we will see below. Paralysed by internal rivalries, whether ideological, territorial or personal, Paris Métropole vegetated and became marginalized.

### *Government: mobilizing around the "world city"*

With the creation of the office of secretary of state for the development of the capital region in 2008, central government returned to centre stage. First of all, through a vision described as "anti-graviériste" (Béhar 2012: 3) that was reflected in the image of the Grand 8, a colossal infrastructure conceived for a world city, serving a dozen clusters, several of them world-ranked, and thereby combining polycentrism and globalism. The mission that the president of the Republic assigned to the new secretary of state was unambiguous. It stated that

> the purpose of the creation of a State Secretariat for the Development of the Capital Region is to enable France to hold its own in the competition of territories, by making its capital an open, dynamic and attractive "world city", which creates wealth and jobs, and is a crucial asset for the nation in the economic competition of the twenty-first century. [...] The vision must precede the project, and the project must lead to the choice of organization and of governance.

Second, the government would give itself the means and instruments to act: the State Secretariat, endowed with a high-level administrative and technical team and a panoply of tools of different kinds that would be assigned to it by the legislation on Grand Paris. Indeed, in 2010 the government imposed the so-called "Grand Paris Act" on Île-de-France's local authorities, a measure that in principle gave it the means and the tools to govern the development of the capital region. This act created a new public company, the Société du Grand Paris (SGP), introduced new development contracts, the territorial development contracts (CDTs: described in the previous chapter) and put the government in charge of the Saclay operation by the creation of a public development corporation under its control.

As previously mentioned, SGP is a public company chaired by the government, which holds a majority on its board of directors. Its mission is to construct the Grand 8 but also to plan and develop the areas around the dozens of stations on the line, which gives it immense power over a significant proportion of regional land. With the CDTs, conceived as contractual tools to develop the areas around the stations, the government also acquired some very binding instruments, since they take precedence over planning documents, including the SDRIF. In addition, since the sole signatories are the government and municipalities or EPCIs, they make it possible to bypass potential opposition from parties such as the region and certain *départements*. As for the Saclay operation, it is headed by a public development corporation (EPA) on which the government holds a majority on the board of directors and appoints the CEO.

Through its vision of Grand Paris and the instruments available to it via the legislation, the government was able to interest a large number of actors in its project: the business community, right-leaning local authorities, municipalities and *départements* (mainly in the west of the region). So MEDEF Île-de-France, PICE and CCIP welcomed the creation of the State Secretariat, as did the right on the regional council: "The need for a State Secretariat for the Development of the Capital Region has emerged as a result of the Region's failure under socialist leadership. It has not been doing its job for a number of years. A recovery instrument is therefore needed to maintain our ranking among world metropolises" (CRIF 2008: 38).

In addition, the business community was seduced by the emphasis placed on competitiveness and openness to the world, as indicated in article 1 of the act ("the Grand Paris project includes an objective of economic growth in order to remain competitive with other world cities") and the importance assigned to serving the business clusters.

Nonetheless, the government also succeeded in uniting many stakeholders against its project, notably the left-wing general councils, which strongly rejected the president's and his secretary of state's vision of Île-de-France.

Christian Favier, chairman of the Val-de-Marne *départemental* council, was positively virulent in his opposition:

> The vision for Île-de-France cannot be about whether or not, for example, it should be the world's leading stock market. That is not the fundamental issue, which is whether Île-de-France is going to be the region where we are really going to be able to work towards an in-depth transformation of the quality of life of its inhabitants and its workers.
>
> (Favier at the "meeting of the agglomeration", Saint-Denis, 25 June 2008)

In June 2008 the five left-wing *départements* – including Val-d'Oise, before it shifted to the right in 2011 – published a joint declaration, which quite simply left out the questions of competitiveness and attractiveness:

> Sharing the same vision of the future of Île-de-France, the presidents of the Départemental Councils seek to promote a new, more ambitious and fairer approach to the development of the region, in order to break with the processes of exclusion, both social and geographical, which severely disadvantage certain populations ... The first challenge is the issue of financial solidarity ... The second issue is mobility ... The third issue is housing. The fourth issue is the protection of the environment and natural resources.

Finally, the Grand Paris Act was considered by many, including certain right-wing individuals and authorities, as a challenge to decentralization. For the region and the left in general, the creation of the SGP was, quite simply, a backward step. Whereas the region had been in charge of the transport organizing authority, STIF, since 2005, the Grand Paris Act imposed a company that was not only beyond the region's control but that also possessed considerable powers that could undermine regional policies relating to transport.

Nonetheless, central government's attempt to take back control of the planning and development of Île-de-France would prove a failure, for three reasons. First, it encountered strong opposition from local players, not only on the left but also on the right of the political chessboard. Second, the government did not have sufficient financial resources to implement it and needed the resources of the local authorities (in particular of the region when it came to transport). And, third, the government would not have the time to do it, since the right lost the presidential and parliamentary elections in 2012. Indeed, after 2012, under the socialists, the new government would seek compromise: in the battle over the SDRIF, as we saw earlier; over the CDT, for which it gave signatory powers to the *départements* and the region; and over the SGP, which it ultimately agreed to return to the fold of the region.

### *The region's incapacity to play a unifying role: aspirations without resources*

"The metropolis is the region": since the beginning of the 2000s the presidents of the regional council continually played on the leitmotif that the region is the natural and legitimate leader of governance in Île-de-France.

The Île-de-France region has many advantages in this respect. First of all, there is its area of jurisdiction, which more or less covers the functional territory of the metropolis and which makes it, according to experts and many researchers, an institution that is well suited to producing policies commensurate with the challenges raised by globalization. Then there is its politico-institutional dynamics, since the decentralization laws have made it a strategic and unifying authority and, over the years, have strengthened its powers and financial and human resources, thereby giving it greater capacity for action.

In fact, immediately following the election of Jean-Paul Huchon, the new socialist president of CRIF, in 1998, initiatives were taken to establish leadership, in particular with the holding of the Conference for Jobs, in which the region successfully brought together numerous local authorities and representatives of the business world to debate economic development. It was following this conference that the Regional Development Agency (ARD)[1] was created to take charge of regional strategy. Gradually, CRIF would acquire new powers and a unifying and leadership role recognized in the 2004 legislation, in which it was made "coordinator of economic development actions". In 2005 it took control of the Île-de-France Transport Authority (STIF) and launched its first master plan, the SDRIF, since the law gave it this right "in association with central government". In 2014 it replaced central government as the authority responsible for managing European structural funds. The NOTRe Act of 2015 declared it "responsible for economic development policy" and made the regional economic development, internationalization and innovation strategy (SRDEII) compulsory and binding on the other parties, local authorities and businesses alike.

Until 2015, albeit timidly, CRIF advanced a vision of the future of Île-de-France based on the need for an economic, social and ecological transition – i.e. a new development model, thus affirming its goal of making Île-de-France

1. Initially conceived as a strategic agency, headed by the regional council, ARD went on to become simply a regional promotion structure as a result of the conflicts caused by its creation with the chambers of commerce and the *départements*.

Europe's first eco-region. This vision was shared by many players, mainly left-wing local authorities, including Paris, but did not have political backing from the regional executive, and CRIF was accused of being incapable of making choices, of identifying priorities – in short, of going beyond fine words. It was unable to play the coordinating and unifying role to which it aspired and that was legitimately its own. Beyond the lack of political backing that would have given a coherence to regional action, the region did not commit enough resources, particularly human resources, to becoming a genuine source of unity and mobilization.

Nonetheless, as we have seen, both the revision of the master plan and the regional strategies triggered general outcry from the business community, the right-wing *départements* and municipalities, and central government, at least until 2012 in the latter case. This coalition of actors was waiting for just one thing: for the region to move rightwards in the 2010 elections, which would inevitably lead to a U-turn in the regional council's strategies and policies. But that is not what happened, and the victory of the left in the regional elections then opened the way for negotiations. This victory did not create the political momentum in the regional executive that would enable it to establish the legitimate leadership over Île-de-France to which it laid claim, however.

The question of political leadership is crucial here. The regional executive was in fact always timorous in its responses to the initiatives of other potential leaders, whether the mayor of Paris or central government. The region always adopted a defensive standpoint. It opposed the Metropolitan Conference, dragging its feet over taking part, but was finally obliged to join in order to avoid giving Paris a free hand (Lefèvre 2017). At this conference, as subsequently in Paris Métropole, it was never proactive in advancing proposals and proved incapable of embodying its leadership ambitions. The same was true of its relations with central government, in particular over the Grand Paris Act, which de facto deprived it of some of its powers in the sphere of mobility and spatial planning. In response to governmental attacks, it made no proposals, undertook no initiatives, being content to protest about an assault on decentralization and hoping that its allies would win the next national elections. We will see that this attitude would be maintained in the ensuing struggle between Île-de-France's players over institutional reform.

## Impossible and pointless institutional reform

It was the government, in the person of president of the Republic, Nicolas Sarkozy, which initiated this process in his "Roissy speech" in June 2007. Almost incidentally, during the opening of a new airport terminal, Sarkozy commented in a speech that "what is now needed is an organization of powers ... Paris is the only metropolitan area in France not to have an urban community [*communauté urbaine*]". This was a real stick poked into Île-de-France's politico-institutional hornets' nest, and it sparked reactions and reform proposals that would culminate in the creation of a new institution, Métropole du Grand Paris, that none of the actors would know what to do with.

### *Institutional proposals*

Three parallel processes were launched in the mid-2000s to improve the governance of Île-de-France: the report by Philippe Dallier, the Planchou Commission and the work of Paris Métropole.

In April 2008 Philippe Dallier, a right-wing senator and mayor of the municipality of Pavillons-sous-Bois in Seine-Saint-Denis, published a Senate report entitled "Les perspectives d'évolution institutionnelle du Grand Paris" ("Prospects of institutional change for Greater Paris"). It recommended the amalgamation of four *départements* in the inner ring and the creation of a *sui generis* authority headed by a president elected by direct universal suffrage. The main argument revolved around questions of financial solidarity between territories, democracy and the effectiveness of public policies (housing, transport, economic development, environment).

On its side, the regional council launched a commission, headed by the socialist Jean-Paul Planchou, tasked with proposing "scenarios for tomorrow's Paris Île-de-France metropolis", which submitted its report in April 2008. With regard to institutions, the Planchou Commission proposed a strengthening of the role and powers of the region in two important domains: transport and housing. Already in the hands of the region, the Île-de-France transport syndicate (STIF), the public transport organizing authority, would become the Île-de-France mobility syndicate (Syndicat des déplacements d'Île-de-France: SDIF), notably taking responsibility for the region's motorways (800 km of roads) and logistics transport. For housing, the commission suggested the creation of an Île-de-France housing syndicate (Syndicat du logement d'Île-de-France), modelled on STIF, which would give the region a greater role in this sphere.

Set up in June 2009, Paris Métropole also very quickly instituted a debate on the governance of Île-de-France. In May 2012 it published a report entitled *Livre (ou)vert: Pour une métropole durable: Quelle gouvernance?* (*Open/Green Book: For a Sustainable Metropolis: What Governance?*), which states that a sustainable metropolis must tackle three challenges: becoming (1) a metropolis of solidarity, (2) a polycentric metropolis and (3) a metropolis that is democratic for all players. To take account of the three challenges, the report proposed three scenarios for governance.

The first, called "the integrated metropolis", envisaged institutional unification for the central conurbation – broadly, the inner ring area. This unification would be brought about by the creation of a new local authority created by the amalgamation of the *départements*, including Paris. An alternative could be the establishment of an urban community to replace the intermunicipal joint authorities set up after the 1999 legislation on intermunicipal arrangements. The second scenario, christened "the concerted metropolis", argued for governance that would be flexible and with a geometry that varied according to its competences. It was based on the quest for a consensus between local authorities. Finally, the third, called "the articulated or confederate metropolis", placed the polycentric nature of the metropolis at the core of its approach. It called for the creation of a confederation of local authorities (region, *départements*, intermunicipal structures and municipalities) as appropriate. It set no specific perimeter but would rely on strong intermunicipal structures (larger and endowed with more powers and resources).

The idea was that Paris Métropole would select a preferred scenario. This proved impossible, however, because of the conflicts between its members, with territorial interests taking precedence over public policy issues. Paris Métropole then went its own way, exposing in the process its internal conflicts.

### *The question of the "dense zone" and the creation of the Greater Paris metropolis*

From the start of the revision of the SDRIF, in 2005/6, the question of the core area of the region raised its head. Because it accounted for 47 per cent of Île-de-France's population, 60 per cent of the region's jobs and 80 per cent of public transport trips in only 4 per cent of the regional territory, there were calls from several quarters for this area to receive special treatment and in particular targeted governance. In November 2005 the city of Paris prevailed upon the region to create a "dense zone" task force among the thematic and territorial task forces involved in the drafting of the SDRIF. In so doing, the region accepted that the core area should enjoy a special role in the deliberations on the governance of Île-de-France, and in particular special treatment on the institutional issue, primarily for political reasons (Gilli 2014: 244).

The new government elected in May 2012 placed institutional reform on the agenda as part of a more general reform of France's territorial organization. The Loi MAPTAM[2] that created the Métropole du Grand Paris was promulgated in January 2014. It established a new public institution, MGP,

2. Modernization of Territorial Public Action and Strengthening of Metropolitan Areas Act.

**Map 7.1** MGP and its 12 EPTs

which broadly covered the inner ring area – i.e. a large part of the "dense zone". Home to some 7 million people across 131 municipalities, MGP was given some powers relating to economic development, the environment, housing and planning.

MGP was divided into 11 territorial public corporations (établissements publics territoriaux) (see Map 7.1), intermunicipal bodies with no specific powers or fiscal resources, each encompassing between 300,000 and 700,000 inhabitants. In addition to these 11 EPTs came the city of Paris, which retained its status, responsibilities and resources. In this configuration, MGP was relatively powerful, since it possessed numerous powers (planning, environment, economic development) and substantial financial resources, notably its own tax-raising powers, which gave it a budget of several billion euros.

Nonetheless, MGP as defined by the act did not satisfy the economic actors, in so far as it added a further tier to the institutional layer cake. Indeed, it added a new structure alongside the municipalities and *départements* of the inner ring. This is why the business community demanded that *départements* should be eliminated at the same time, in order to avoid a pile-up of structures and the expenditure and taxes that go with them. Unsuccessful in this attempt, they indicated that they would nevertheless accept MGP provided that it was a strong institution endowed with clear responsibilities. It was on this precise point that the conflicts re-emerged, however.

### *Local authorities against central government: dismantling the MAPTAM Act*

As soon as the act was passed, local authorities set themselves to dismantling it. In an unprecedented consensus between right and left, the process of weakening MGP was put in train. The idea was to endow the 11 EPTs with real powers and their own tax resources, by transferring to them some of the powers and resources of MGP. MGP would then become simply a federation of intermunicipal structures, the EPTs. This idea was supported by Paris Métropole, which had become the voice of the local authorities, but was rejected by central government, which wished to maintain an "integrated" MGP, as provided for in the act. In the debates that followed the drafting of the NOTRe Act, the third decentralization law of François Hollande's five-year term, elected local officials in Île-de-France undertook to dismantle everything associated with Métropole du Grand Paris. They proposed a strengthening of the powers and resources of the EPTs and therefore a weakening of MGP, which the government finally granted.

This was when the business community took a stand. In a press release on 7 October 2014, MEDEF Île-de-France expressed "its total disagreement with the dismantlement of the MAPTAM Act". In March 2015 the chairman of CCI Paris-Île-de-France condemned "a metropolis with weak foundations", stating that, "with respect to the objectives of development and economic attractiveness, the projects in progress correspond in no way to the terms of reference". Despite the enactment of the legislation in August 2015, the business community did not lay down its arms. Taking advantage of the campaign in the run-up to the regional elections in December that year, MEDEF Île-de-France, CCI Paris-Île-de-France and the Confédération générale des petites et moyennes entreprises (CGPME) published a joint document under the title "Businesses take action! Programmatic proposals, 2015 regional elections: let Île-de-France breathe" (MEDEF Île-de-France, CCI Paris-Île-de-France & CGPME 2015). In it, they called on the future regional council to reopen the file on Île-de-France's governance, arguing that "the current territorial reform does not fulfil the promises that were made" (MEDEF Île-de-France, CCI

Paris-Île-de-France & CGPME 2015: 17). The main two candidates in the running seemed to be on the same wavelength, since the region had never been particularly satisfied with the creation of an institutional structure in the heart of its territory. Immediately on her election as president of the region, Valérie Pécresse denounced the "shrunken Greater Paris" represented by MGP. In June 2016 she told the magazine *Grand Paris Développement*:

> I think that the right scale for this metropolitan process today is Île-de-France. Greater London, or the big Asian Metropolitan regions, cover between 8 and 15 million inhabitants. If we take Île-de-France as a whole, i.e. 12 million inhabitants, we would be in the top tier of all the international rankings. On the other hand, with a Metropolis, what I call the "shrunken Greater Paris", we are at 7 million inhabitants and situated at the bottom of those rankings!
> (*Grand Paris Développement* 2016)

After around a decade of debates and conflicts, in 2015 Île-de-France's system of actors hatched a complex institutional arrangement, described by some as "chaos" or as a "gimmick". With no fewer than five tiers of government (region, MGP, *départements*, EPTs and EPCIs, municipalities), it satisfied no one. The arguments about building an institutional organization for a twenty-first-century metropolis, capable of rivalling the world's greatest cities in the economic, cultural, environmental and social arenas, seemed to have dissolved into sterile quarrels between territorial authorities, dominated by local issues. If Paris Île-de-France is a "world city", its stakeholders find it hard to think beyond their local backyards and are unable to agree on a shared vision of its future, thereby leaving in place a highly conflictual system that seems incapable of regulation (Lefèvre 2012). Recent politico-institutional developments confirm this view.

### *An institutional imbroglio that solves nothing, 2015–20*

Métropole du Grand Paris officially became operational on 1 January 2016. Its powers were wide in theory: spatial planning, economic development, environment and living conditions, flood prevention, housing. It was also responsible for strategic planning. Some of these responsibilities, such as spatial planning, economic development, the environment and strategic planning, were also the responsibilities of other authorities, such as the intermunicipal structures or the region, notably with the SDRIF in the latter case. Achieving coexistence between MGP's powers and those of the other local governments was thus no simple matter.

To perform all its different roles, MGP in principle had a significant budget: around €3.5 billion in 2019. This budget came from taxation and central government contributions. Under the NOTRe Act, however, almost the whole of this budget was transferred to the EPTs. In fact, almost 97 per cent of MGP's resources are transferred in this way. Ultimately, MGP's real budget, the money it has to spend, consists of just a few tens of millions of euros. In financial terms, therefore, it is an authority virtually without resources.

MGP's governance depends primarily on the municipalities, since they are the entities that send their delegates to the Metropolitan Council, the main political body. This structure is made up of 209 members, all of them elected municipal councillors, and each municipality sends the number of councillors proportional to its population. It is this council that elects the chairman of MGP and the board, a small body of 30 people, which has the task of setting strategy and deciding the main orientations of the metropolis. In addition, MGP has an assembly of mayors, an advisory structure comprising the 131 mayors of the member municipalities, and the "conference of presidents of territories", a coordination and harmonization structure made up of the chair of MGP and the 11 presidents of the EPTs, including the mayor of Paris. These two entities are consultative. In addition to these structures, there is the "conference of adjacent EPCIs", which has the role of maintaining relations between MGP and the authorities in the rest of the regional territory. In other words, this is a complicated system of governance that has the effect of diluting MGP's powers and capacity for action.

Since its establishment in 2016, Métropole du Grand Paris has launched several projects, mainly in the planning sphere. In 2018, for example, it approved a metropolitan climate, air and energy plan (Plan climat, air, énergie métropolitain: PCAEM), which sets the goals for combating climate change and protecting the environment (see Chapter 6). A metropolitan housing and accommodation plan (Programme métropolitain de l'habitat et de l'hébergement: PMHH) is also in preparation. These two plans have no legal value – unlike the metropolitan plan, a framework for the other plans, which is binding on local authorities. It should be noted, however, that this metropolitan plan must be consistent with the SDRIF, which substantially restricts it.

Outside these planning projects, MGP's actions are heavily limited by its lack of resources. This situation is the result, first, of the dismantling that followed the NOTRe Act and, second, of the actions and initiatives of many local authorities, which are opposed to the creation of MGP and would like to see it abolished.

Following the creation of Métropole du Grand Paris the *départements* took a stand to defend not only their powers and resources but their very existence. Indeed, calls for the elimination of the *départements*, particularly those in inner Paris, proliferated between the proposals in the 2008 Dallier Report, which wanted to see them merged, the demands of the business community in 2015 and the support for this idea expressed by the new president of the Republic, Emmanuel Macron, in his 2017 presidential campaign. To counter this trend, the *départements*, united regardless of political orientation, campaigned to show the extent of their usefulness, notably with respect to social and territorial solidarity. They warned the government against the idea of a merger and their disappearance by absorption into MGP, and denounced the latter's creation as a mistake that had simply added to the clatter of the existing institutional arrangements.

Moreover, some *départements* developed their own initiatives. For example, the *départements* of Hauts-de-Seine and Yvelines, the richest in Île-de-France apart from Paris, embarked on a merger process in 2016 to create a single authority. Little by little, the two *départements* have been pooling their services and have been making veiled appeals to the government to approve the project. Considered by other authorities to be a "wedding of the rich", the merger of Hauts-de-Seine and Yvelines, if it happened, would challenge the very existence of MGP, since the Yvelines *département* is located outside the perimeter of the Métropole (see Map 1.1).

Calls for the elimination of MGP can also be heard among authorities that are members of it, however. In 2018 the presidents of the 11 EPTs, as well as all the mayors in the *départements* within the inner ring area, set up an informal structure called the "alliance of territories". Since its creation this entity has been campaigning vigorously for the abolition of MGP and its replacement by a territorially flexible structure, with "light" powers, similar to those of the former Paris Métropole. They are calling for the EPTs to become intermunicipal public corporations with their own tax-raising powers and numerous competences.

In a unitary state as centralized as France, it is up to central government to take a position. During the presidential campaign in 2017 Macron took the view that the governance of the Paris metropolitan region needed to be reformed. Nonetheless, since his election, the government has been strangely silent, postponing its decision several times, refusing to adopt a position on the merger of Hauts-de-Seine and Yvelines, refusing to express a view on the merger of the *départements* and the possible elimination of MGP. Given the gravity of the stakes and the political risks, it would seem that the government considers it urgent to wait until the next elections, thereby following the same strategy as the other actors in Île-de-France.

As of 2021 the system of governance in Île-de-France seems at a standstill. It is unlikely that the 2021 regional elections won by the right and the next national elections in 2022 will enable Île-de-France's actors to overcome their differences and commit to processes of negotiation and cooperation, the only way in which the system can be unblocked. Indeed, all the ingredients and sources of conflict are still in place. In addition, the absence of forums for discussion and dialogue between the protagonists, the only way in which antagonisms might be overcome, contributes to the persistence of the status quo.

# Conclusion

From a reading of this book, Paris Île-de-France emerges as a metropolitan region similar in many ways to other world cities with which it is generally compared, such as London and New York. Like them, it has to deal with problems of transport and mobility, a housing crisis and difficult environmental conditions. Like them, but to lesser degrees, it is characterized by significant and growing poverty and sometimes ostentatious wealth.

Like the other big metropolitan regions in democratic countries, Île-de-France tackles these problems and manages this territory by means of a system of governance that is complex and calls upon multiple actors, both public and private, at different scales. Whether as providers of skills and responsibilities or of finance, this multitude of actors operates within a web of relationships marked often by significant conflict but also by extensive cooperation. Within this crowd of actors, the state stands out through the resources it holds, be they political, legal, technical or financial. Contrary to a popular view that has spread since the 1980s, the state has not disappeared, and, if remodelling there has been, this is to maintain an often crucial presence in the conduct of metropolitan affairs. The 2008 financial crisis and the recent Covid-19 health crisis clearly show the extent to which the state remains a central and powerful player, the only one capable of undertaking measures and policies to tackle situations that affect metropolitan regions more severely because of their economic influence and demographic density.

Nevertheless, all these similarities should not lead us to ignore the distinctive features of France's premier metropolitan region – features that have been identified, developed and analysed throughout this book. In many respects, these singularities set Paris apart within the small circle of the Northern Hemisphere's big metropolitan regions. There are at least five main differences that account for this distinctiveness.

First, there is Paris's ultra-dominant position on the national stage and relative to the country's other big cities. This dominance, unrivalled for centuries, is explained, as we have seen, by the history of the construction of the French state, which made Paris – and, by extension, Île-de-France – not only its political capital but also its administrative, economic, social and cultural centre. The few policies that have sought to lessen this predominance, such as those initiated after the Second World War, changed nothing of this. In this respect, we need to look to Asia, with cities such as Seoul and Tokyo, to find comparable conditions. Even London, which is often compared with the French capital in this respect, does not dominate the rest of its national territory to the same extent and leaves a certain amount of room for the other secondary cities, such as Birmingham and Manchester.

Next, there is the predominant role of the public player in the management of this metropolis. Here again, although France and Île-de-France are not exceptions on the international stage, it is the degree of dominance, its institutionalization and its acceptance by society as a whole that set them apart. This is well illustrated, particularly at local scale, by the so-called neocorporatism described in the different chapters of this book. This neocorporatism remains dominant and legitimate, even though it is beginning to be challenged by a number of players, mainly those excluded from it or for whom it is becoming an obstacle (e.g. big companies). If the public sector and neocorporatism do play an essential part in the growth of the Paris region, however, it would be a mistake to underestimate the direct role of firms and companies in this process. By and large, they have been at the forefront of stressing the changes brought about by the globalization process and have thus paved the way in the building of a global metropolis, leading the public sector in this direction.

Third, Île-de-France still enjoys economic diversity – greater diversity, for example, than London or New York – and, notably, the persistence of a significant industrial sector. Indeed, although Île-de-France has undoubtedly been affected by deindustrialization, it has succeeded in maintaining an industrial base, albeit significantly diminished in recent decades. As a corollary, its power in the financial and business services sectors, the flagship spheres of globalization, cannot rival those of London and New York, or even other big cities, such as Hong Kong. Nonetheless, this economic diversity gives it a wider range of strategic choices than are open to the other metropolitan regions, and partly explains why Île-de-France has come through the crises better than other more powerful territories. In this sense, Île-de-France's economic diversity may be an asset in the future.

Fourth, Île-de-France differs in the trajectory of its public policies. In a period marked by globalization and, hence, by an emphasis on territorial competition and competitiveness, France's capital region, though not deaf to the sirens of competition, also prioritizes the struggle against social and territorial inequalities, highlighting its ambivalence regarding the different actors' perceptions of globalization.

Finally, whereas the development of Île-de-France has been nurtured partly by foreign immigration, as it has in other metropolitan regions (with the relative exception of certain Asian cities), migration is not a factor that is considered by most of the region's policy-makers. Immigration remains an unspoken issue, a phenomenon that – although it is visible and salient both economically and socially – receives little attention, positive or otherwise, in discussion or in the formulation of policies to tackle the problems of the region. Indeed, there is a significant gap between the positive role played by immigration in the economic development of the Paris region as a global metropolis and the ways this phenomenon is considered and dealt with in the political arena. As such, Paris stands in strong contrast to cities such as London and New York, where immigration is acknowledged, praised and desired. Although the Paris situation can be explained, once again, by a political culture strongly committed to the principle of republican equality, this lack of interest sets the region apart from the other big cities of the Global North: London and New York, of course, but also smaller cities, such as Toronto and Manchester.

These five points of singularity complement each other and overlap to form a unique global metropolis, through a sort of alchemy that can be explained only by the historical processes that contributed to its shaping.

# References

Aguilera, T., F. Artioli & C. Colomb 2019. "Explaining the diversity of policy responses to platform-mediated short-term rentals in European cities: a comparison of Barcelona, Paris and Milan". *Environment and Planning A*: doi 10.1177/0308518X19862286.

Airbnb 2015. "Paris, première destination pour Airbnb, accueillera 6000 hôtes pour l'événement Airbnb Open". 26 February. Available at www.airbnb.fr/press/news/paris-premiere-destination-pour-airbnb-accueillera-6000-hotes-pour-l-evenement-airbnb-open.

Airparif 2018. "Qualité de l'air en Île-de-France en 2017: une situation similaire à 2016, avec une légère amélioration", communiqué de presse. 31 January. Paris: Airparif.

Airparif 2019. "Bilan 2018 de la qualité de l'air". 4 April.

Anon. 1960. "L'aménagement de la région parisienne", Notes et études documentaires 2708. Paris: Documentation française.

Assemblée Nationale 2018. "Déposé sur l'évaluation de l'action de l'État dans l'exercice de ses missions régaliennes en Seine-Saint-Denis", Rapport d'information 1014. Paris: Assemblée Nationale. Available at www.assemblee-nationale.fr/dyn/15/rapports/cec/l15b1014_rapport-information.

Auzannet, P. 2012. "Rapport de la mission sur le calendrier pluriannuel de réalisation et de financement du projet de Grand Paris Express". Paris: Ministère de l'égalité des territoires et du logement. Available at https://images.derstandard.at/2013/03/07/Rapport_C_Duflot_Version_Finalex.pdf.

Béhar, D. 2012. "L'État et la gouvernabilité métropolitaine: une apologie conceptuelle". Paper presented at conference "Gouverner les métropoles: bilan et nouvelles directions de recherché", Paris, 30 November.

Béhar D. & P. Estèbe 2007. "Faut-il un gouvernement à l'Île-de-France?". *Pouvoirs locaux* 73: 98–102.

Bellanger, E. 2008. "Gouverner le Grand Paris: le poids de l'histoire". Mouvements, 19 November. Available at https://mouvements.info/gouverner-le-grand-paris-le-poids-de-lhistoire.

Bellanger, E. 2010. "De De Gaulle à Pompidou, lorsque l'État s'opposait aux élus locaux: l'exemplarité du Grand Paris". In *Le grand dessein parisien de Georges Pompidou: l'aménagement de Paris et de la région capitale*, P. Nivet *et al.* (eds), 43–53. Paris: Somogy.

Bellanger, E. 2012. "Le Grand Paris bienfaiteur et ses dynamiques de coopération sous la Troisième République". In *Agrandir Paris au 19è et 20è siècles*, A. Fourcaut & F. Bourillon (eds), 55–74. Paris: Publications de la Sorbonne.

Brenner, N. 2004. *New State Spaces, Urban Governance and the Rescaling of Statehood.* Oxford: Oxford University Press.

Bruitparif 2019. *Impacts sanitaires du bruit des transports dans la zone dense de la région Île-de-France.* Paris: Bruitparif.

CCIP 2007. "Paris-La Défense, moteur d'attractivité internationale de l'Île-de-France". Paris: CCIP.

CCI Paris Île-de-France, Institut Paris Région & INSEE Île-de-France 2008. "Chiffres-clés de la région Île-de-France 2008". Paris: CCI Paris Île-de-France.

CCI Paris Île-de-France, Institut Paris Région & INSEE Île-de-France 2019. "Chiffres-clés de la région Île-de-France 2019". Paris: CCI Paris Île-de-France.

CCI Paris Île-de-France, Institut Paris Région & INSEE Île-de-France 2020. "Chiffres-clés de la région Île-de-France 2020". Paris: CCI Paris Île-de-France. Available at www.cci-paris-idf.fr/sites/default/files/crocis/wysiwyg/Chiffres.cl.

CESER 2011. "Avis relatif à la Stratégie régionale de développement économique et d'innovation (SRDEI)", Avis 2011-05. Paris: CESER. Available at www.banquedesterritoires.fr/sites/default/files/ra/Consulter%20I%27avis%20du%20CESER%20Ile-de-France.pdf.

CESER 2013. "Avis relatif au projet de schéma directeur de la région Île-de-France arrêté par le Conseil régional le 25 Octobre 2012", Avis 2013-01. Paris: CESER.

Choose Paris Region 2020. "Paris Region facts and figures 2020". Paris: Choose Paris Region. Available at www.chooseparisregion.org/sites/default/choose_wp/uploads/2020/04/Paris-Region-Facts-and-Figures.-2020-Edition.pdf.

Conférence des présidents des 8 régions du basin parisien 2011. "Débat public Arc Express", cahier d'acteurs. Paris: Commission nationale de débat public. Available at https://cpdp.debatpublic.fr/cpdp-grandparis/site/DEBATPUBLIC_GRANDPARIS_ORG/_SCRIPT/NTSP_DOCUMENT_FILE_DOWNLOADB3139.PDF?document_id=2338&document_file_id=2464.

Cottour, C. 2008a. "Du district à la région l'Île-de-France". In *Une brève histoire de l'aménagement de Paris et sa région*, 75–96. Paris: DREIF. Available at: www.driea.ile-de-france.developpement-durable.gouv.fr/IMG/pdf/Chapitre5_de_Breve_histoire_de_amenagement_de_Paris_DREIF_Auteur_Claude_Cottour_cle0344bc.pdf.

Cottour, C. 2008b. "Le schéma directeur de la région Île-de-France de 1994". In *Une brève histoire de l'aménagement de Paris et sa région*, 117–26. Paris: DREIF. Available at: www.driea.ile-de-france.developpement-durable.gouv.fr/IMG/pdf/Chapitre7_de_Breve_histoire_de_amenagement_de_Paris_DREIF_Auteur_Claude_Cottour_cle0344bc.pdf.

Cour des comptes 2010. *Rapport sur les transports ferroviaires régionaux en Île-de-France*. Paris: Cour des comptes.

Cour des comptes 2014. "Rapport d'observations définitives et sa réponse: région Île-de-France: Contrat de projet État–région: exercices 2007 et suivants". Paris: Cour des comptes.

Cour des comptes 2015. *Le logement en Île-de-France: Donner de la cohérence à l'action publique*. Paris: Cour des comptes.

Cour des comptes 2017. *La Société du Grand Paris*. Paris: Cour des comptes. Available at www.ccomptes.fr/sites/default/files/2018-01/20170117-rapport-societe-grand-Paris_1.pdf.

CRIF 2007. "Schéma Régional de Développement Economique, SRDE". Paris: CRIF.

CRIF 2008. "Scenarii pour la métropole Paris–Île-de-France demain", rapport 3. Paris: CRIF.

CRIF 2011. "Schéma Régional de Développement Economique et d'Innovation, SRDEI". Paris: CRIF.

CRIF 2013. "Schéma Directeur de la Région Ile de France, SDRIF". Paris: CRIF.

CRIF 2016. "Schéma Régional de Développement Economique, d'Innovation et d'Internationalisation, SRDEII". Paris: CRIF.

Dallier P. 2008. "Le Grand Paris: un vrai projet pour un enjeu capital", Rapport d'information du Sénat 07–262. Paris: Sénat. Available at www.senat.fr/rap/r07-262/r07-2621.pdf.

Damon, J. 2016. "Politique de la ville: un bilan nécessairement contrasté". *Constructif* 45: 68–71.

DIRECCTE Île-de-France 2008. "Chiffres clés 2008". Paris: DIRECCTE Île-de-France. Available at https://idf.direccte.gouv.fr/Chiffres-cles,4570.

DIRECCTE Île-de-France 2019. "Près de la moitié des emplois du numérique localisés en Île-de-France", Synthèse thématique 91. Paris: DIRECCTE Île-de-France. Available at https://idf.drieets.gouv.fr/sites/idf.drieets.gouv.fr/IMG/pdf/synthese_thematique_91_insee_v7web.pdf.

DIRECCTE Île-de-France 2020. "Chiffres clés 2008". Paris: DIRECCTE Île-de-France. Available at https://idf.direccte.gouv.fr/Chiffres-cles,4570.

DRIEA 2020. "La construction de logements en Île-de-France: note de conjoncture trimestrielle". Paris: DRIEA. Available at www.driea.ile-de-france.developpement-durable.gouv.fr/IMG/pdf/sitadel_-_note_de_conjoncture_-_octobre_2020.pdf.

*Echos, Les* 2007. "Île-de-France: polémique autour du schéma directeur, voté par le Conseil de Paris". 17 July. Available at www.lesechos.fr/2007/07/ile-de-france-polemique-autour-du-schema-directeur-vote-par-le-conseil-de-paris-552645.

Flonneau, M. 2003. "L'action du district de la région parisienne et les 'dix glorieuses' de l'urbanisme automobile". *Vingtième siècle: revue d'histoire* 79: 93–104.

Forray, J.-B. 2007. "Deux projets de transport, deux conceptions de l'aménagement". *Gazette des communes*, 30 July.

Fourcaut, A., E. Bellanger & M. Flonneau 2006. *Paris/banlieues: Conflits et solidarités*. Paris: Créaphis.

François-Poncet, J. 2003. "L'exception territoriale: un atout pour la France", Rapport d'information du Sénat 02–241. Paris: Sénat. Available at www.senat.fr/rap/r02-241/r02-2411.pdf.

Gilli, F. 2014. *Grand Paris: L'émergence d'une métropole*. Paris: Presses de Sciences Po.

GPSO 2013. "Ville numérique, créative et durable". Paris: GPSO. Available at www.seineouest.fr/app/uploads/2020/04/CDT_GPSO_01_25635_compressed.pdf.

*Grand Paris Développement* 2016. "Grand entretien avec Valérie Pécresse: 'la Métropole est une création politicienne'". 9 June.

Gravier, J.-F. 1947. *Paris et le désert français*. Paris: Le Portulan.

Guieysse, J.-A. 1986. "L'industrie en Île-de-France depuis 1965". *Villes en parallèle* 11: 134–61.

Higonnet, P. 2005. *Paris: capitale du monde*. Paris: Tallandier.

IAU 2001. *40 ans en Ile-de-France: rétrospective 1960–2000*. Paris: IAURIF.

IAU 2005. "Population: modes de vie", Note rapide 401. Paris: IAURIF. Available at www.institutparisregion.fr/fileadmin/NewEtudes/Etude_375/nr_401_le_revenu_des_franciliens.pdf.

IAU 2013a. *Atlas des Franciliens*. Paris: IAU.

IAU 2013b. *La circulation routière en Île-de-France en 2010*. Paris: IAU. Available at www.institutparisregion.fr/fileadmin/NewEtudes/Etude_997/La_circulation_routiere_en_IdF_en_2010.pdf.

IAU 2015. *L'environnement en Île-de-France: Mémento 2015*. Paris: IAU.

IAU 2016a. "Recherche et innovation: l'Île-de-France en quête de reconnaissance mondiale", Note rapide 733. Paris: IAU. Available at www.fnau.org/wp-content/uploads/2016/12/nr_733_recherche_innov.pdf.

IAU 2016b. *Les trajectoires de l'économie francilienne: Constats et enjeux*. Paris: IAU. Available at www.iau-idf.fr/fileadmin/DataStorage/user_upload/Les_trajectoires_de_l_economie_francilienne.pdf.

IAU 2017a. "Inégalités sociales et environnementales sont étroitement liées en Île-de-France", Note rapide 749. Paris: IAU. Available at www.iau-idf.fr/fileadmin/NewEtudes/Etude_1379/NR_749_WEB.pdf.

IAU 2017b. *Les conditions du logement en Île-de-France: Édition 2017*. Paris: IAU. Available at www.driea.ile-de-france.developpement-durable.gouv.fr/IMG/pdf/enl_web_lien_compresse_2.pdf.

IAU 2018a. "Territoire inondable: l'aléa inondation en Île-de-France". 25 January. Available at www.institutparisregion.fr/environnement/risques-naturels-et-technologiques/territoire-inondable.html.

IAU 2018b. "Poursuivre l'effort du logement en faveur des ménages modestes", Note rapide 790. Paris: IAU. Available at www.iau-idf.fr/fileadmin/NewEtudes/Etude_1733/NR_790_web.pdf.

IAU 2018c. *L'industrie aéronautique, spatiale et de défense en Île-de-France*. Paris: IAU. Available at www.institutparisregion.fr/fileadmin/NewEtudes/Etude_1441/Etude_aero_V3def28fevrier2018.pdf.

IAU 2019a. *Gentrification et paupérisation au cœur de l'Île-de-France: Évolutions 2001–2015*. Paris: IAU. Available at www.institutparisregion.fr/fileadmin/NewEtudes/Etude_1807/Gentrification_et_pauperisation_complet.pdf.

IAU 2019b. *Bilan de la mise en œuvre du SDRIF*, part 1, *Quelle atteinte des objectifs? Analyse des indicateurs régionaux de l'aménagement*. Paris: IAU. Available at www.institutparisregion.fr/fileadmin/NewEtudes/Etude_1818/Partie1-Objectifs-2019-06-26.pdf.

IAU 2021. "Covid 19: un choc qui oblige à transformer le modèle économique francilien", Note rapide 883. Paris: IAU. Available at www.institutparisregion.fr/fileadmin/NewEtudes/000pack2/Etude_2572/NR_883_web.pdf.

IAU & MGP 2018. *Métropolisation et habitat: Contribution au diagnostic du programme métropolitain de l'habitat et de l'hébergement (PMHH)*. Paris: IAU. Available at www.institutparisregion.fr/fileadmin/NewEtudes/Etude_1646/MetropolisationHabitat.pdf.

INSEE 2020. "L'équipement automobile des ménages en 2017: comparaisons regionales et départementales". 29 June. Available at www.insee.fr/fr/statistiques/2012694.

INSEE n.d. "L'essentiel sur … les immigrés et les étrangers". Available at www.insee.fr/fr/statistiques/3633212 [last accessed 19 May 2021].

INSEE Île-de-France 2003. "Ile-de-France, region capitale", Insee À la page hors-série. Paris: INSEE Île-de-France. Available at www.epsilon.insee.fr/jspui/bitstream/1/4406/1alap_hs.pdf.

INSEE Île-de-France 2017a. "Une population immigrée aujourd'hui plus répartie sur le territoire regional", Insee Analyse 70. Paris: INSEE Île-de-France. Available at http://recherche-naf.insee.fr/fr/statistiques/3136640.

INSEE Île-de-France 2017b. "Les quartiers de la politique de la ville en Île-de-France", Insee Analyse 57. Paris: INSEE Île-de-France. Available at www.insee.fr/fr/statistiques/2658852.

Institut Paris Région 2019. "L'industrie de la santé en Île-de-France, panorama statistique". Paris: Institut Paris Région. Available at www.institutparisregion.fr/fileadmin/NewEtudes/000pack2/Etude_2197/EtudeSante_MEP_06122019.pdf.

Institut Paris Région 2020a. *Diagnostic de l'Île-de-France: Dans le cadre de la préparation du contrat de plan État–région et du programme opérationel régional*. Paris: Institut Paris Région. Available at www.institutparisregion.fr/fileadmin/NewEtudes/000pack2/Etude_2362/Diag-PO-CPER_complet-VF-2020-05-25.pdf.

Institut Paris Région 2020b. *Impact de la crise Covid 19 sur l'économie francilienne: Mars à Octobre 2020: Dossier technique*. Paris: Institut Paris Région. Available at www.institutparisregion.fr/fileadmin/NewEtudes/000pack2/Etude_2477/Eco_Covid_web.pdf.

International Organization for Migration 2015. *World Migration Report 2015: Migrants and Cities: New Partnerships to Manage Mobility*. Geneva: IOM.

*Journal du Dimanche* 2017. "Dix solutions pour mettre fin aux bouchons en Île-de-France". 26 February.

Larroque, D. & G. Jigaudon 1980. "Industrialisation et équipements urbains à Paris, 1830–1914". *Annales de la recherche urbaine* 8: 49–86.

Lefèvre, C. 2012. "Paris-Île-de-France, unregulated competitive decentralization". In *Struggling Giants: City Region Governance of London, New York, Paris, and Tokyo*, P. Kantor *et al.* (eds), 171–89. Minneapolis: University of Minnesota Press.

Lefèvre, C. 2017. *Paris, métropole introuvable*. Paris: PUF.

Lefèvre, C. 2020. "The governance of megacities: searching for the collective actor". In *Handbook of Megacities and Megacity-Regions*, D. Labbé & A. Sorensen (eds), 78–91. Cheltenham: Edward Elgar.

Lillo, N. *et al.* 2009. "Île-de-France, histoire et mémoire des immigrations depuis 1789". *Hommes & migrations* 1278: 18–31.

Mansat, P. & C. Lefèvre 2021. *Ma vie rouge: Meurtre au Grand Paris*. Grenoble: Presses Universitaires de Grenoble.

Marchand, B. 1993. *Paris, histoire d'une ville: XIXe–XXe siècle*. Paris: Le Seuil.

MEDEF Île-de-France 2010. "Débat public Arc Express", cahier d'acteurs. Paris: Commission nationale de débat public. Available at https://cpdp.debatpublic.fr/cpdp-grandparis/site/DEBATPUBLIC_GRANDPARIS_ORG/_SCRIPT/NTSP_DOCUMENT_FILE_DOWNLOADBE31.PDF?document_id=75&document_file_id=145.

MEDEF Île-de-France, CCI Paris Île-de-France & CGPME 2015. "Les entreprises se mobilisent! Réflexions programmatiques, élections régionales 2015: faisons respirer l'Île-de-France". Paris: MEDEF Île-de-France/CCI Paris Île-de-France/CGPME. Available at www.medef-idf.fr/wp-content/uploads/2015/09/MEDEF_Les-Entreprises.pdf.

Merlin, P. 1982. *L'aménagement de la région parisienne et les villes nouvelles*. Paris: Documentation française.

MGP 2017. *Document de synthèse du Plan climat, air et énergie de la métropole du Grand Paris*. Paris: MGP.

Ministère de la cohésion des territoires 2017. "Bilan triennal SRU 2014–2016". Paris: Ministère de la cohésion des territoires.

Nivet, P. 2004. "L'histoire des institutions parisiennes, d'Étienne Marcel à Bertrand Delanoë". *Pouvoirs* 3(110): 5–18.

OMNIL 2010. "Enquête globale transport". Paris: OMNIL. Available at http://omnil.fr/IMG/pdf/egt2010_enquete_globale_transports_-_2010.pdf.

OMNIL 2019. "La nouvelle enquête globale transport: présentation des premier résultats 2018". Paris: OMNIL. Available at http://omnil.fr/IMG/pdf/presentation_egt_v_publique_vf.pdf.

Parilla, J., N. Marchio & J. Leal Trujillo 2016. *Global Paris: Profiling the Region's International Competitiveness and Connections*. Washington, DC: Brookings Institution.

Paris Métropole 2012. *Livre (ou)vert: Pour une métropole durable: Quelle gouvernance?* Paris: Paris Métropole. Available at www.ekopolis.fr/node/14445/printable/print.

*Parisien, Le* 2016. "Charles de Gaulle Express à nouveau sur les rails". 7 July.

PICE 2010. "Débat public Arc Express", cahier d'acteurs. Paris: Commission nationale de débat public. Available at https://cpdp.debatpublic.fr/cpdp-grandparis/site/DEBATPUBLIC_GRANDPARIS_ORG/_SCRIPT/NTSP_DOCUMENT_FILE_DOWNLOADB39.PDF?document_id=601&document_file_id=605.

PICE & CCI Paris Île-de-France 2014. *Compétitivité et attractivité: Le double défi des global cities: Comment réinventer le modèle économique de Paris Île-de-France*. Paris: PICE/CCI Paris Île-de-France.

*Pouvoirs locaux* 2007. "Paris Île-de-France: comment gouverner la métropole régionale". 73 (special issue).

PRIF & CRIF 2007. "Contrat de plan État-région Île-de-France, 2007–2014". Paris: PRIF.

PRIF & CRIF 2015. "Contrat de plan État-région 2015–2020 Île-de-France". Paris: PRIF. Available at www.iledefrance.fr/sites/default/files/medias/2019/05/cper_2015-2020_0.pdf.

PRIF & DRIHL 2019. *Bilan 2018: Comité régional de l'habitat et de l'hébergement*. Paris: PRIF. Available at www.drihl.ile-de-france.developpement-durable.gouv.fr/IMG/pdf/bilan-2018-lecture-etat.pdf.

Rey-Lefebvre, I. 2019. "Paris, les prix de l'immobilier cassent la baraque". *Le Monde*, 30 August.

Sarkozy, N. 2007. "Inauguration du satellite no. 3 Roissy Charles-de-Gaulle", speech. 26 June. Available at https://observatoiregrandparis.org/2007/06/26/discours-de-nicolas-sarkozy.

STIF 2014. *Plan de déplacements urbains d'Île-de-France*. Paris: STIF.

STIF 2016. *Évaluation en continu du PDUIF: Éléments à mi-parcours, 2010–2015*. Paris: STIF. Available at https://omnil.fr/IMG/pdf/pduif_2010-2015_mel_light_2.pdf.

Stromboni, C. 2017. "La Cour des comptes appelle à sortir de l'impasse à Saclay". *Le Monde*, 8 February.

Subra, P. 2012. *Le Grand Paris: Géopolitique d'une métropole mondiale*. Paris: Armand Colin.

*Tribune, La* 2007. "Le Schéma directeur de la région Île-de-France critiqué". 7 July.

Union Routière de France 2019. *Faits et chiffres 2019: Statistiques de mobilité en France et en Europe*. Paris: URF.

V-Traffic n.d. "L'état du trafic en Île-de-France".

Vadelorge, L. 2012. "Du District de la région parisienne au Conseil régional d'Île-de-France: la loi de 1972 en miroir". *Pour mémoire* (hors série): 42–54.

# List of illustrations

## Figures



## Tables

## Maps



## Photos

# Index